SEX CRIMINALS

ONE WEIRD TRICK

MATT FRACTION
CHIP ZDARSKY

BECKA KINZIE
CHRISTOPHER SEBELA
COLOR FLATTING

THOMAS K
EDITING

DREW GILL
PRODUCTION

IMAGE COMICS, INC.
Robert Kirkman – Chief Operating Officer
Erik Larsen – Chief Financial Officer
Todd McFarlane – President
Marc Silvestri – Chief Executive Officer
Jim Valentino – Vice-President

Eric Stephenson – Publisher
Ron Richards – Director of Business Development
Jennifer de Guzman – Director of Trade Book Sales
Kat Salazar – Director of PR & Marketing
Jeremy Sullivan – Director of Digital Sales
Emilio Bautista – Sales Assistant
Branwyn Bigglestone – Senior Accounts Manager
Emily Miller – Accounts Manager
Jessica Ambriz – Administrative Assistant
Tyler Shainline – Events Coordinator
David Brothers – Content Manager
Jonathan Chan – Production Manager
Drew Gill – Art Director
Meredith Wallace – Print Manager
Monica Garcia – Senior Production Artist
Jenna Savage – Production Artist
Addison Duke – Production Artist
Tricia Ramos – Production Assistant
IMAGECOMICS.COM

SEX CRIMINALS, VOL. 1: ONE WEIRD TRICK. Second printing. June 2014. Published by Image Comics, Inc. Office of publication: 2001 Center Street, Sixth Floor, Berkeley, CA 94704. Contains material originally published as Sex Criminals #1-5. Printed in the USA. For information regarding the CPSIA on this printed material call: 203-595-3636 and provide reference #RICH–566956. For international rights, contact: foreignlicensing@imagecomics.com. ISBN: 978-1-60706-946-1

To anyone, anywhere, at
literally any time in human
history who ever rubbed one
out: you are the real heroes.

MATT

To my darling Jessica,
wherever you may b—ah!
You were behind me!
What the fuck?

CHIP

1
SUZIE
DOWN
IN THE
QUIET

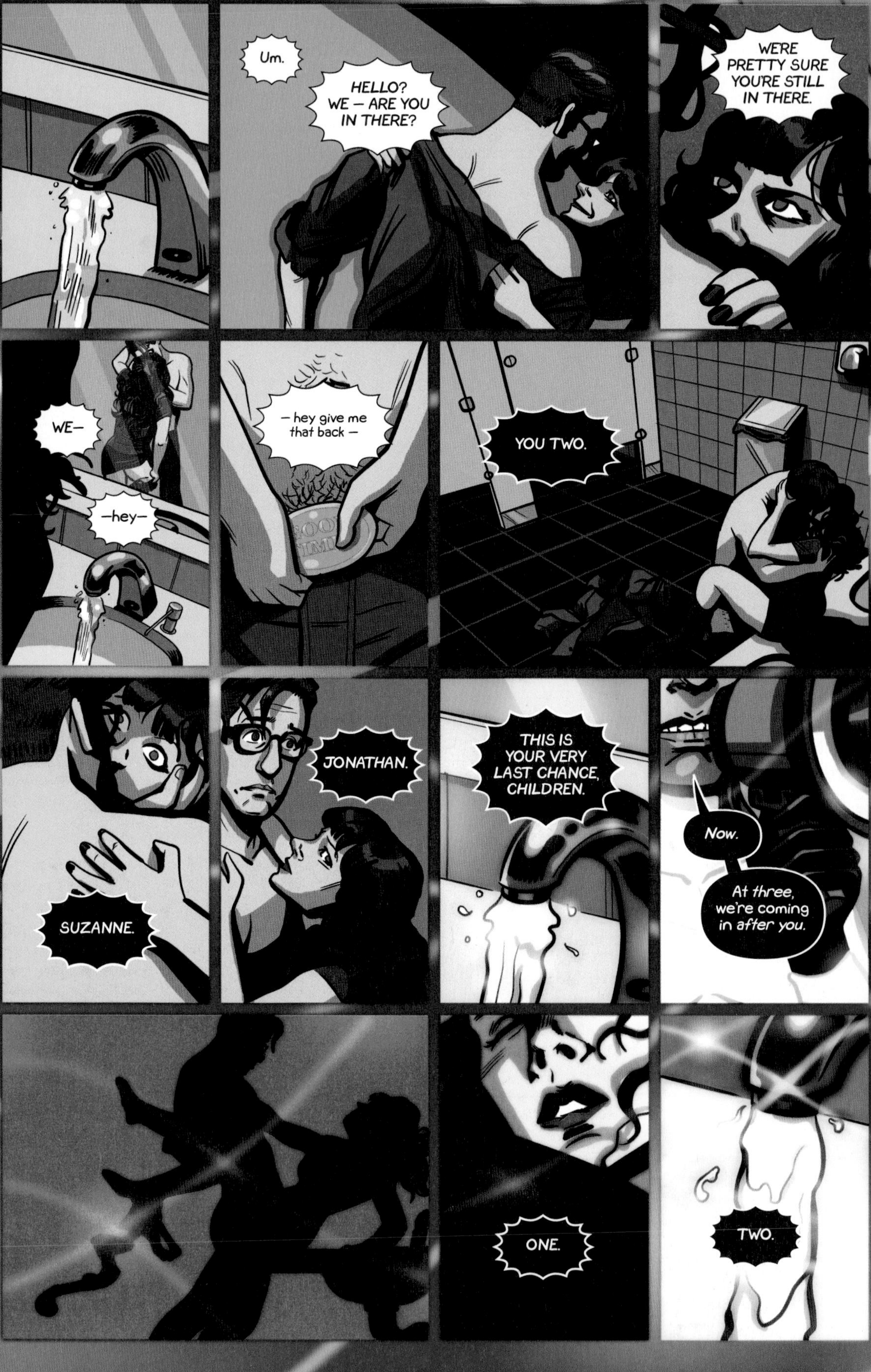
Um.
HELLO? WE — ARE YOU IN THERE?
WE'RE PRETTY SURE YOU'RE STILL IN THERE.
WE—
—hey—
— hey give me that back —
YOU TWO.
SUZANNE.
JONATHAN.
THIS IS YOUR VERY LAST CHANCE, CHILDREN.
Now.
At three, we're coming in after you.
ONE.
TWO.

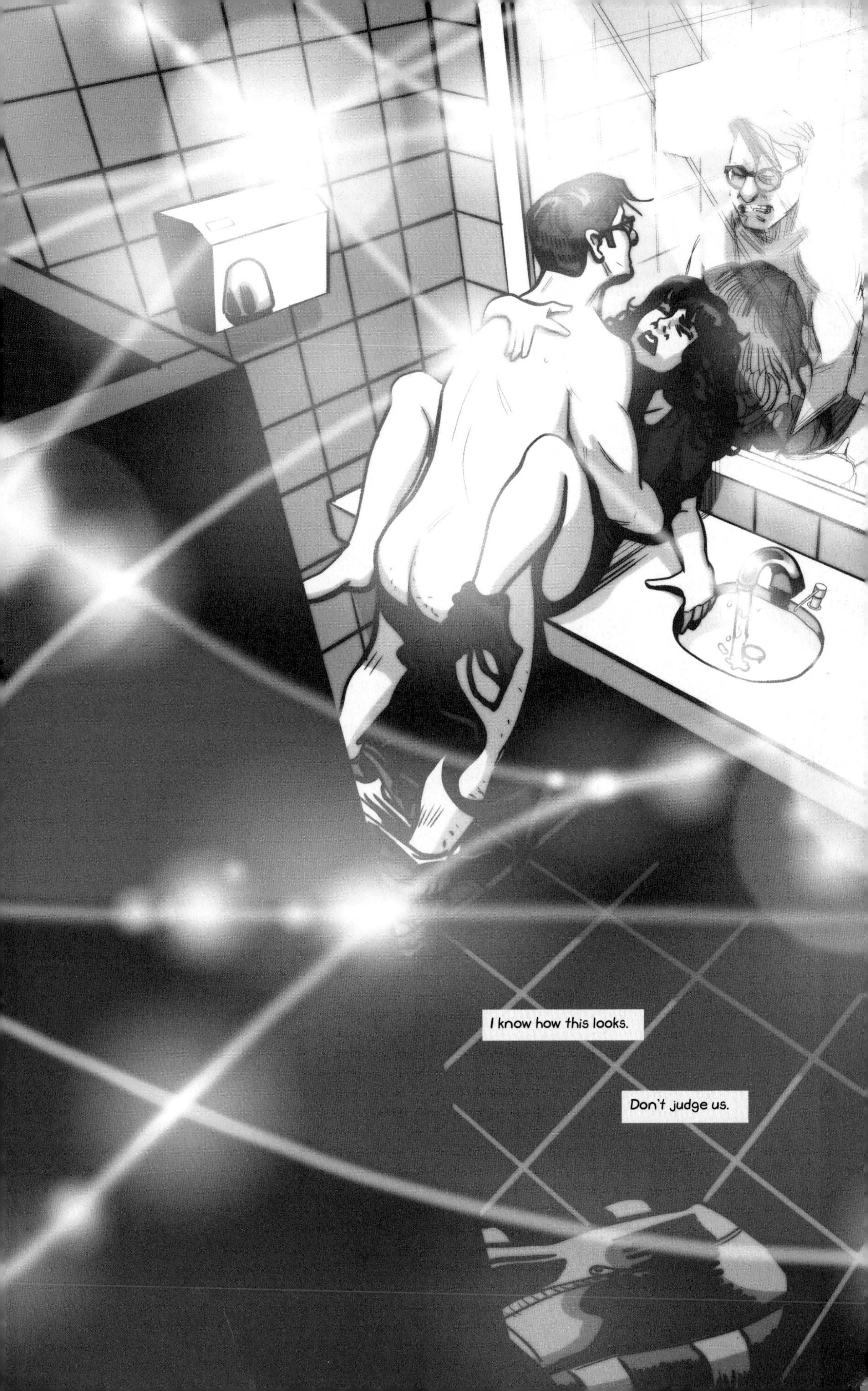
I know how this looks.
Don't judge us.

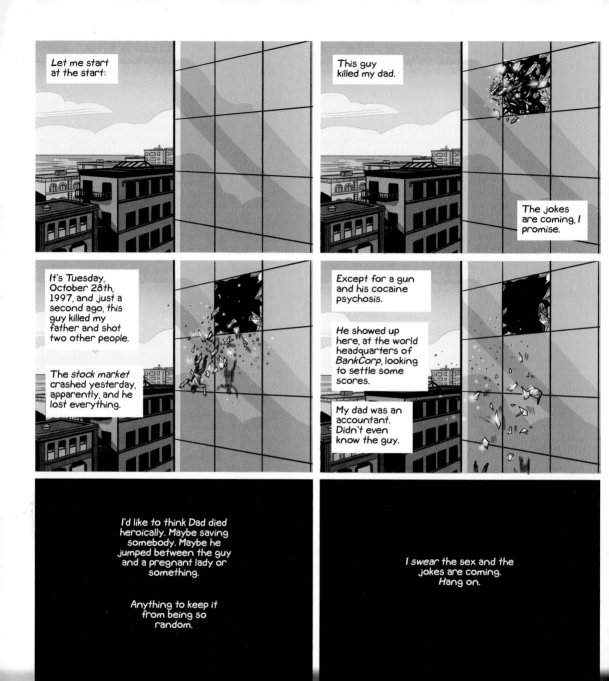

Let me start at the start:

This guy killed my dad.

The jokes are coming, I promise.

It's Tuesday, October 28th, 1997, and just a second ago, this guy killed my father and shot two other people.

The stock market crashed yesterday, apparently, and he lost everything.

Except for a gun and his cocaine psychosis.

He showed up here, at the world headquarters of BankCorp, looking to settle some scores.

My dad was an accountant. Didn't even know the guy.

I'd like to think Dad died heroically. Maybe saving somebody. Maybe he jumped between the guy and a pregnant lady or something.

Anything to keep it from being so random.

I swear the sex and the jokes are coming. Hang on.

There. That's me.

With the hair.

My whole world's about to end.

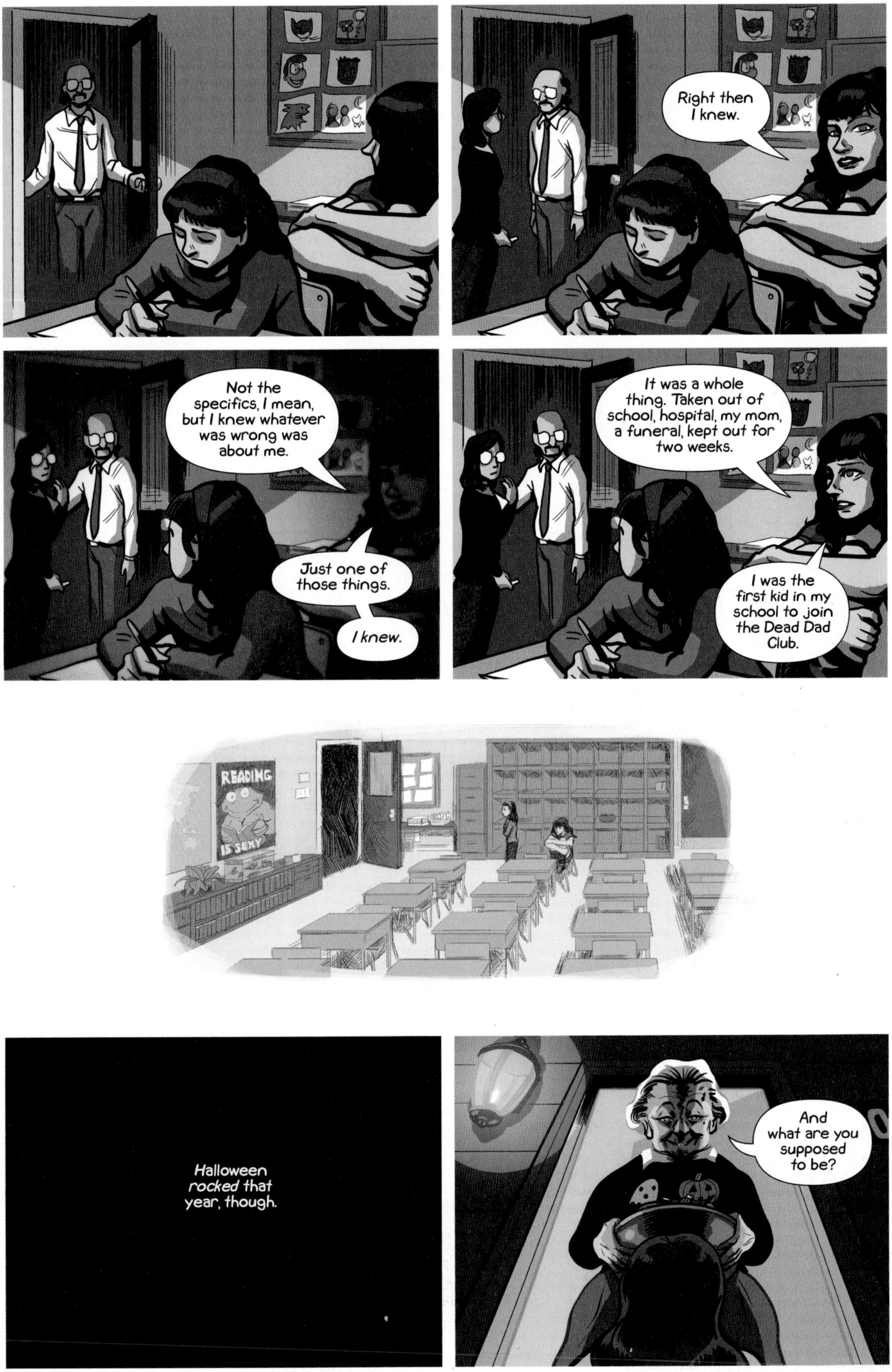
Right then I knew.
Not the specifics, I mean, but I knew whatever was wrong was about me.
Just one of those things.
I knew.
It was a whole thing. Taken out of school, hospital, my mom, a funeral, kept out for two weeks.
I was the first kid in my school to join the Dead Dad Club.
READING IS SEXY
Halloween rocked that year, though.
And what are you supposed to be?

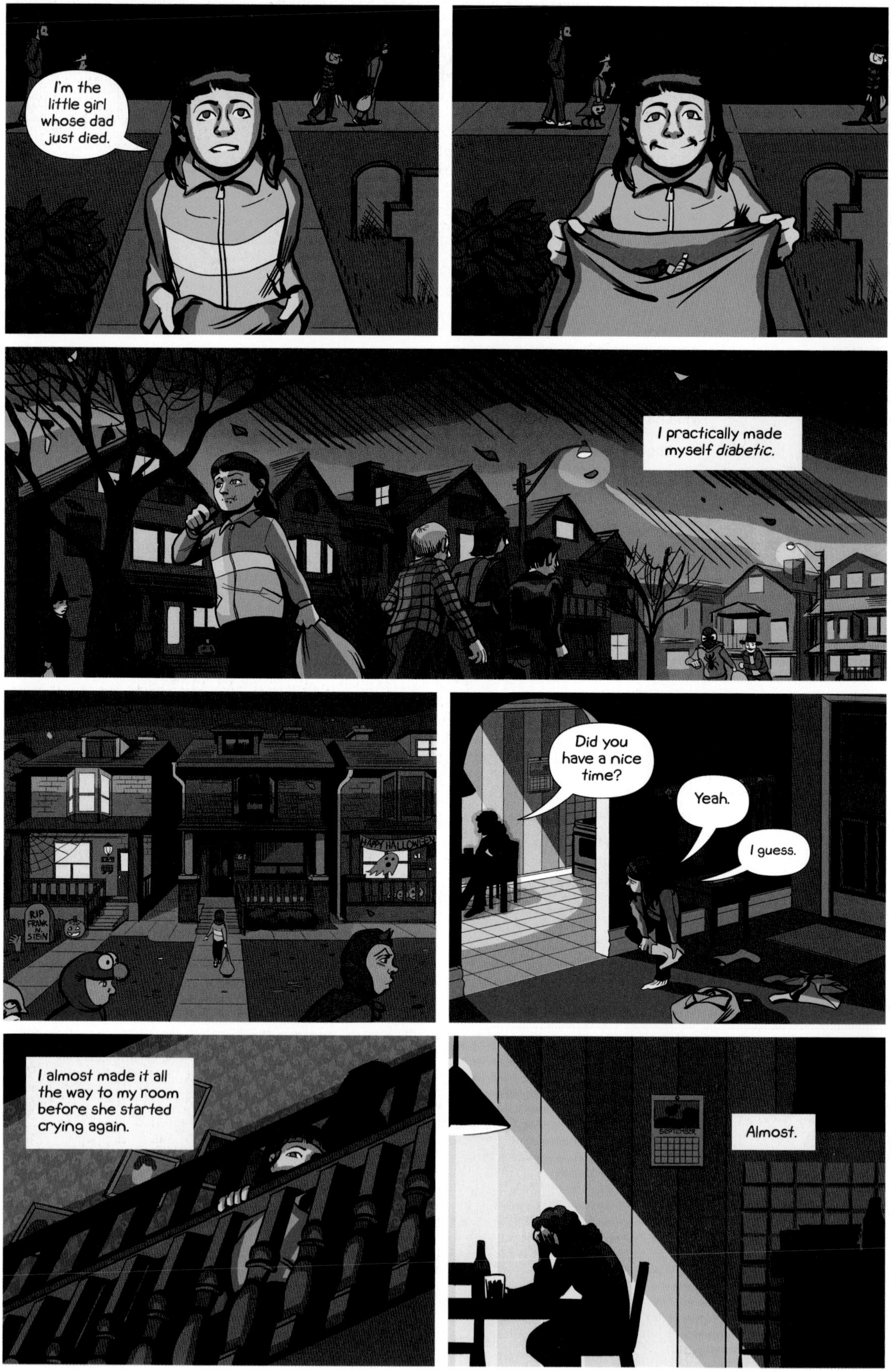
I'm the little girl whose dad just died.
I practically made myself *diabetic.*
RIP FRANK N STEIN
Did you have a nice time?
Yeah.
I guess.
I almost made it all the way to my room before she started crying again.
Almost.

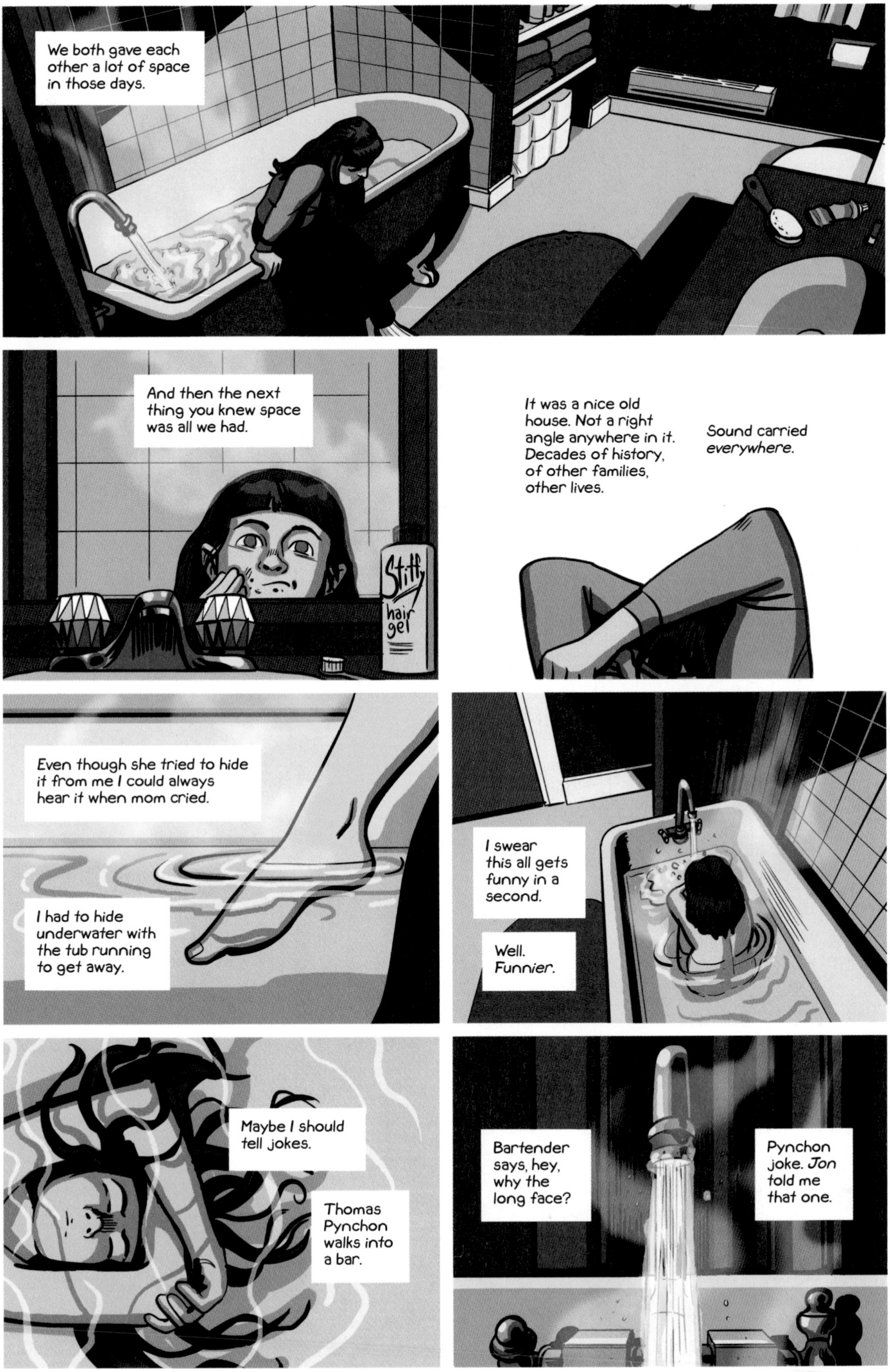
We both gave each other a lot of space in those days.
And then the next thing you knew space was all we had.
Stiffy hair gel
It was a nice old house. Not a right angle anywhere in it. Decades of history, of other families, other lives.
Sound carried *everywhere.*
Even though she tried to hide it from me I could always hear it when mom cried.
I had to hide underwater with the tub running to get away.
I swear this all gets funny in a second.
Well. *Funnier.*
Maybe I should tell jokes.
Thomas Pynchon walks into a bar.
Bartender says, hey, why the long face?
Pynchon joke. *Jon* told me that one.

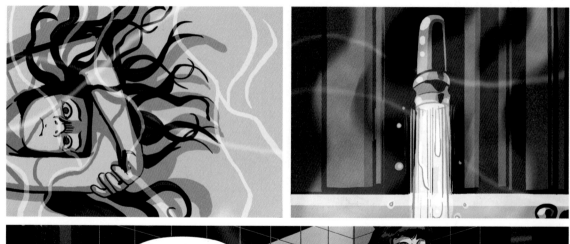

I knew, of course, what was happening when it started to happen. Even though I didn't really know.

You know?

I wasn't the *first* girl in my class and I wasn't the *last*, but I suppose, until then, I thought it was something that only the *Dirty Girls* did.

Time stopped.

Literally.

And I knew —

You know what, scratch that.

I had *no idea* what was happening to me whatsoever.

On so *many* levels.

I even left the water on.

It wasn't going anywhere.

That's how weird it all was.

I was enveloped in *silence* and *color*.

An *ocean* of warm silence and color that I could, apparently, make explode out from inside me.

It felt so amazing that...

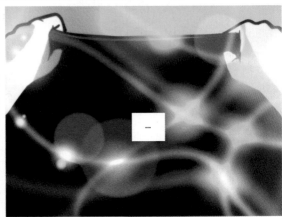

...

...that I was terrified.

I was confused and terrified.

How could anything feel so good?

How could anything make everything get so *quiet*?

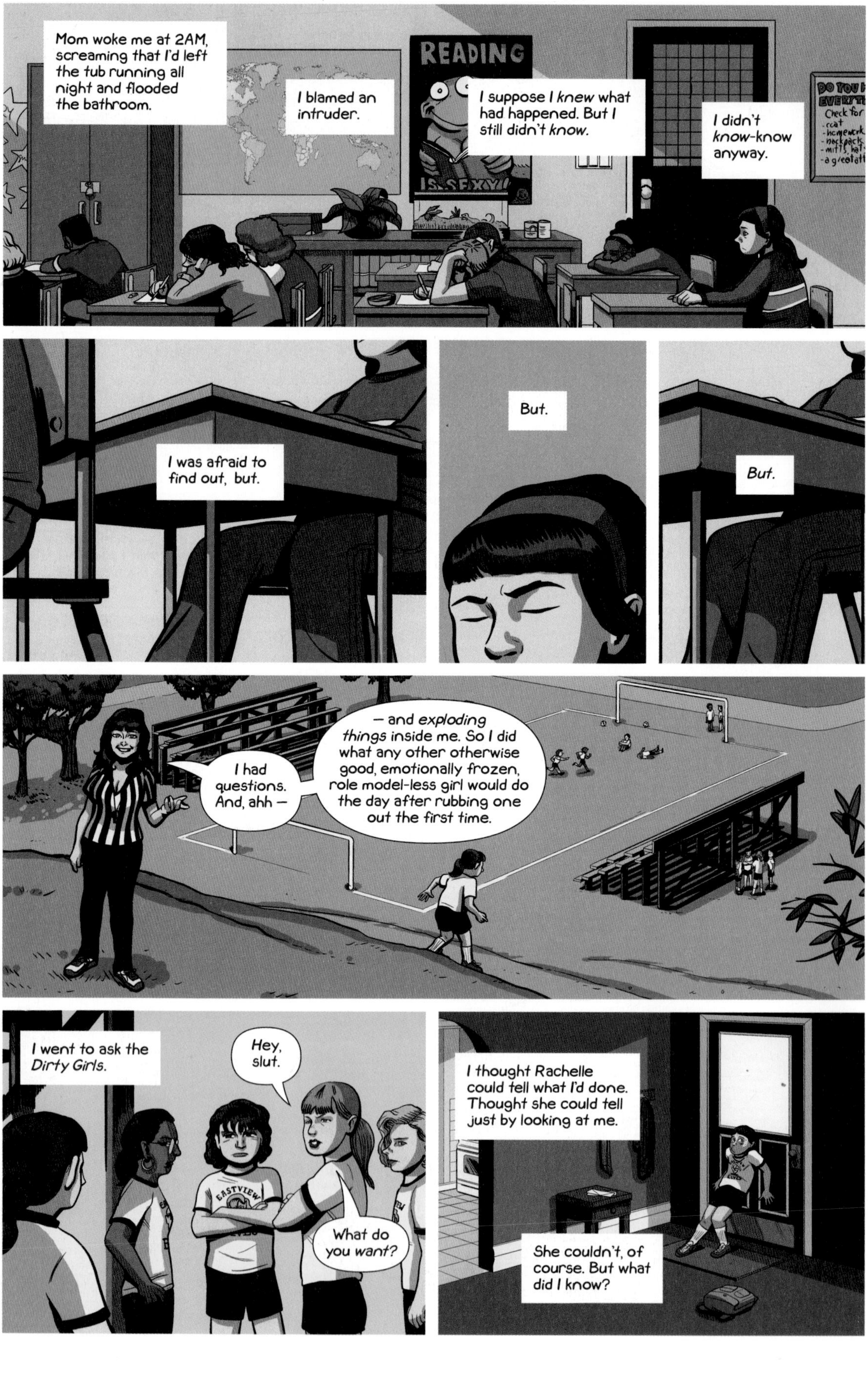

Mom woke me at 2AM, screaming that I'd left the tub running all night and flooded the bathroom.
READING
I blamed an intruder.
I suppose I *knew* what had happened. But I still didn't *know*.
I didn't *know*-know anyway.
I was afraid to find out, but.
But.
But.
I had questions. And, ahh —
— and *exploding things* inside me. So I did what any other otherwise good, emotionally frozen, role model-less girl would do the day after rubbing one out the first time.
I went to ask the *Dirty Girls*.
Hey, slut.
EASTVIEW
What do you *want?*
I thought Rachelle could tell what I'd done. Thought she could tell just by looking at me.
She couldn't, of course. But what did I know?

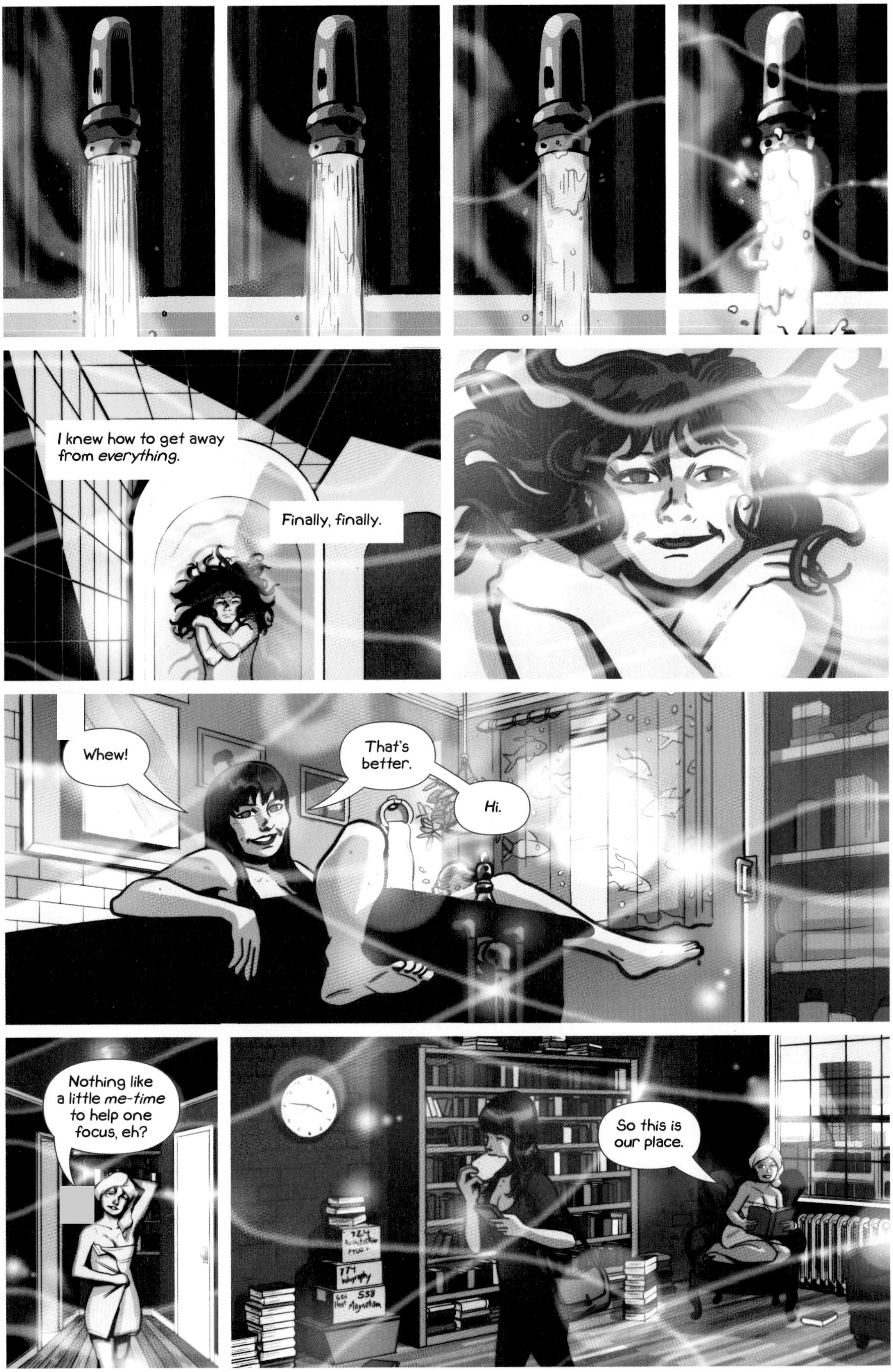
I knew how to get away from *everything.*
Finally, finally.
Whew!
That's better.
Hi.
Nothing like a little *me-time* to help one focus, eh?
So this is our place.

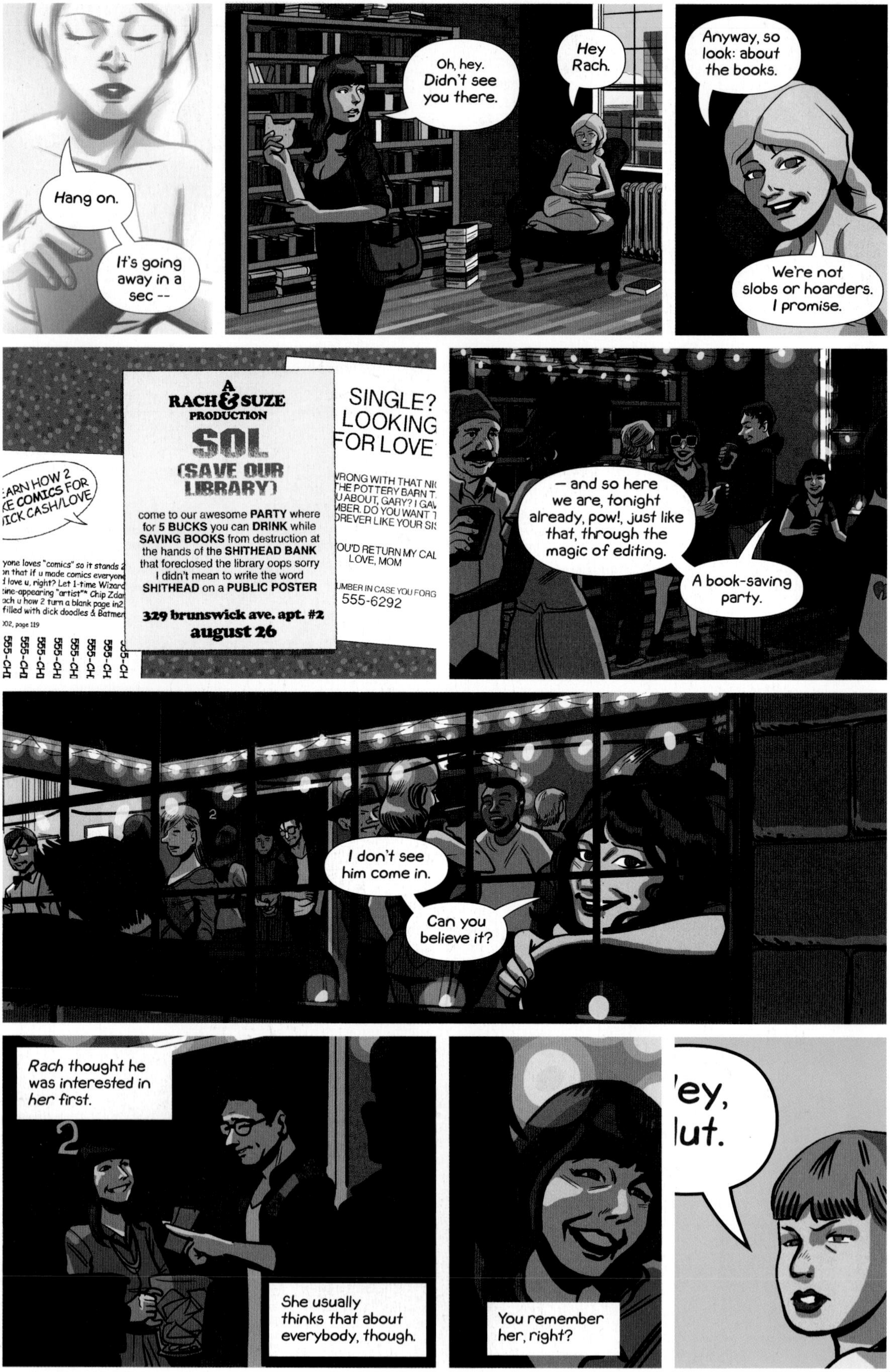
Hang on.
It's going away in a sec --
Oh, hey. Didn't see you there.
Hey Rach.
Anyway, so look: about the books.
We're not slobs or hoarders. I promise.
A RACH & SUZE PRODUCTION
SOL (SAVE OUR LIBRARY)
come to our awesome PARTY where for 5 BUCKS you can DRINK while SAVING BOOKS from destruction at the hands of the SHITHEAD BANK that foreclosed the library oops sorry I didn't mean to write the word SHITHEAD on a PUBLIC POSTER
329 brunswick ave. apt. #2
august 26
SINGLE? LOOKING FOR LOVE
555-6292
— and so here we are, tonight already, pow!, just like that, through the magic of editing.
A book-saving party.
I don't see him come in.
Can you believe it?
Rach thought he was interested in her first.
She usually thinks that about everybody, though.
You remember her, right?

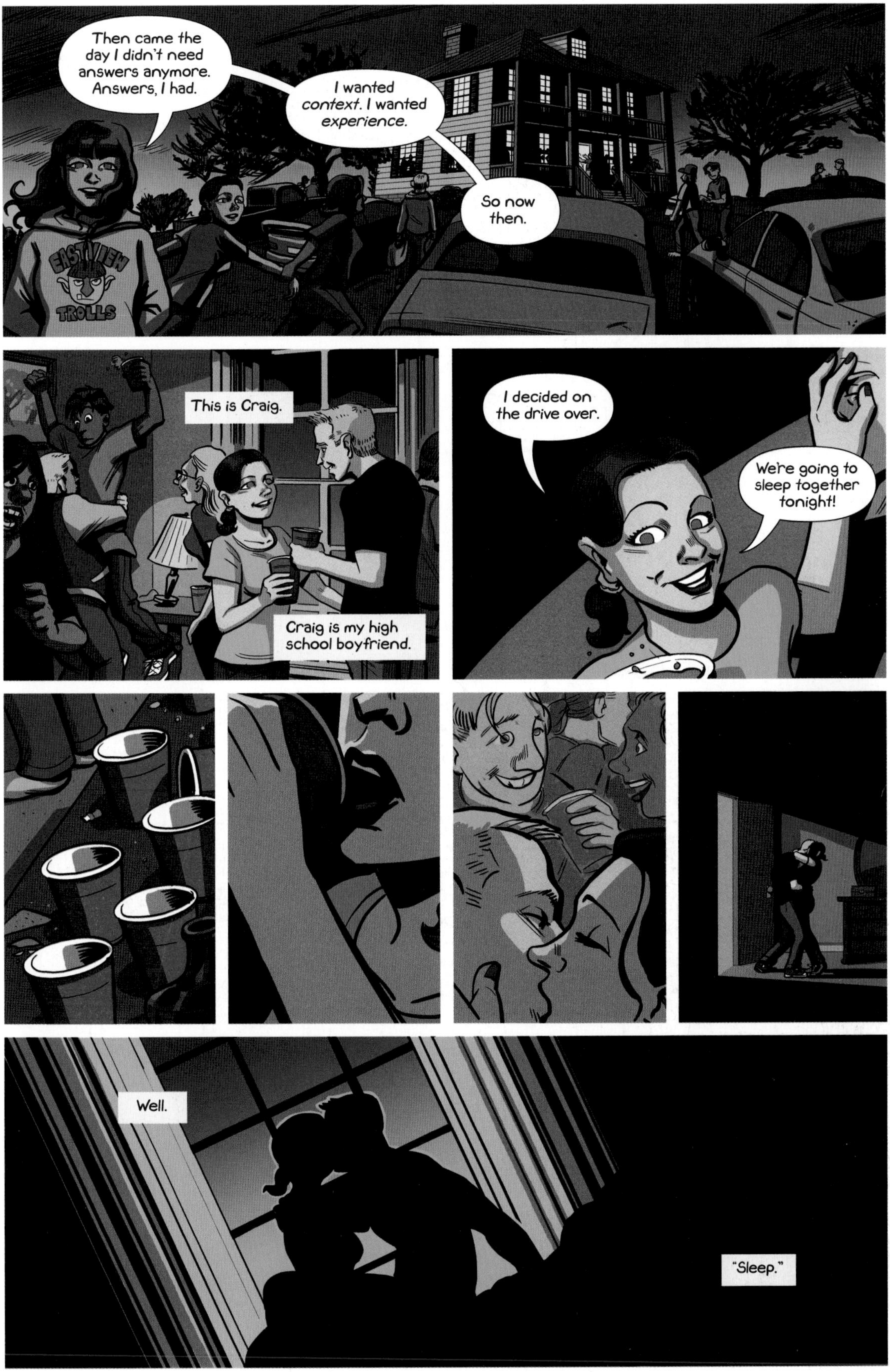
Then came the day I didn't need answers anymore. Answers, I had.
I wanted *context*. I wanted *experience*.
So now then.
This is Craig.
Craig is my high school boyfriend.
I decided on the drive over.
We're going to sleep together tonight!
EASTVIEW TROLLS
Well.
"Sleep."

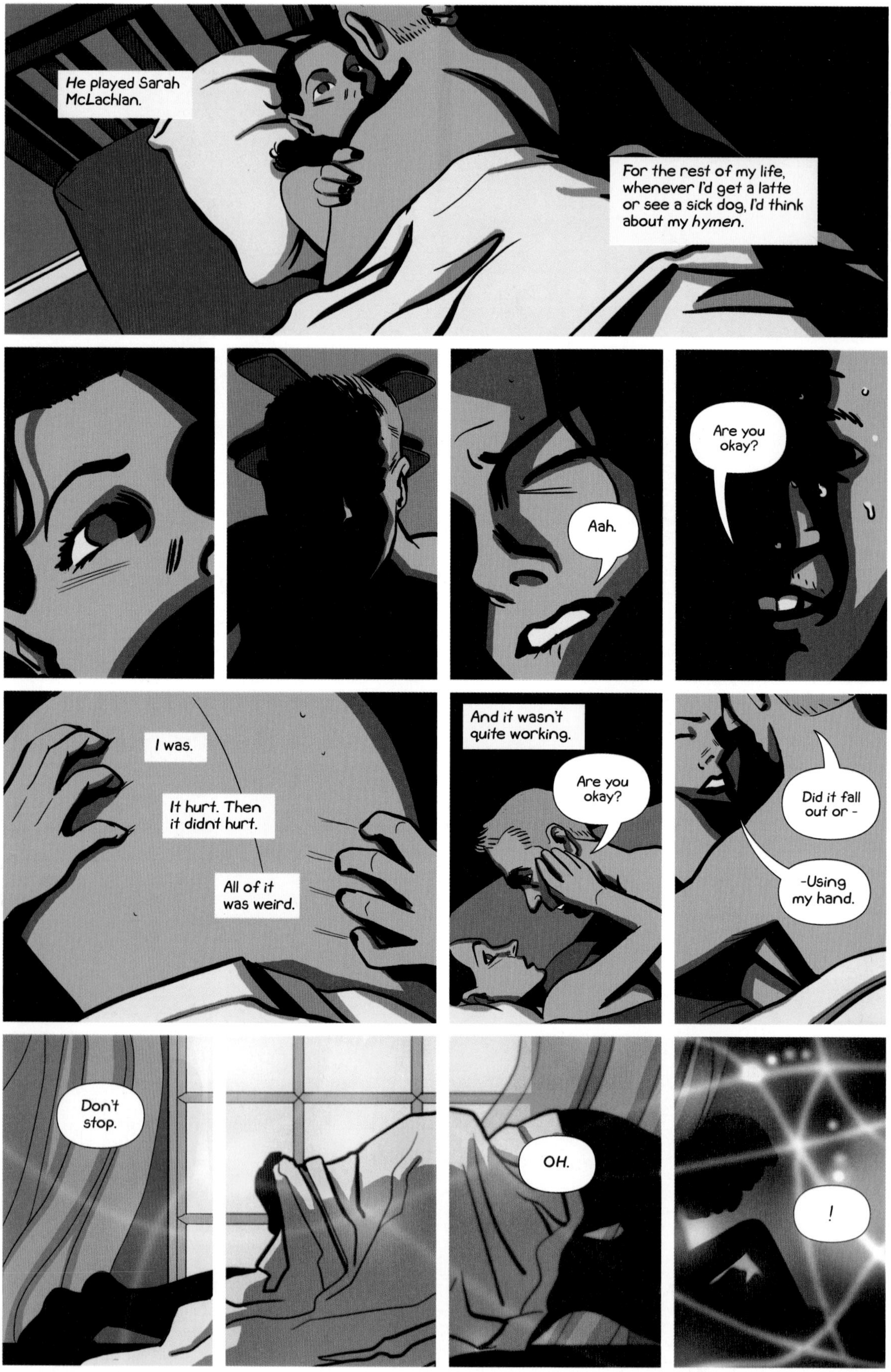
He played Sarah McLachlan.
For the rest of my life, whenever I'd get a latte or see a sick dog, I'd think about my *hymen*.
Aah.
Are you okay?
I was.
It hurt. Then it didnt hurt.
All of it was weird.
And it wasn't quite working.
Are you okay?
Did it fall out or -
-Using my hand.
Don't stop.
OH.
!

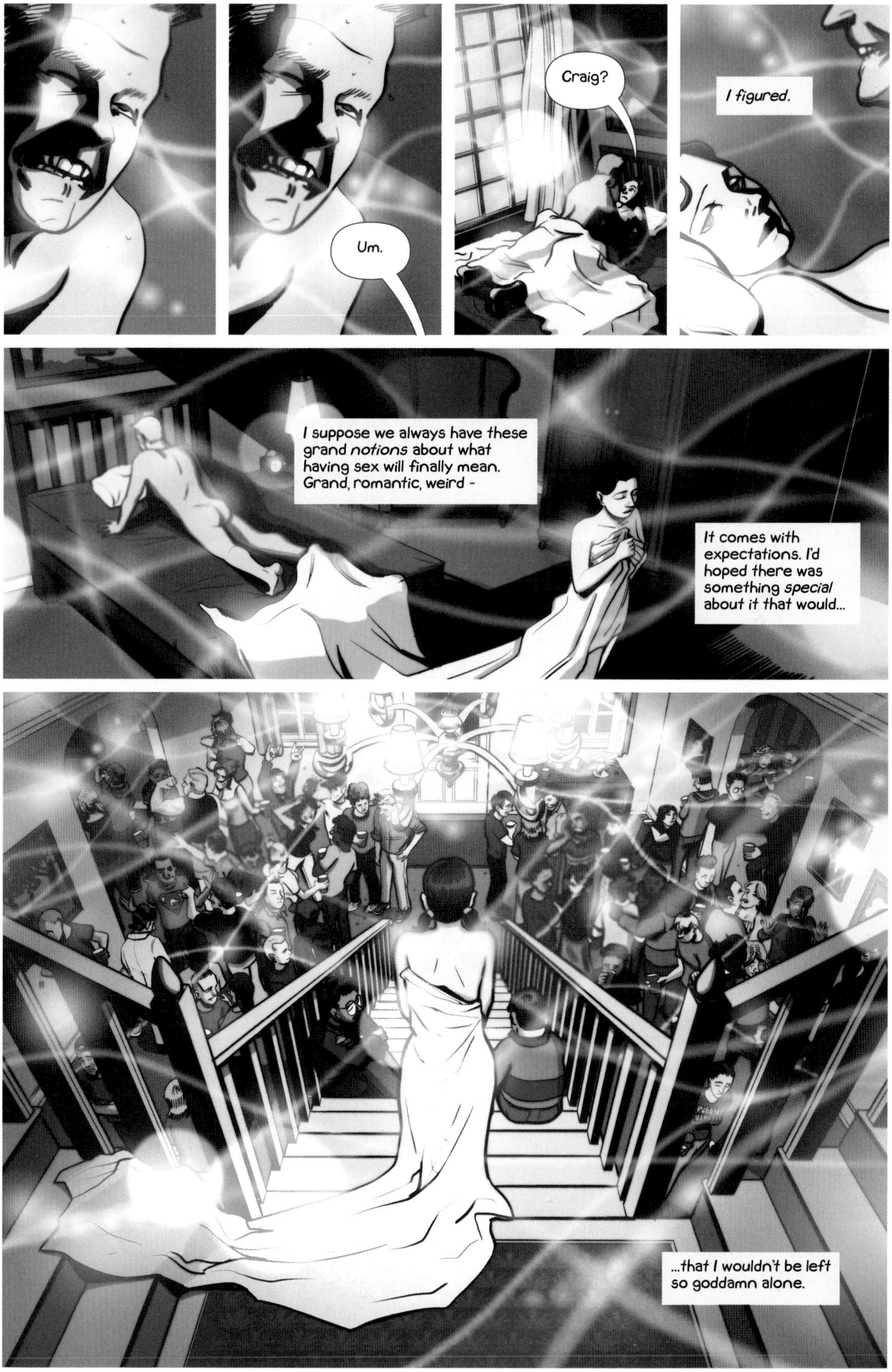
Um.
Craig?
I figured.
I suppose we always have these grand notions about what having sex will finally mean. Grand, romantic, weird -
It comes with expectations. I'd hoped there was something special about it that would...
...that I wouldn't be left so goddamn alone.

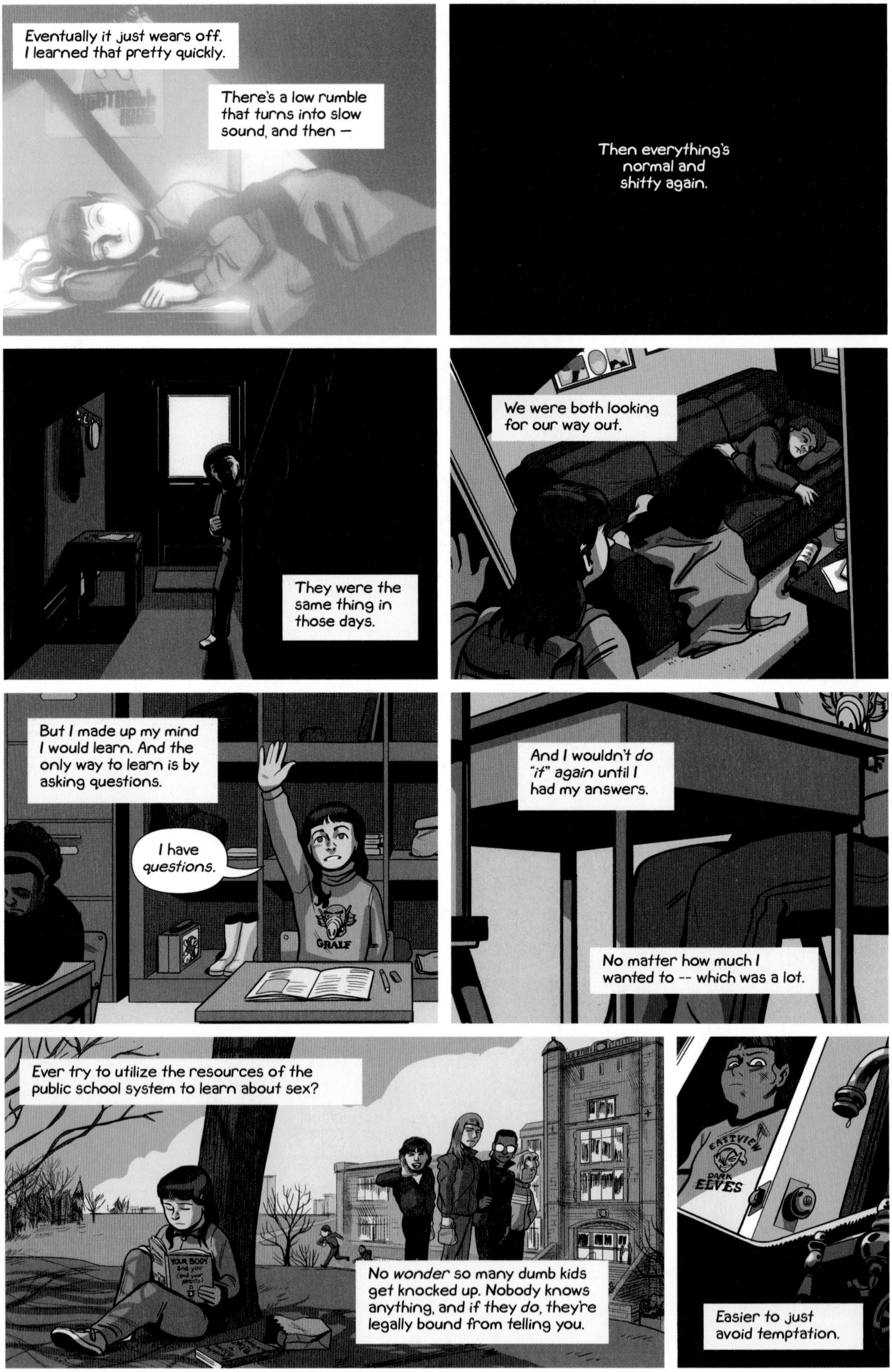

Eventually it just wears off. I learned that pretty quickly.
There's a low rumble that turns into slow sound, and then —
Then everything's normal and shitty again.
They were the same thing in those days.
We were both looking for our way out.
But I made up my mind I would learn. And the only way to learn is by asking questions.
I have *questions*.
GRALF
And I wouldn't *do* *"it"* again until I had my answers.
No matter how much I wanted to -- which was a lot.
Ever try to utilize the resources of the public school system to learn about sex?
YOUR BODY and you (and your parents)
No *wonder* so many dumb kids get knocked up. Nobody knows anything, and if they *do*, they're legally bound from telling you.
EASTVIEW DARK ELVES
Easier to just avoid temptation.

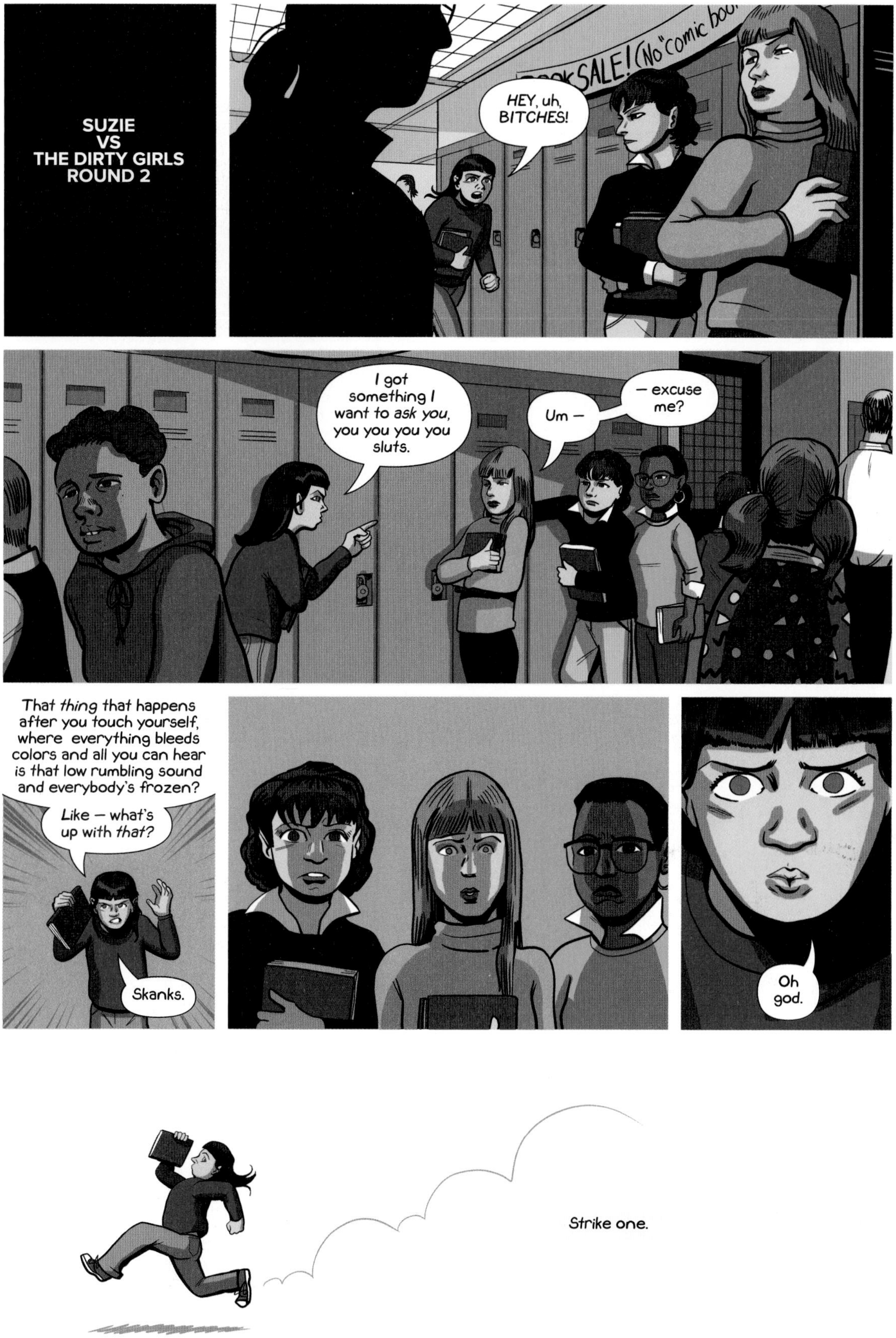
SUZIE VS THE DIRTY GIRLS ROUND 2
HEY, uh, BITCHES!
I got something I want to *ask you*, you you you you sluts.
Um —
— excuse me?
That *thing* that happens after you touch yourself, where everything bleeds colors and all you can hear is that low rumbling sound and everybody's frozen?
Like — what's up with *that?*
Skanks.
Oh god.
Strike one.

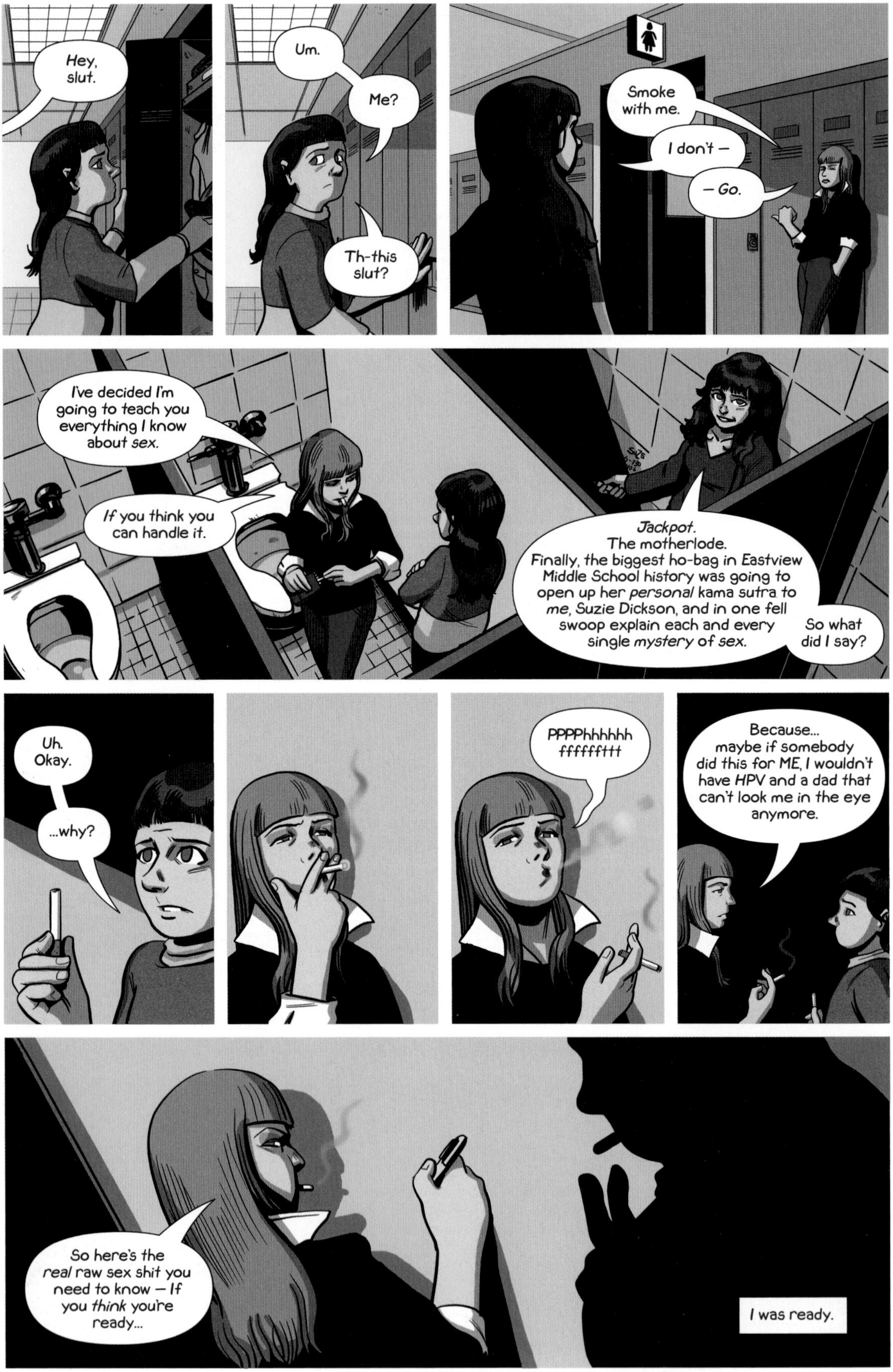
Hey, slut.
Um.
Me?
Th-this slut?
Smoke with me.
I don't –
– Go.
I've decided I'm going to teach you everything I know about *sex.*
If you think you can handle it.
Jackpot. The motherlode. Finally, the biggest ho-bag in Eastview Middle School history was going to open up her *personal* kama sutra to *me,* Suzie Dickson, and in one fell swoop explain each and every single *mystery* of *sex.*
So what did I say?
Uh. Okay.
...why?
PPPPhhhhhh ffffffttt
Because... maybe if somebody did this for *ME,* I wouldn't have *HPV* and a dad that can't look me in the eye anymore.
So here's the *real* raw sex shit you need to know – *If* you *think* you're ready...
I was ready.

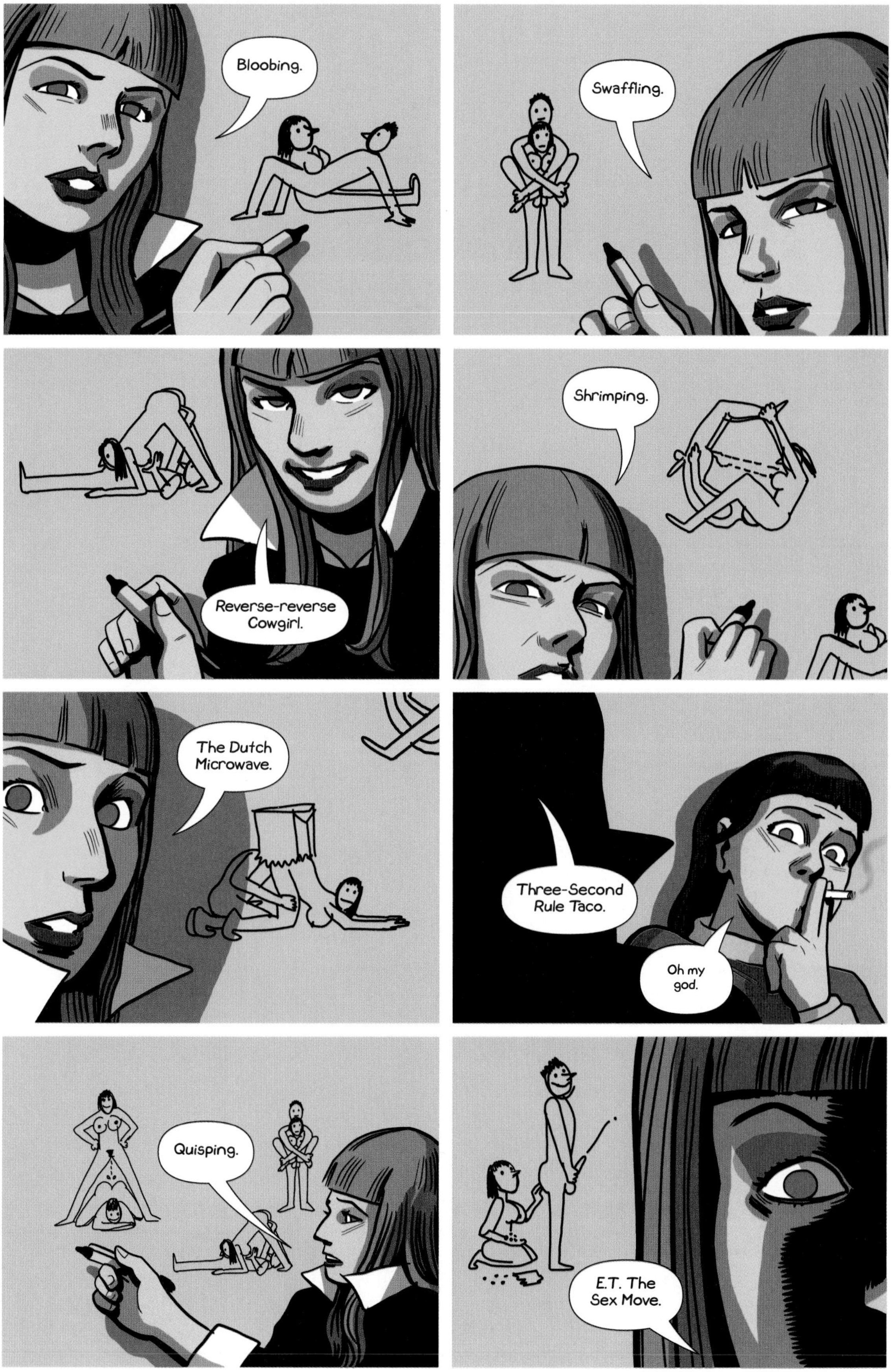
Bloobing.
Swaffling.
Reverse-reverse Cowgirl.
Shrimping.
The Dutch Microwave.
Three-Second Rule Taco.
Oh my god.
Quisping.
E.T. The Sex Move.

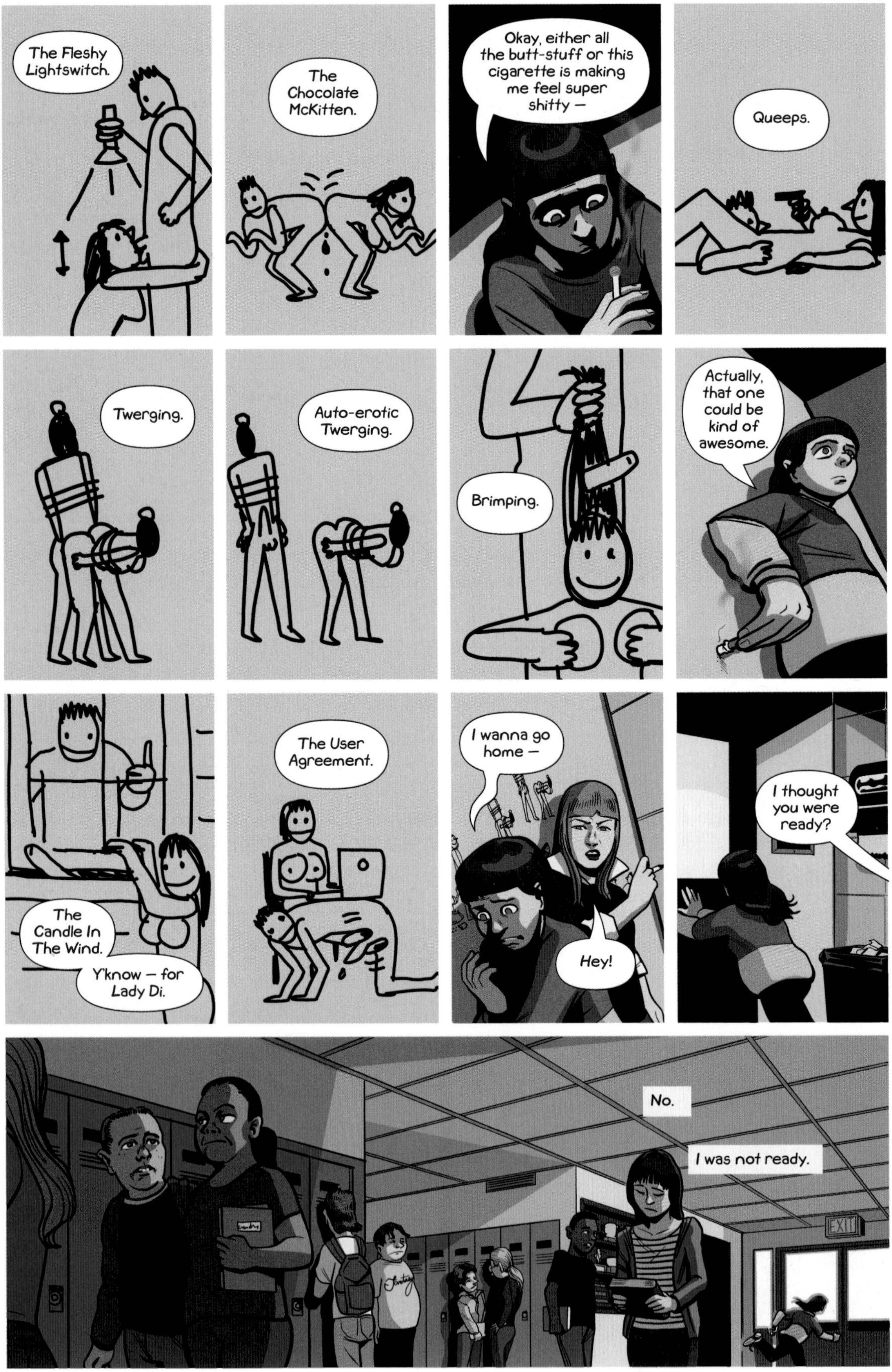
The Fleshy Lightswitch.
The Chocolate McKitten.
Okay, either all the butt-stuff or this cigarette is making me feel super shitty —
Queeps.
Twerging.
Auto-erotic Twerging.
Brimping.
Actually, that one could be kind of awesome.
The Candle In The Wind.
Y'know — for Lady Di.
The User Agreement.
I wanna go home —
Hey!
I thought you were ready?
No.
I was not ready.

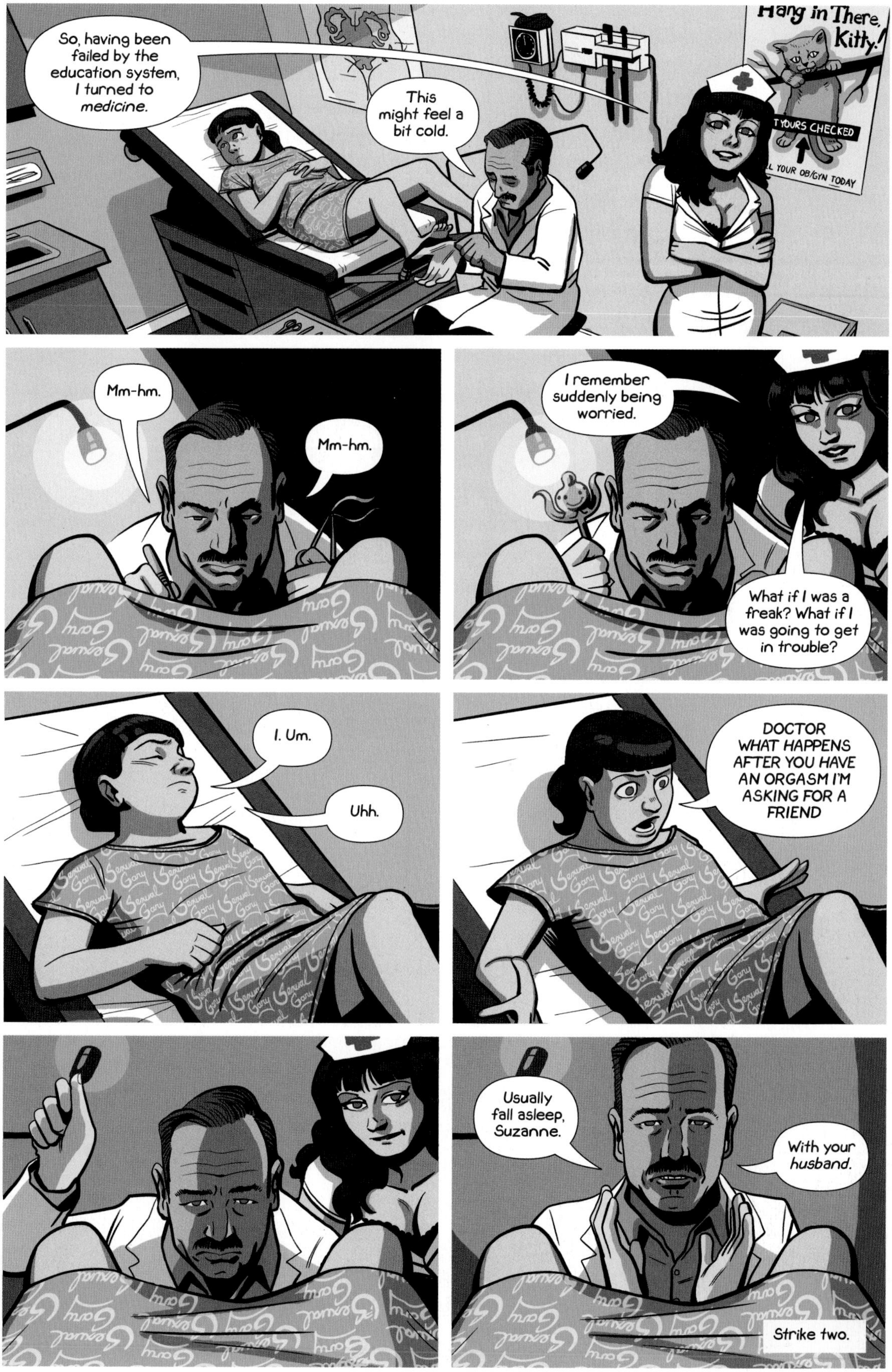
So, having been failed by the education system, I turned to *medicine*.
This might feel a bit cold.
Hang in There, Kitty!
T YOURS CHECKED
LL YOUR OB/GYN TODAY
Mm-hm.
Mm-hm.
I remember suddenly being worried.
What if I was a freak? What if I was going to get in trouble?
I. Um.
Uhh.
DOCTOR WHAT HAPPENS AFTER YOU HAVE AN ORGASM I'M ASKING FOR A FRIEND
Usually fall asleep, Suzanne.
With your *husband*.
Strike two.

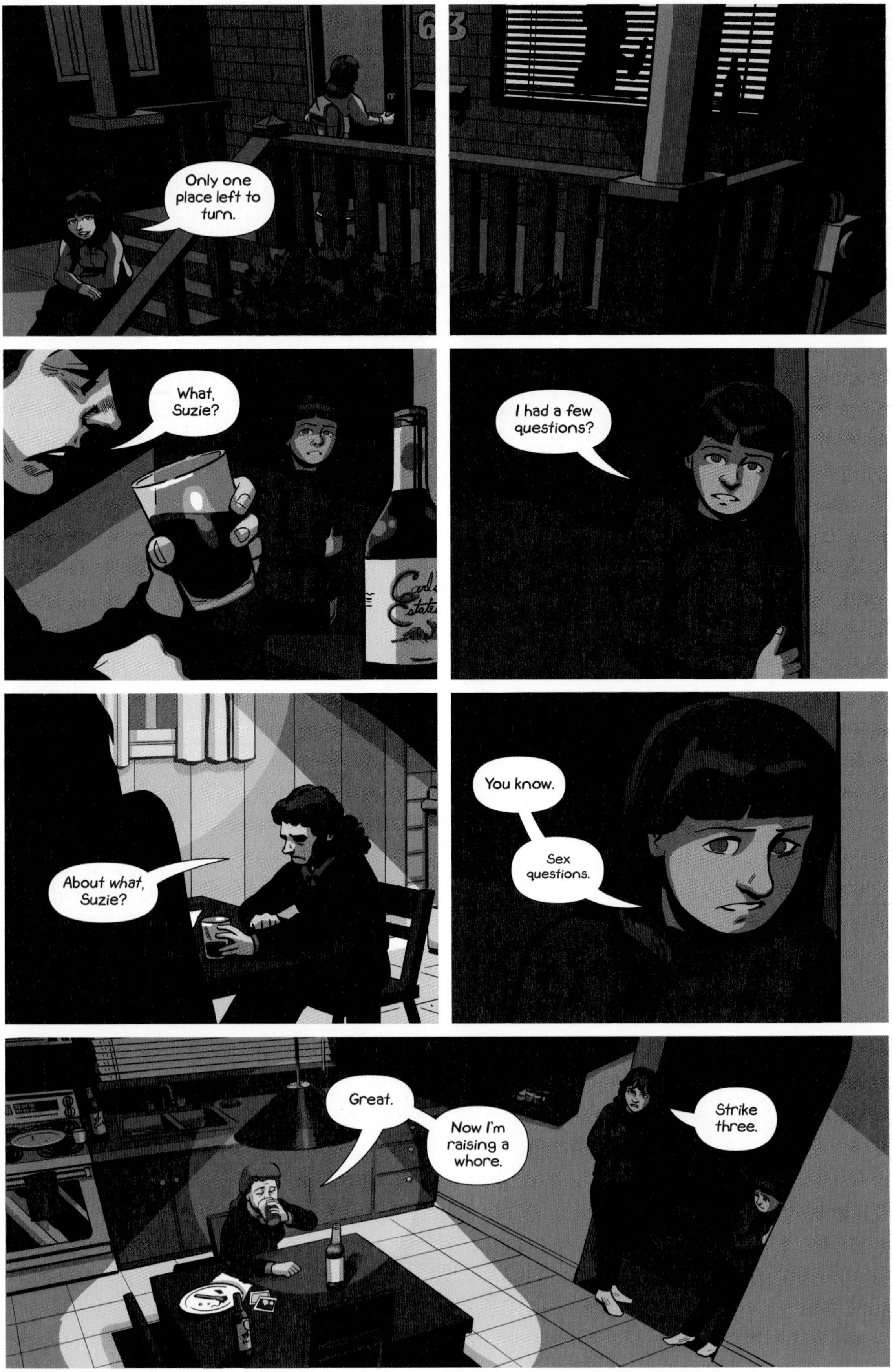
63
Only one place left to turn.
What, Suzie?
Carl's Estates
I had a few questions?
About what, Suzie?
You know.
Sex questions.
Great.
Now I'm raising a whore.
Strike three.

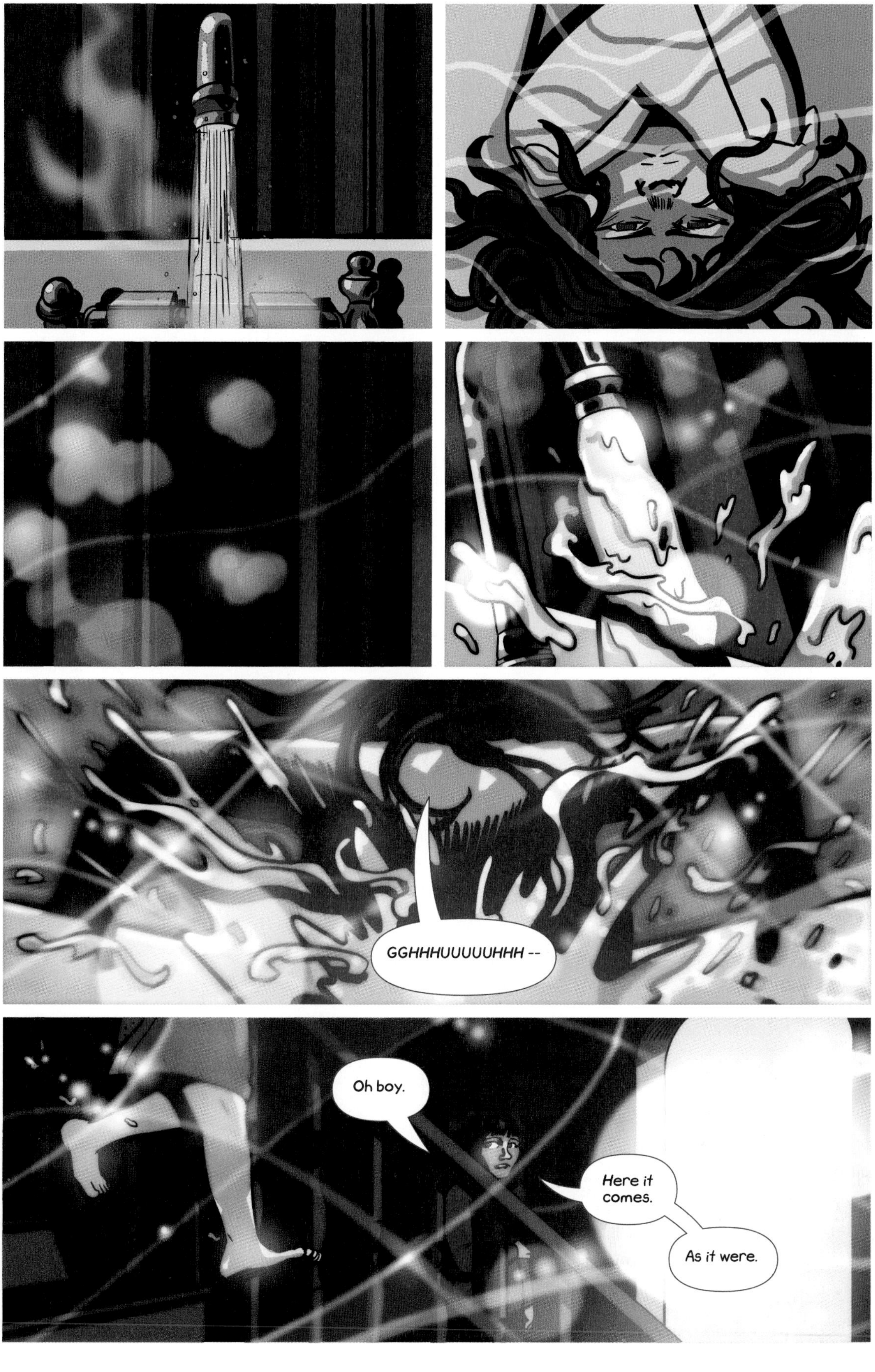
GGHHHUUUUUHHH --
Oh boy.
Here it comes.
As it were.

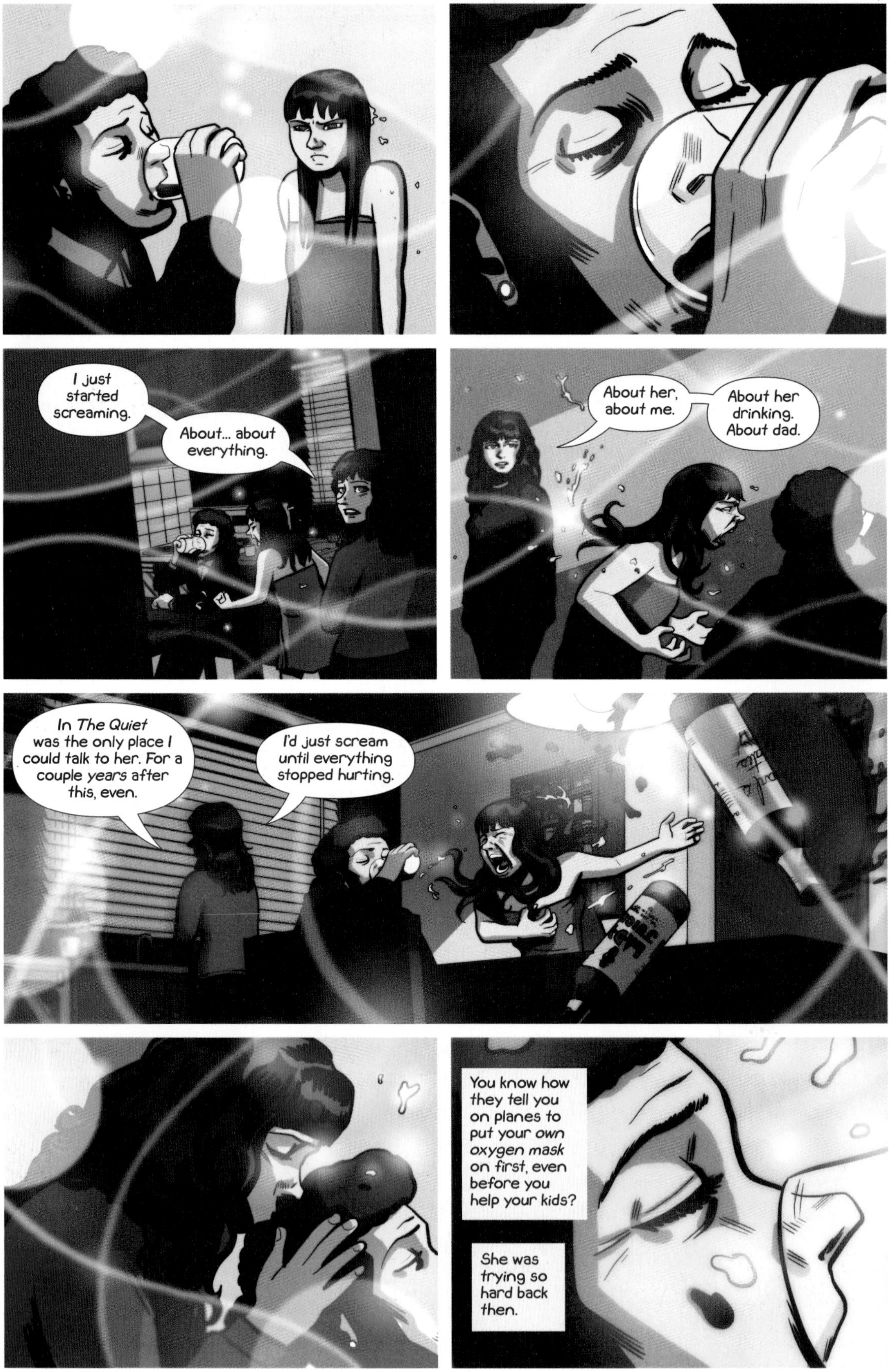

I just started screaming.
About... about everything.
About her, about me.
About her drinking. About dad.
In *The Quiet* was the only place I could talk to her. For a couple *years* after this, even.
I'd just scream until everything stopped hurting.
You know how they tell you on planes to put your *own oxygen mask* on *first*, even before you help your kids?
She was trying so hard back then.

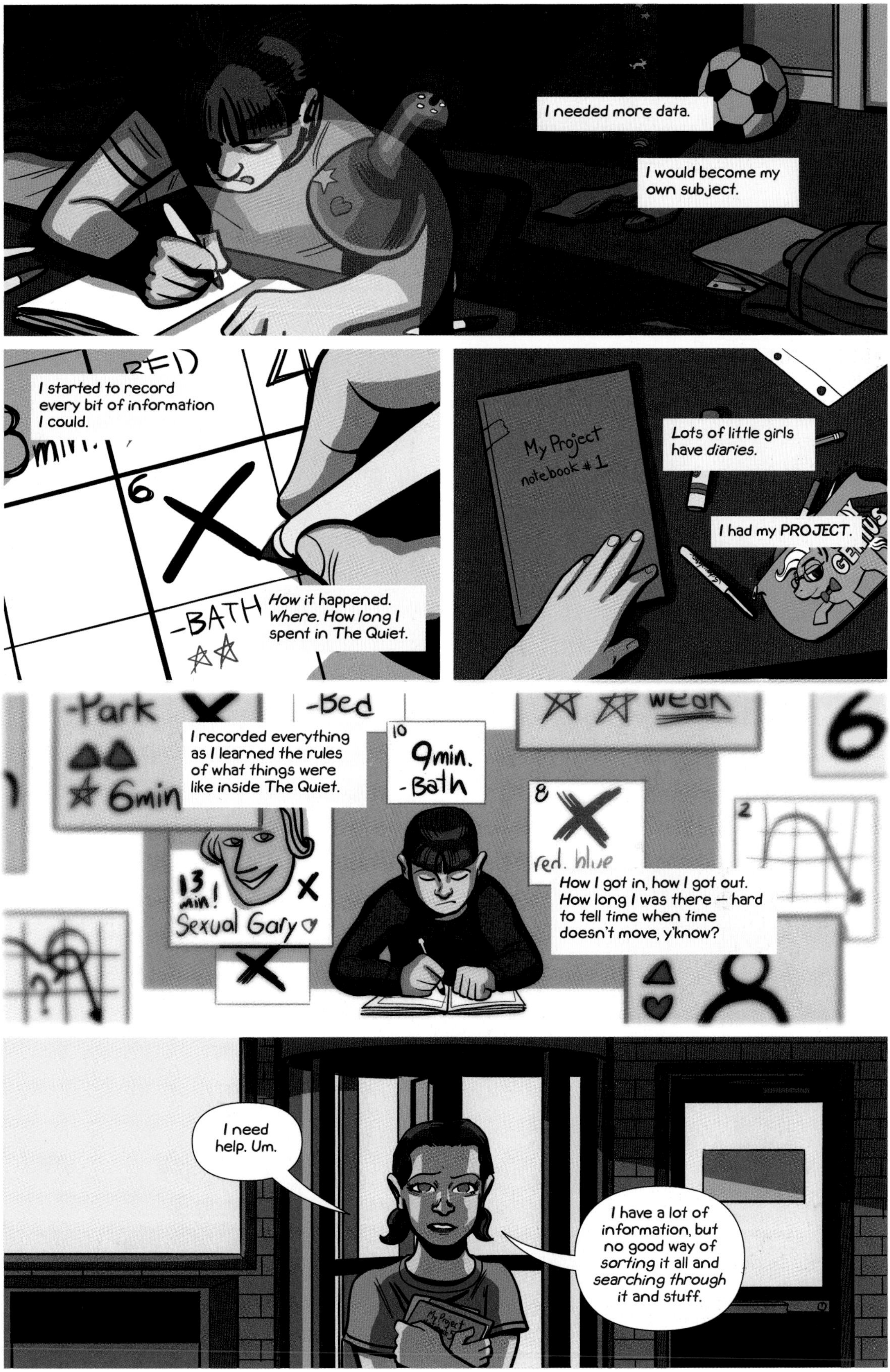

I needed more data.
I would become my own subject.
I started to record every bit of information I could.
How it happened. Where. How long I spent in The Quiet.
My Project notebook #1
Lots of little girls have *diaries*.
I had my PROJECT.
I recorded everything as I learned the rules of what things were like inside The Quiet.
-Park
-Bed
6min
10
9min.
-Bath
8
red. blue
13 min!
Sexual Gary
How I got in, how I got out. How long I was there — hard to tell time when time doesn't move, y'know?
I need help. Um.
I have a lot of information, but no good way of *sorting* it all and *searching through* it and stuff.

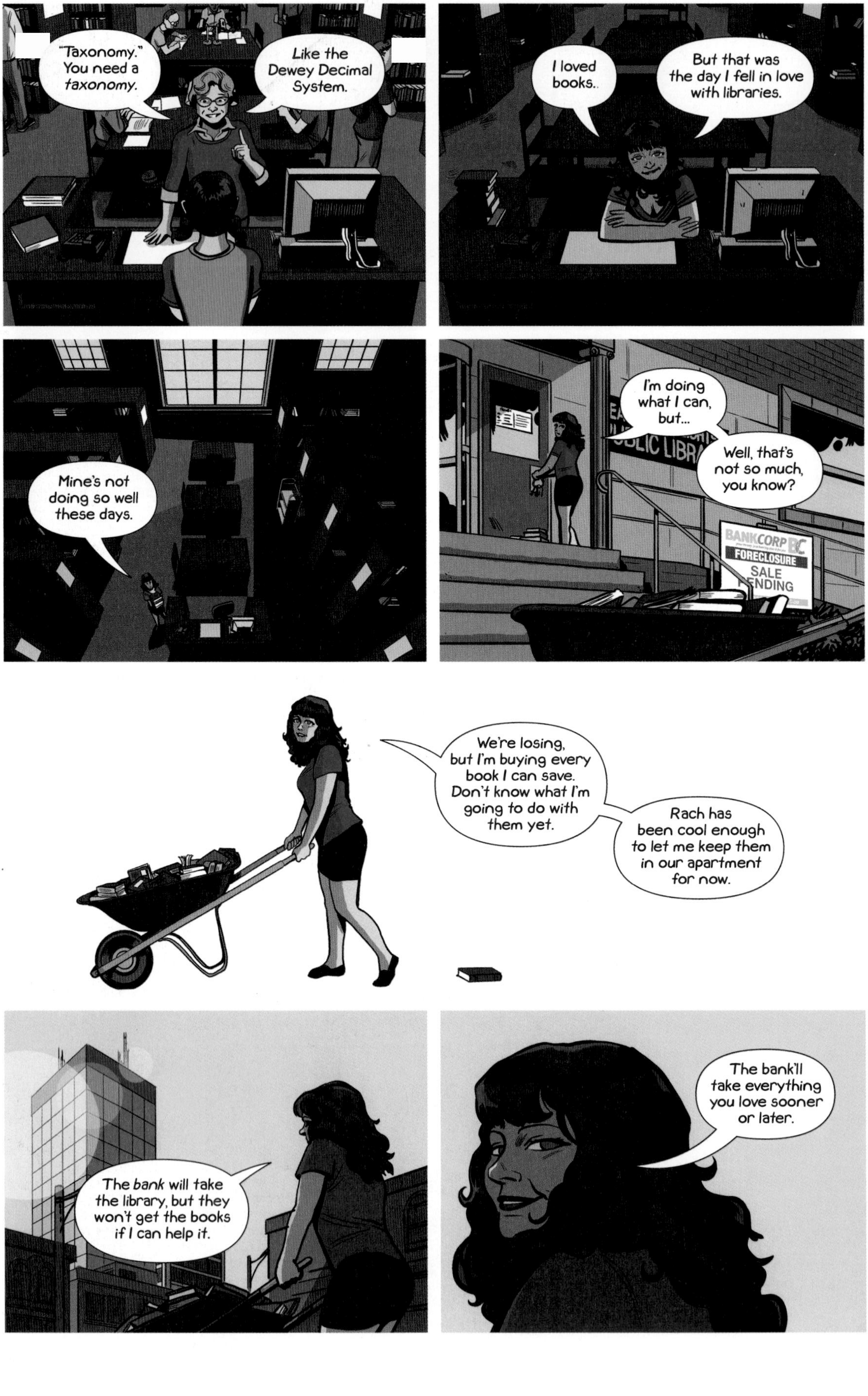
"Taxonomy." You need a *taxonomy.*
Like the Dewey Decimal System.
I loved books..
But that was the day I fell in love with libraries.
Mine's not doing so well these days.
I'm doing what I can, but...
Well, that's not so much, you know?
BANKCORP
FORECLOSURE
SALE
We're losing, but I'm buying every book I can save. Don't know what I'm going to do with them yet.
Rach has been cool enough to let me keep them in our apartment for now.
The *bank* will take the library, but they won't get the books if I can help it.
The bank'll take everything you love sooner or later.

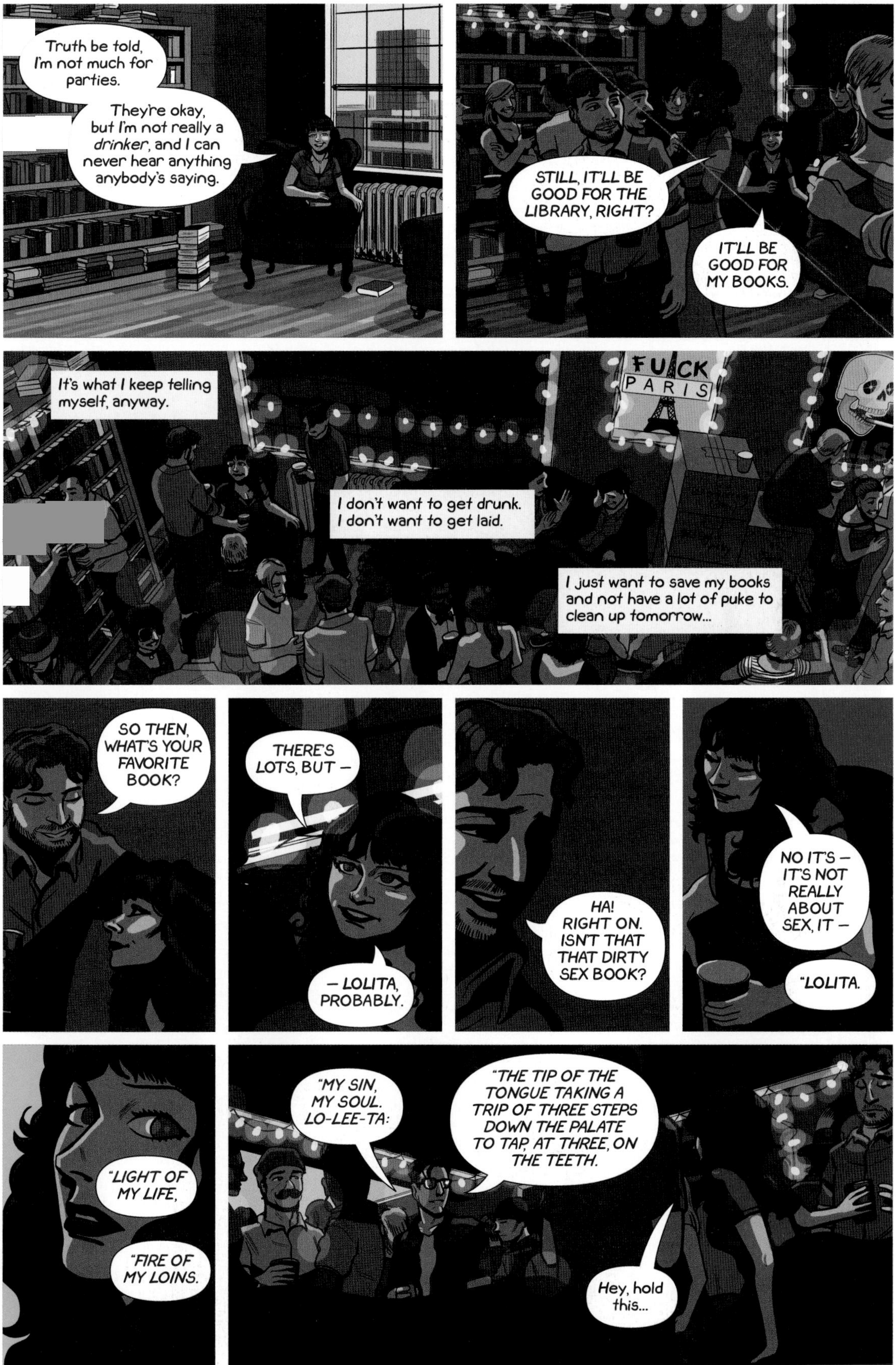

Truth be told, I'm not much for parties.
They're okay, but I'm not really a *drinker*, and I can never hear anything anybody's saying.
STILL, IT'LL BE GOOD FOR THE LIBRARY, RIGHT?
IT'LL BE GOOD FOR MY BOOKS.
It's what I keep telling myself, anyway.
FU CK
PARIS
I don't want to get drunk. I don't want to get laid.
I just want to save my books and not have a lot of puke to clean up tomorrow...
SO THEN, WHAT'S YOUR FAVORITE BOOK?
THERE'S LOTS, BUT —
— LOLITA, PROBABLY.
HA! RIGHT ON. ISN'T THAT THAT DIRTY SEX BOOK?
NO IT'S — IT'S NOT REALLY ABOUT SEX, IT —
"LOLITA.
"LIGHT OF MY LIFE,
"FIRE OF MY LOINS.
"MY SIN, MY SOUL. LO-LEE-TA:
"THE TIP OF THE TONGUE TAKING A TRIP OF THREE STEPS DOWN THE PALATE TO TAP, AT THREE, ON THE TEETH.
Hey, hold this...

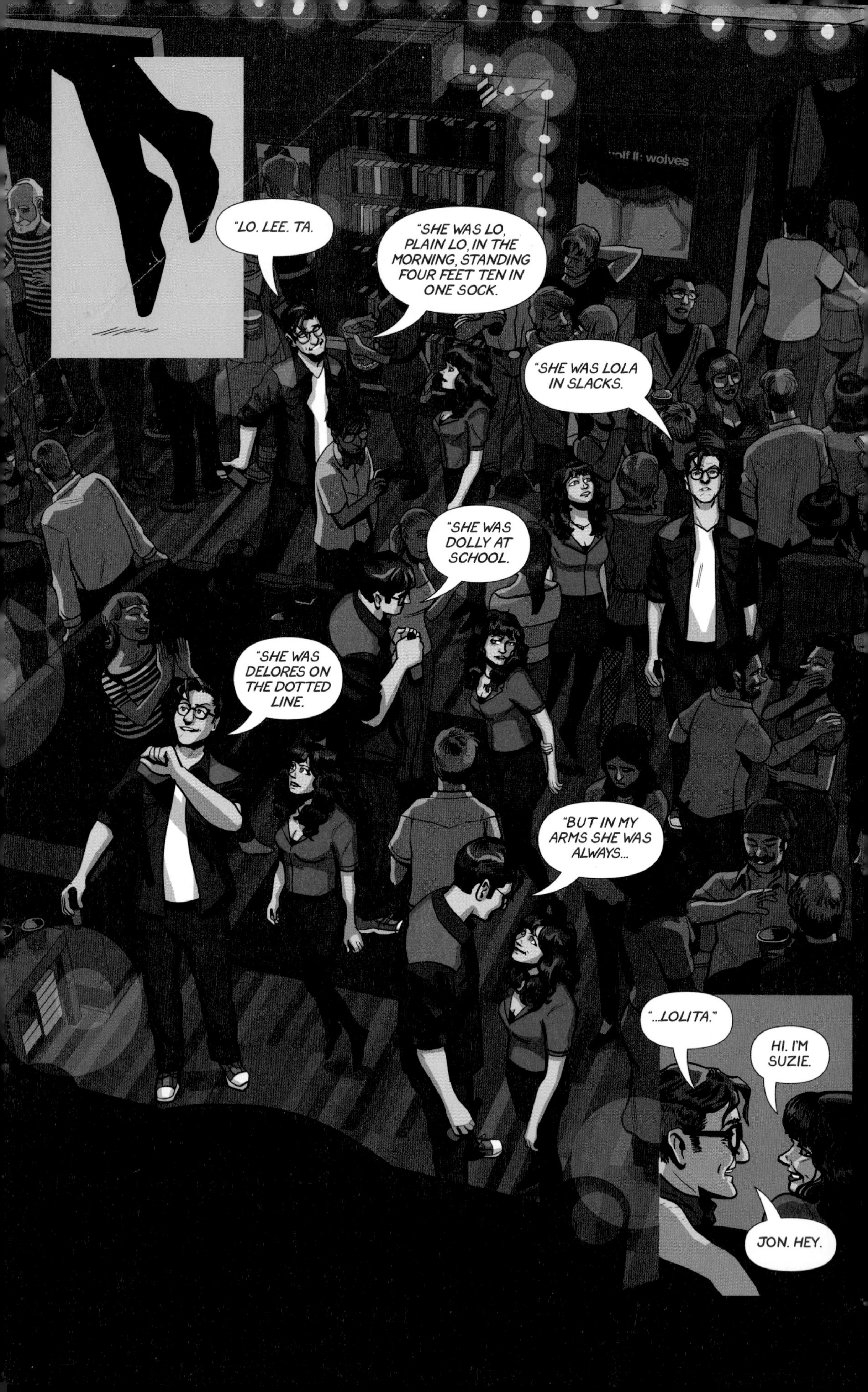
"LO. LEE. TA.
"SHE WAS LO, PLAIN LO, IN THE MORNING, STANDING FOUR FEET TEN IN ONE SOCK.
"SHE WAS LOLA IN SLACKS.
"SHE WAS DOLLY AT SCHOOL.
"SHE WAS DELORES ON THE DOTTED LINE.
"BUT IN MY ARMS SHE WAS ALWAYS...
"...LOLITA."
HI. I'M SUZIE.
JON. HEY.

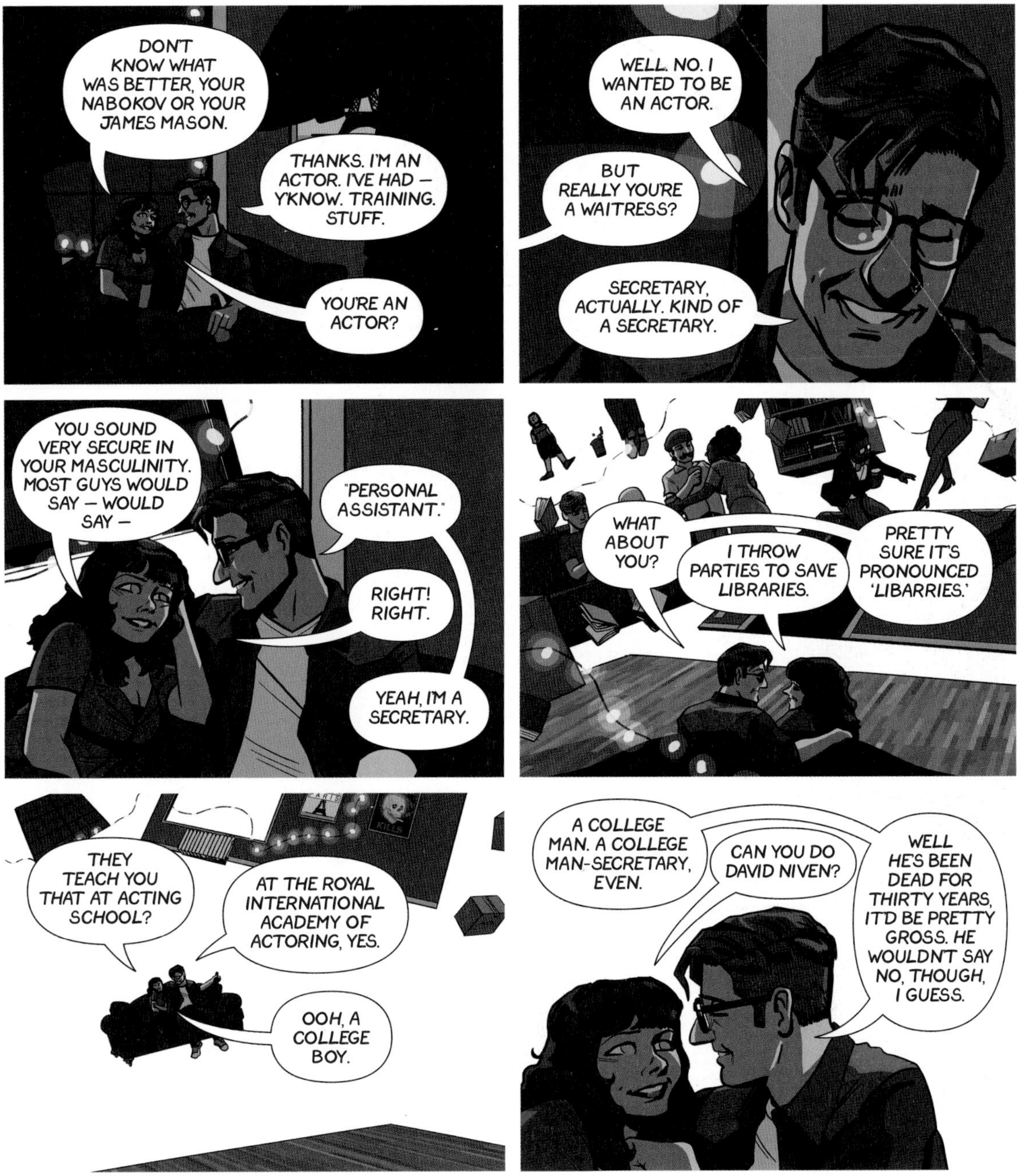

DON'T KNOW WHAT WAS BETTER, YOUR NABOKOV OR YOUR JAMES MASON.
THANKS. I'M AN ACTOR. I'VE HAD — Y'KNOW. TRAINING. STUFF.
YOU'RE AN ACTOR?
WELL. NO. I WANTED TO BE AN ACTOR.
BUT REALLY YOU'RE A WAITRESS?
SECRETARY, ACTUALLY. KIND OF A SECRETARY.
YOU SOUND VERY SECURE IN YOUR MASCULINITY. MOST GUYS WOULD SAY — WOULD SAY —
"PERSONAL ASSISTANT."
RIGHT! RIGHT.
YEAH, I'M A SECRETARY.
WHAT ABOUT YOU?
I THROW PARTIES TO SAVE LIBRARIES.
PRETTY SURE IT'S PRONOUNCED 'LIBARRIES.'
THEY TEACH YOU THAT AT ACTING SCHOOL?
AT THE ROYAL INTERNATIONAL ACADEMY OF ACTORING, YES.
OOH, A COLLEGE BOY.
A COLLEGE MAN. A COLLEGE MAN-SECRETARY, EVEN.
CAN YOU DO DAVID NIVEN?
WELL HE'S BEEN DEAD FOR THIRTY YEARS, IT'D BE PRETTY GROSS. HE WOULDN'T SAY NO, THOUGH, I GUESS.

Because of this.

Because you're funny.

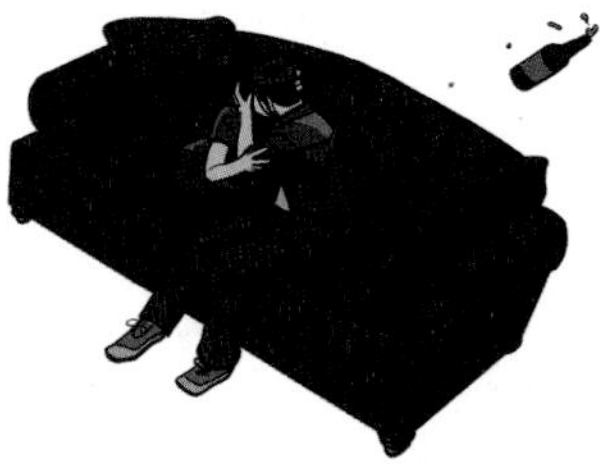

Because you know *Lolita.*

And Nabokov and James Mason too.

Because you're cute and funny and I'm kind of *sad* and you haven't tried *hitting on me* once.

Because you weren't even trying...

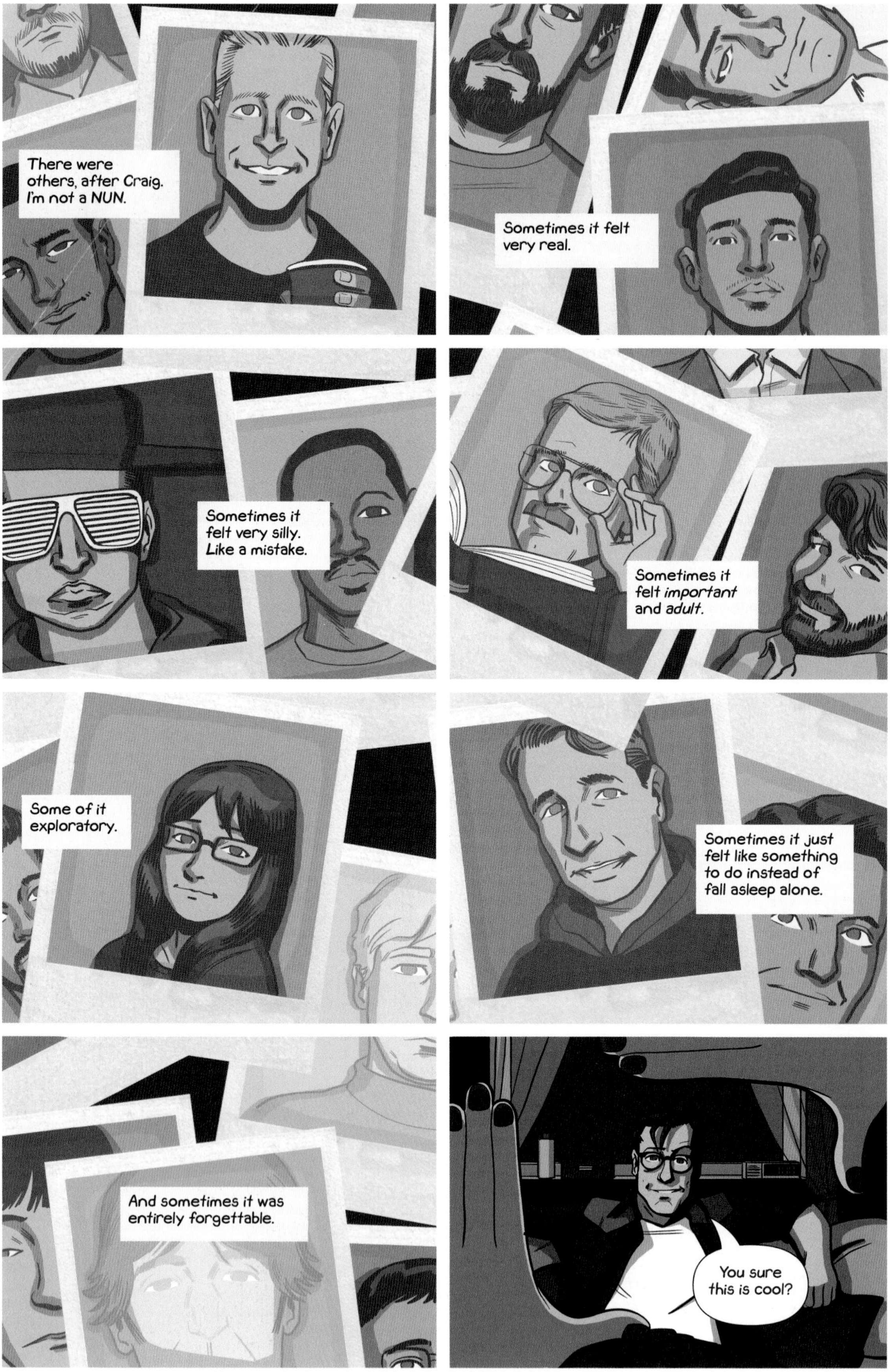
There were others, after Craig. I'm not a NUN.
Sometimes it felt very real.
Sometimes it felt very silly. Like a mistake.
Sometimes it felt *important* and *adult*.
Some of it exploratory.
Sometimes it just felt like something to do instead of fall asleep alone.
And sometimes it was entirely forgettable.
You sure this is cool?

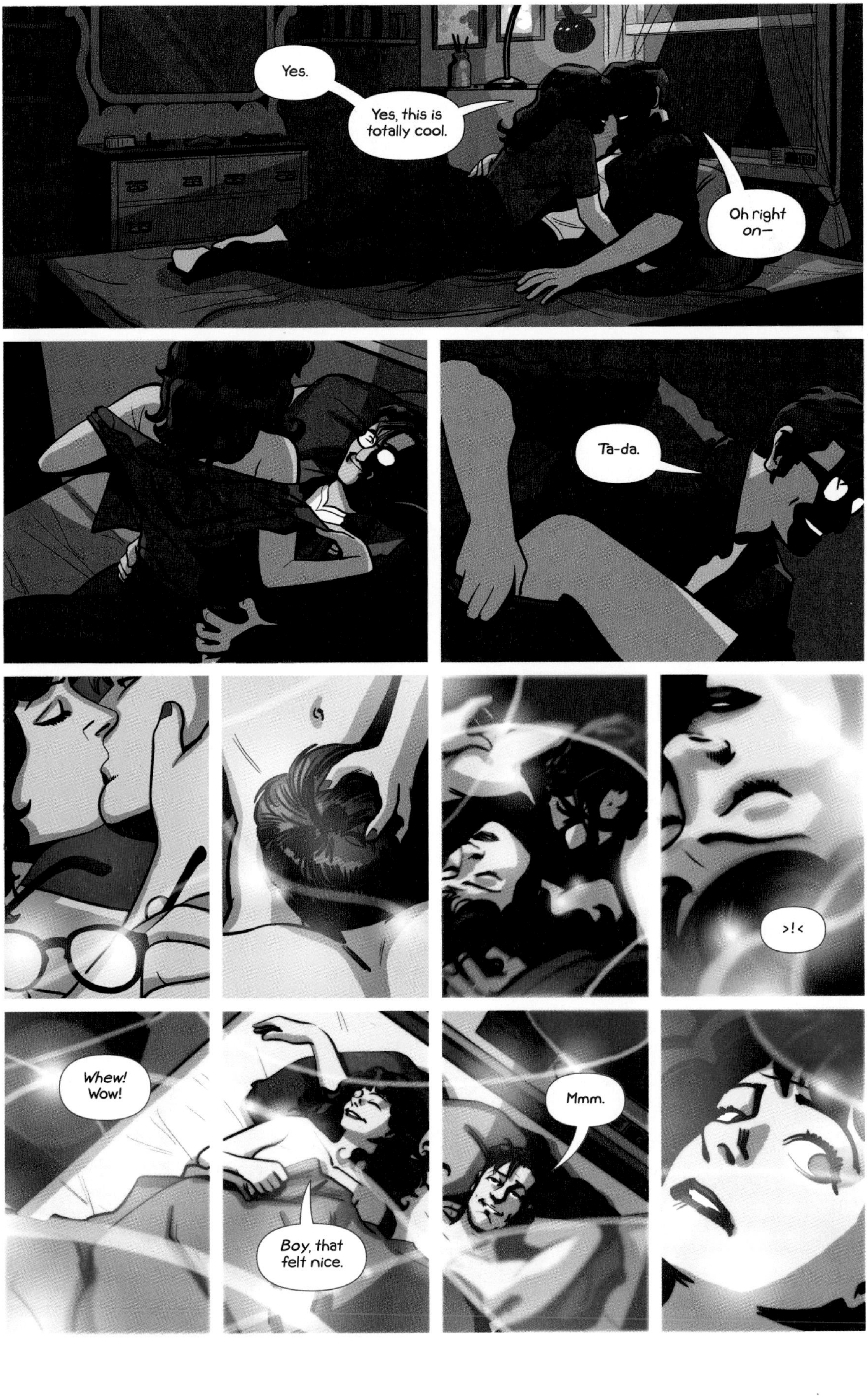

Yes.
Yes, this is totally cool.
Oh right on—
Ta-da.
>!<
Whew! Wow!
Boy, that felt nice.
Mmm.

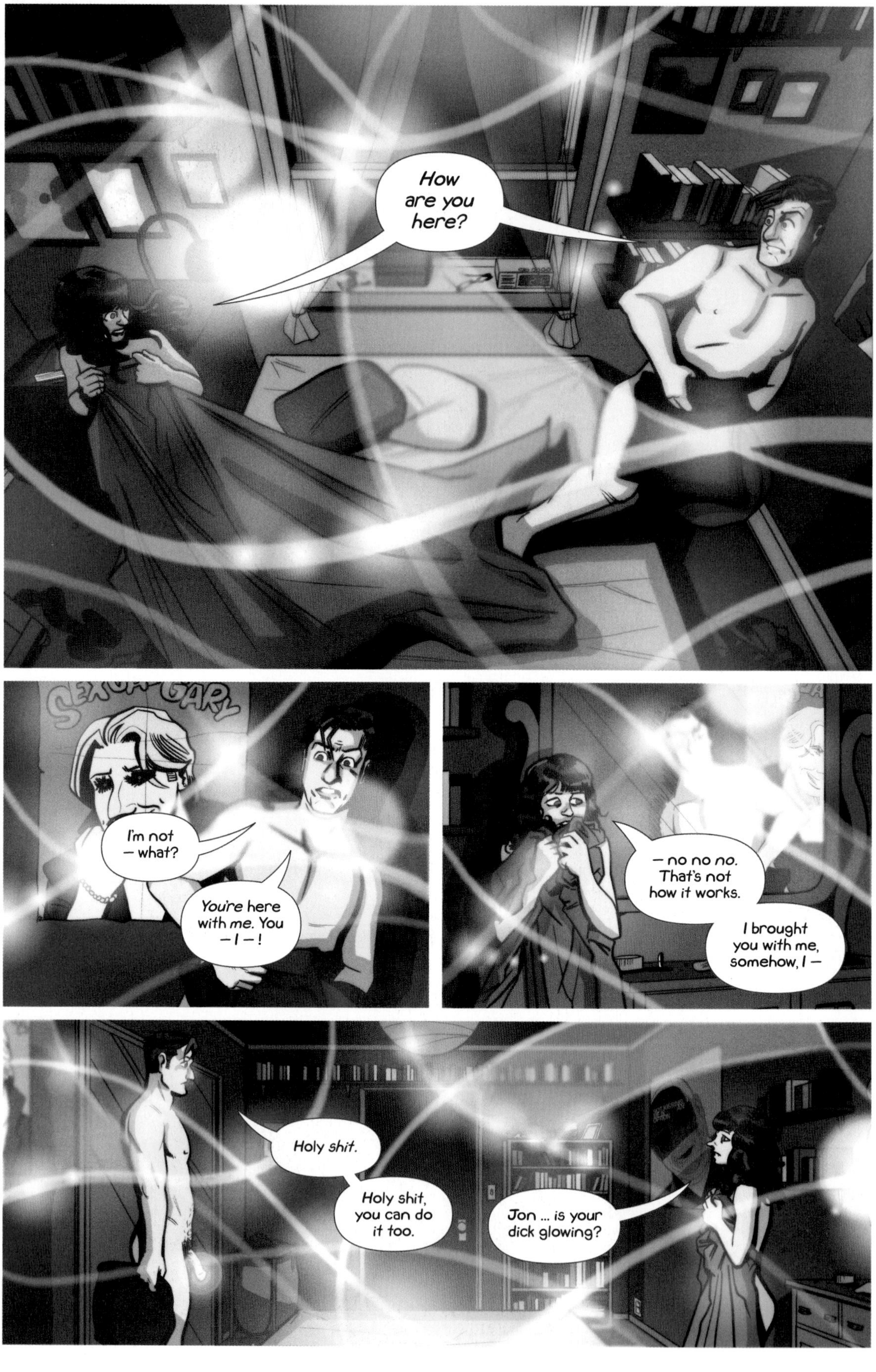
How are you here?
I'm not — what?
You're here with me. You — I — !
— no no no. That's not how it works.
I brought you with me, somehow, I —
Holy shit.
Holy shit, you can do it too.
Jon ... is your dick glowing?

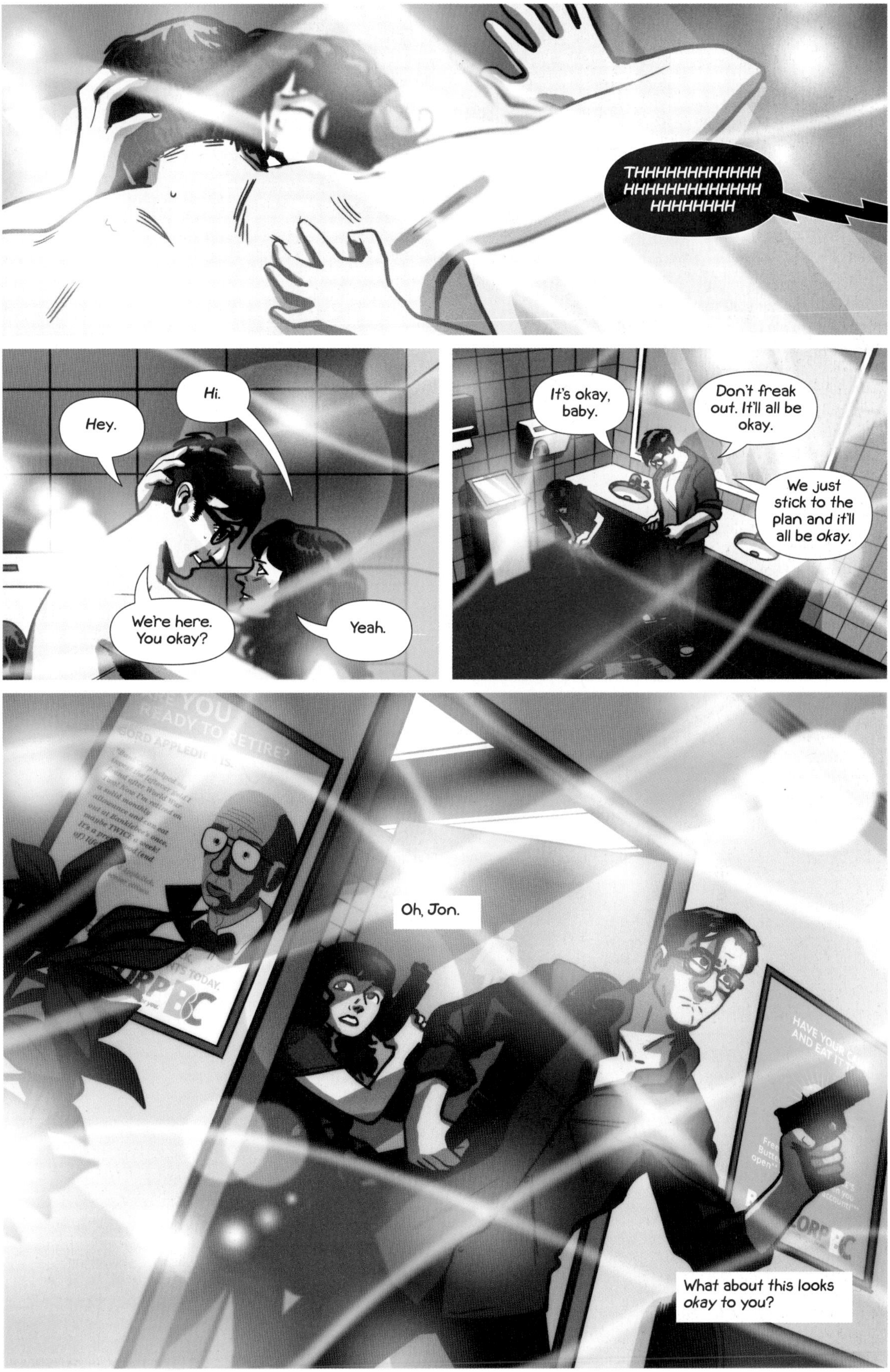
THHHHHHHHHHHH HHHHHHHHHHHHH HHHHHHHH
Hey.
Hi.
We're here. You okay?
Yeah.
It's okay, baby.
Don't freak out. It'll all be okay.
We just stick to the plan and it'll all be *okay*.
Oh, Jon.
What about this looks *okay* to you?

2
COME,
WORLD

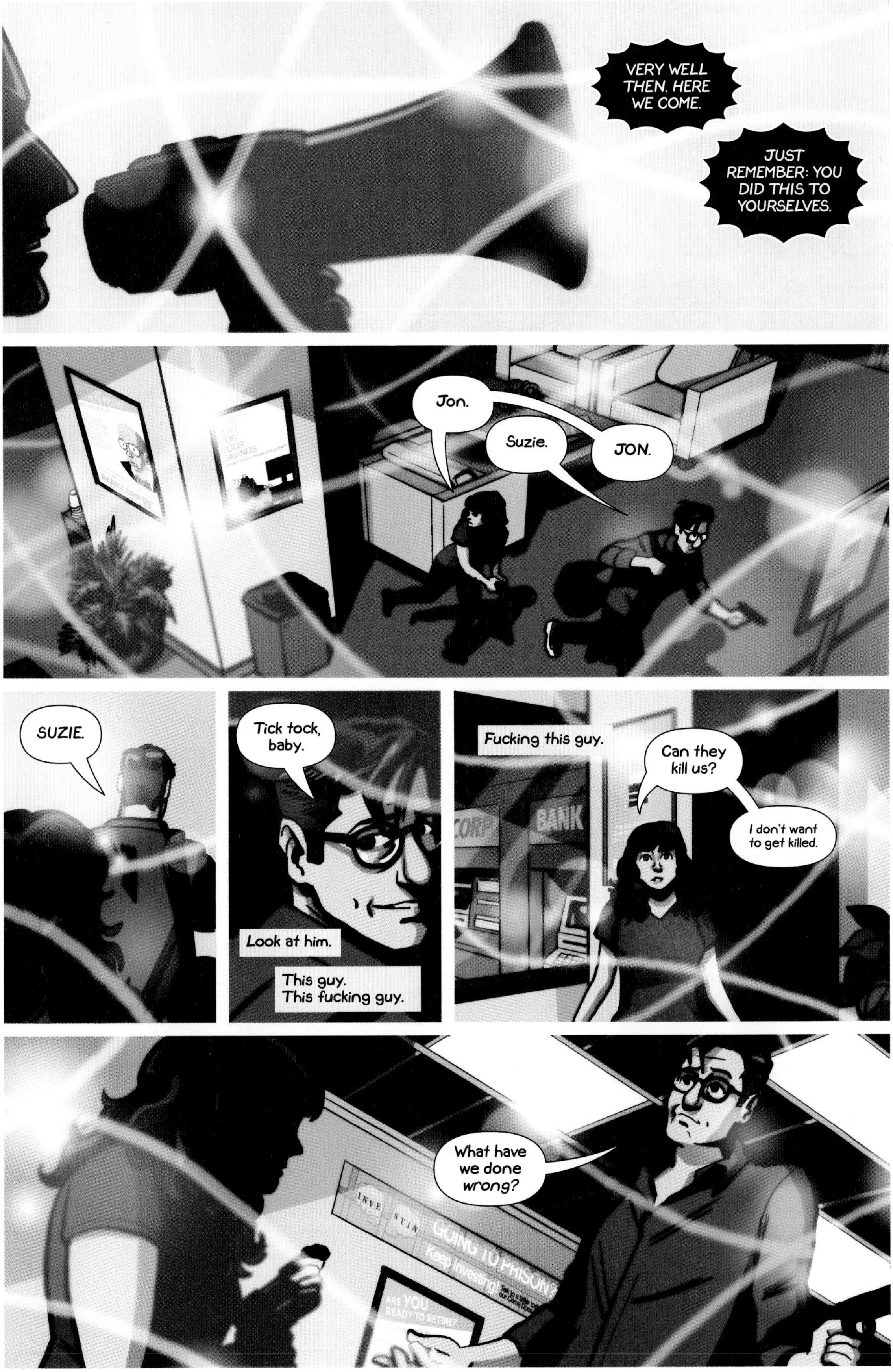
VERY WELL THEN. HERE WE COME.
JUST REMEMBER: YOU DID THIS TO YOURSELVES.
Jon.
Suzie.
JON.
SUZIE.
Tick tock, baby.
Look at him.
This guy. This fucking guy.
Fucking this guy.
Can they kill us?
I don't want to get killed.
BANK
What have we done wrong?
GOING TO PRISON?
Keep investing!
ARE YOU READY TO RETIRE?

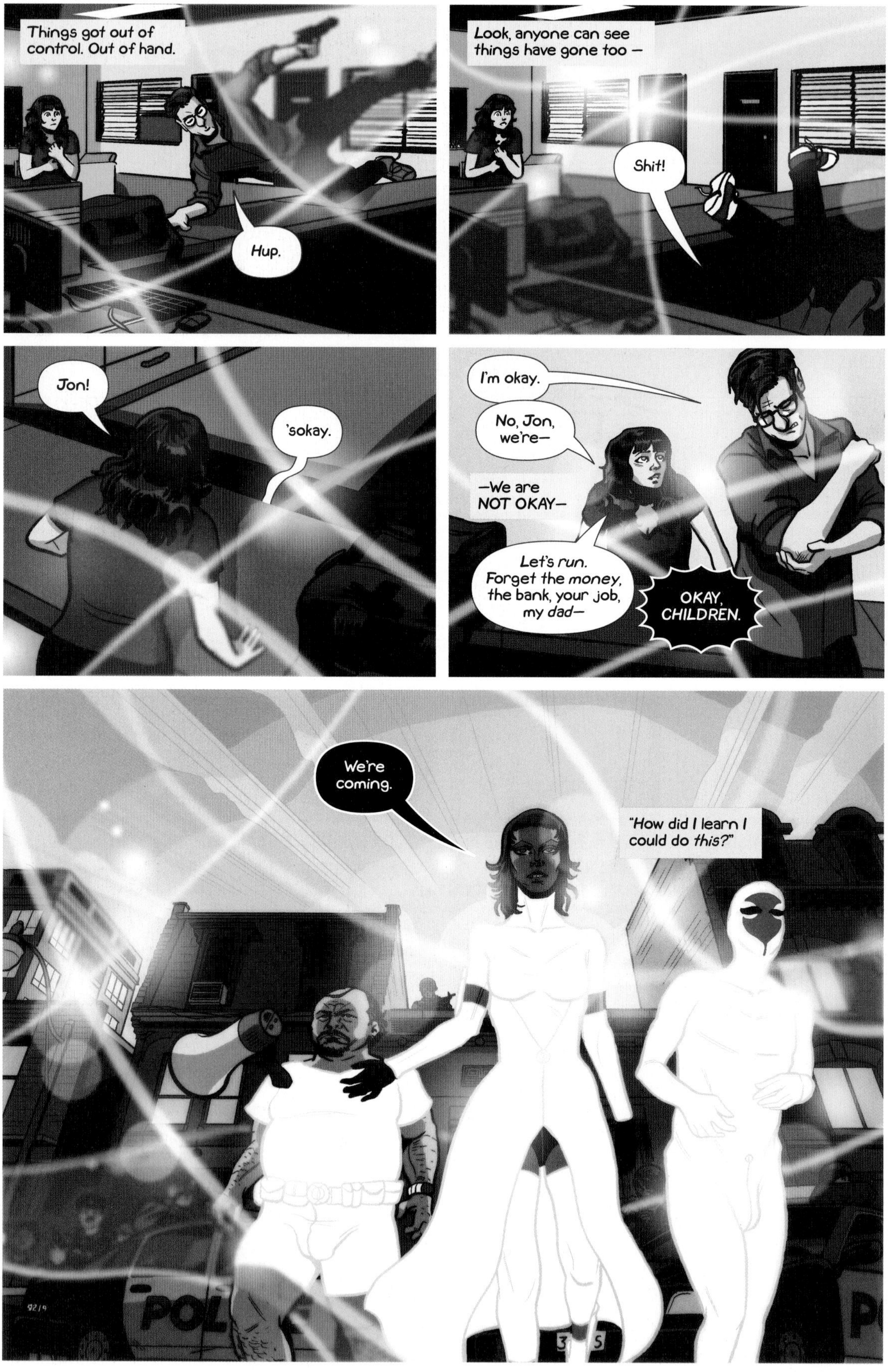
Things got out of control. Out of hand.
Hup.
Look, anyone can see things have gone too —
Shit!
Jon!
'sokay.
I'm okay.
No, Jon, we're—
—We are NOT OKAY—
Let's *run*. Forget the *money*, the bank, your job, my *dad*—
OKAY, CHILDREN.
We're coming.
"How did I learn I could do *this*?"
POL
PO

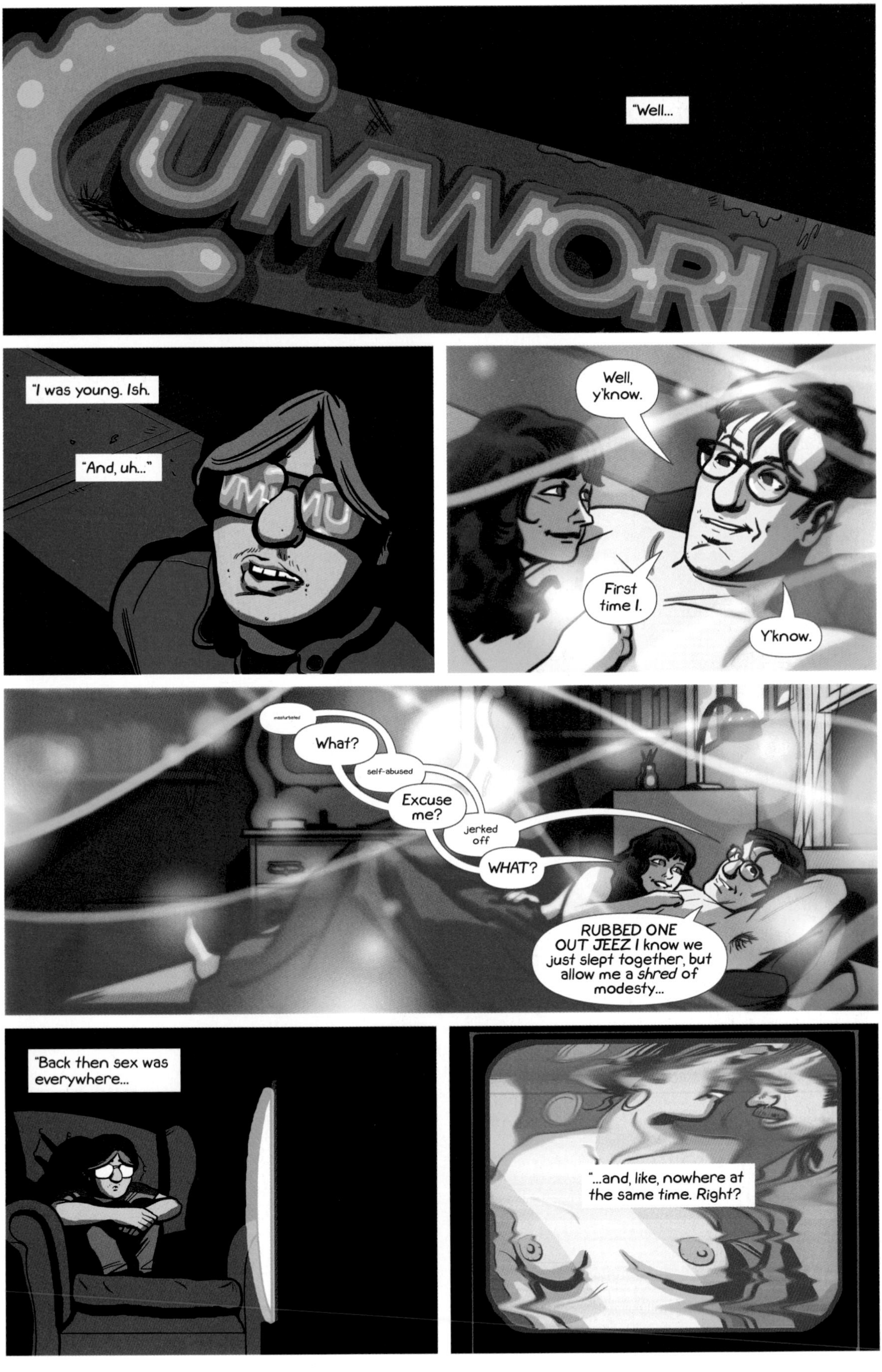

CUMWORLD
"Well...
"I was young. Ish.
"And, uh..."
Well, y'know.
First time I.
Y'know.
masturbated
What?
self-abused
Excuse me?
jerked off
WHAT?
RUBBED ONE OUT JEEZ I know we just slept together, but allow me a *shred* of modesty...
"Back then sex was everywhere...
"...and, like, nowhere at the same time. Right?

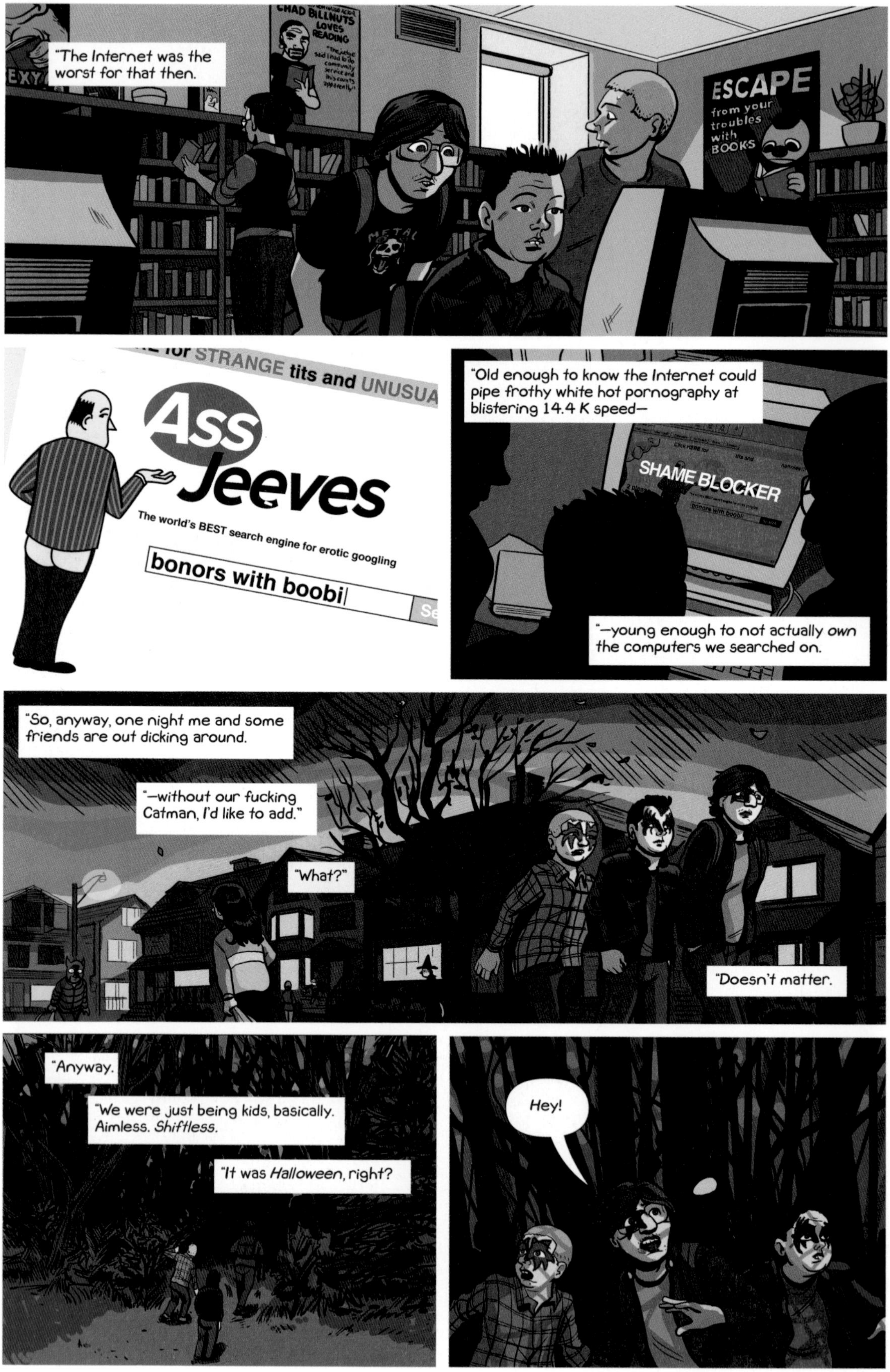

CHAD BILLNUTS LOVES READING
"The Internet was the worst for that then.
ESCAPE from your troubles with BOOKS
for STRANGE tits and
Ass Jeeves
The world's BEST search engine for erotic googling
bonors with boobi
"Old enough to know the Internet could pipe frothy white hot pornography at blistering 14.4 K speed—
SHAME BLOCKER
"—young enough to not actually *own* the computers we searched on.
"So, anyway, one night me and some friends are out dicking around.
"—without our fucking Catman, I'd like to add."
"What?"
"Doesn't matter.
"Anyway.
"We were just being kids, basically. Aimless. *Shiftless.*
"It was *Halloween*, right?
Hey!

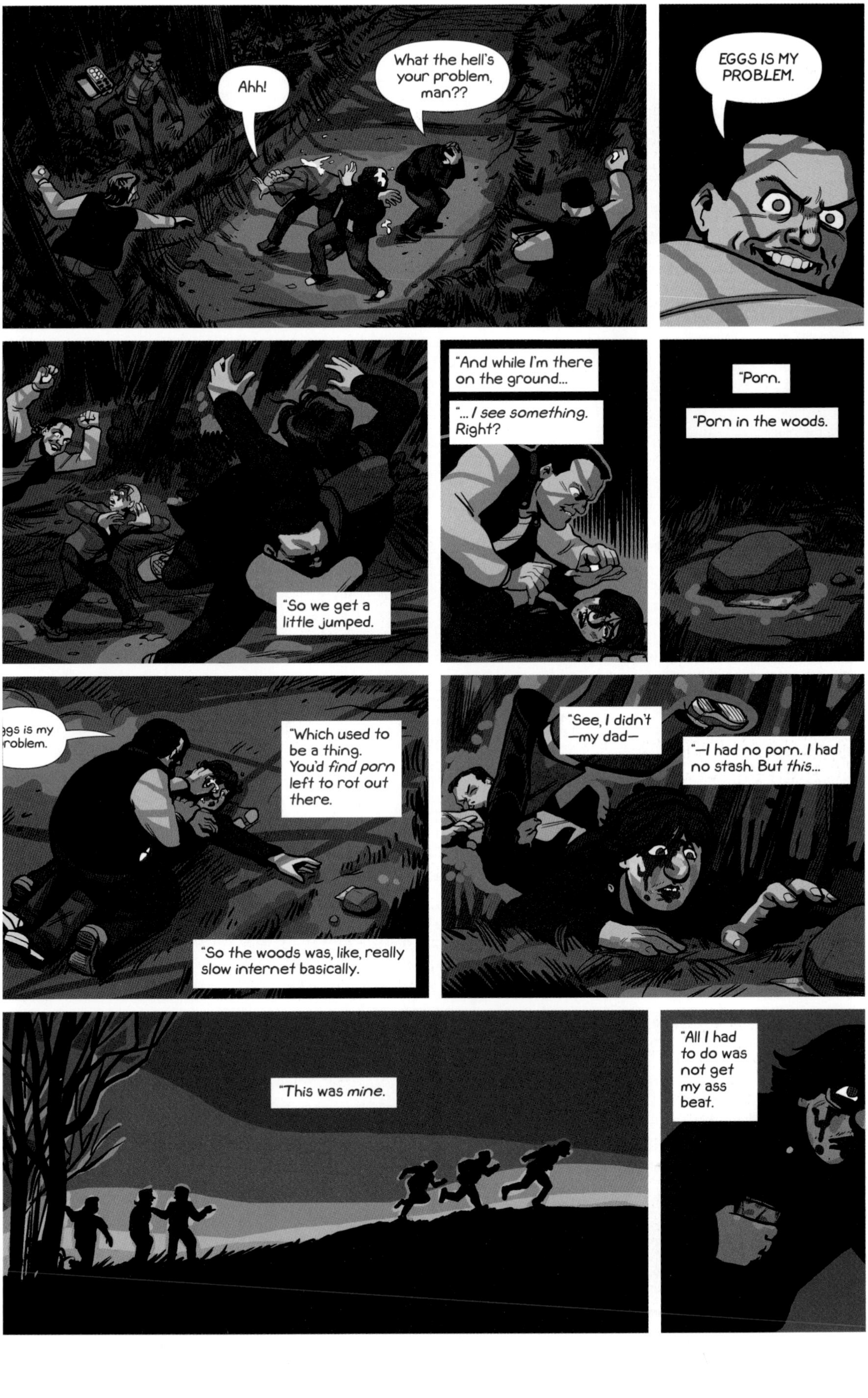
Ahh!
What the hell's your problem, man??
EGGS IS MY PROBLEM.
"So we get a little jumped.
"And while I'm there on the ground...
"...*I see something.* Right?
"Porn.
"Porn in the woods.
ggs is my roblem.
"Which used to be a thing. You'd *find porn* left to rot out there.
"So the woods was, like, really slow internet basically.
"See, I didn't —my dad—
"—I had no porn. I had no stash. But *this*...
"This was *mine.*
"All I had to do was not get my ass beat.

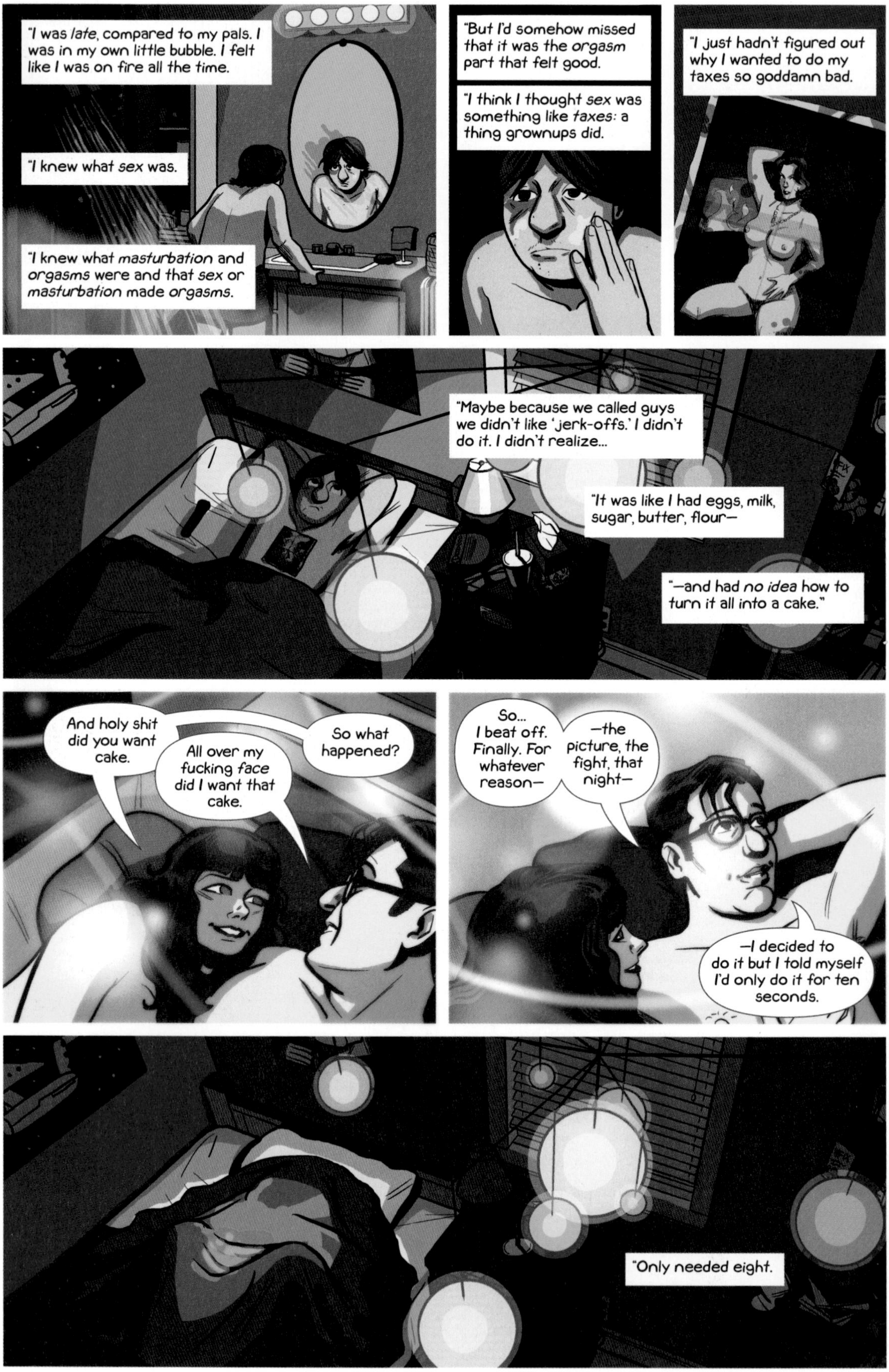
"I was *late*, compared to my pals. I was in my own little bubble. I felt like I was on fire all the time.
"I knew what *sex* was.
"I knew what *masturbation* and *orgasms* were and that *sex* or *masturbation* made *orgasms*.
"But I'd somehow missed that it was the *orgasm* part that felt good.
"I think I thought *sex* was something like *taxes:* a thing grownups did.
"I just hadn't figured out why I wanted to do my taxes so goddamn bad.
"Maybe because we called guys we didn't like 'jerk-offs.' I didn't do it. I didn't realize...
"It was like I had eggs, milk, sugar, butter, flour—
"—and had *no idea* how to turn it all into a cake."
And holy shit did you want cake.
All over my fucking *face* did I want that cake.
So what happened?
So... I beat off. Finally. For whatever reason—
—the picture, the fight, that night—
—I decided to do it but I told myself I'd only do it for ten seconds.
"Only needed eight.

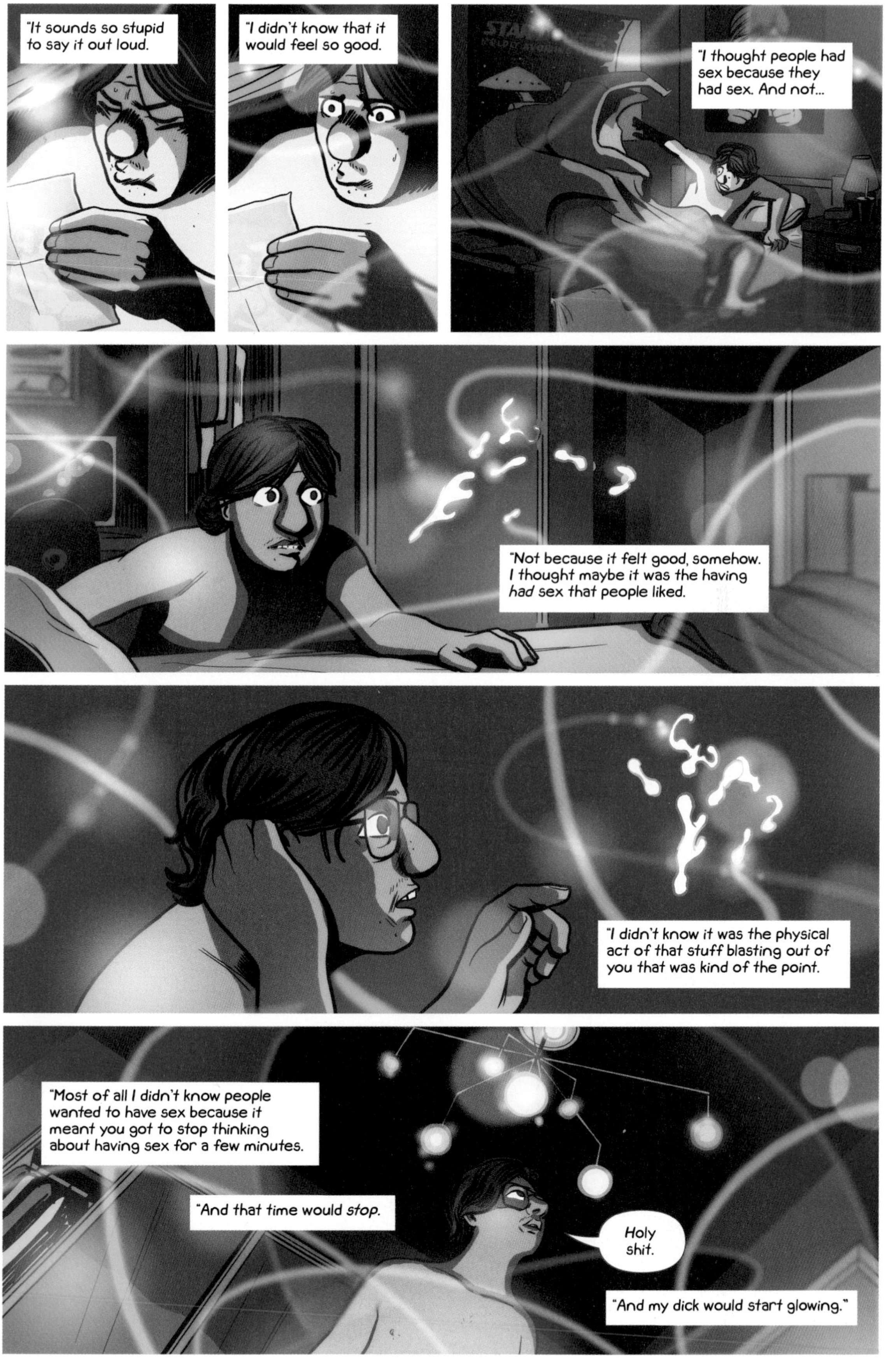
"It sounds so stupid to say it out loud.
"I didn't know that it would feel so good.
"I thought people had sex because they had sex. And not...
"Not because it felt good, somehow. I thought maybe it was the having *had* sex that people liked.
"I didn't know it was the physical act of that stuff blasting out of you that was kind of the point.
"Most of all I didn't know people wanted to have sex because it meant you got to stop thinking about having sex for a few minutes.
"And that time would *stop*.
Holy shit.
"And my dick would start glowing."

Oh my GOD—

—Don't laugh don't *laugh*—

I just—it *glows* like E.T.

Like E.T.'s *dick*, I mean.

See there, now, I don't need this kind of abuse.

I'm gonna go back to sleeping with boring, normal girls who don't freeze time when they fuck and laugh at my dick afterwards.

Does it... *feel*... like anything?

Feels like... y'know. *Like a dick.*

"It's kind of like a timer for how long I get to spend in—"

"The Quiet!"

I call it "The Quiet." What do you call it?

Uh.

Not that.

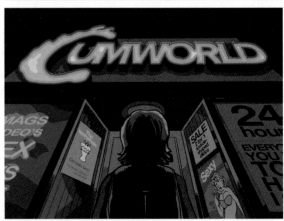

Wait, I want to see if it feels any different—

—No, Suzie, I didn't—

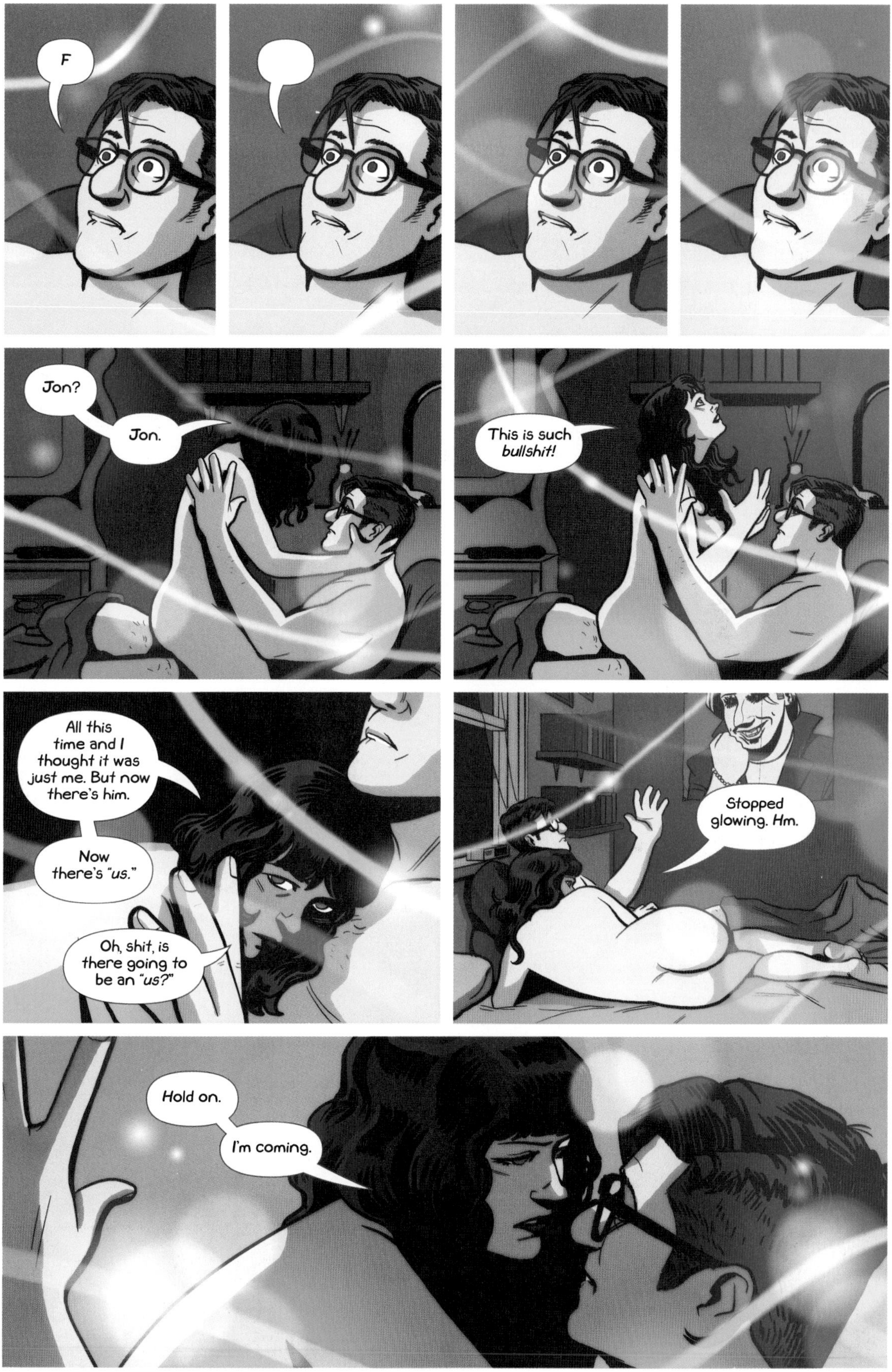
F
Jon?
Jon.
This is such *bullshit!*
All this time and I thought it was just me. But now there's him.
Now there's "*us.*"
Oh, shit, is there going to be an "*us?*"
Stopped glowing. *Hm.*
Hold on.
I'm coming.

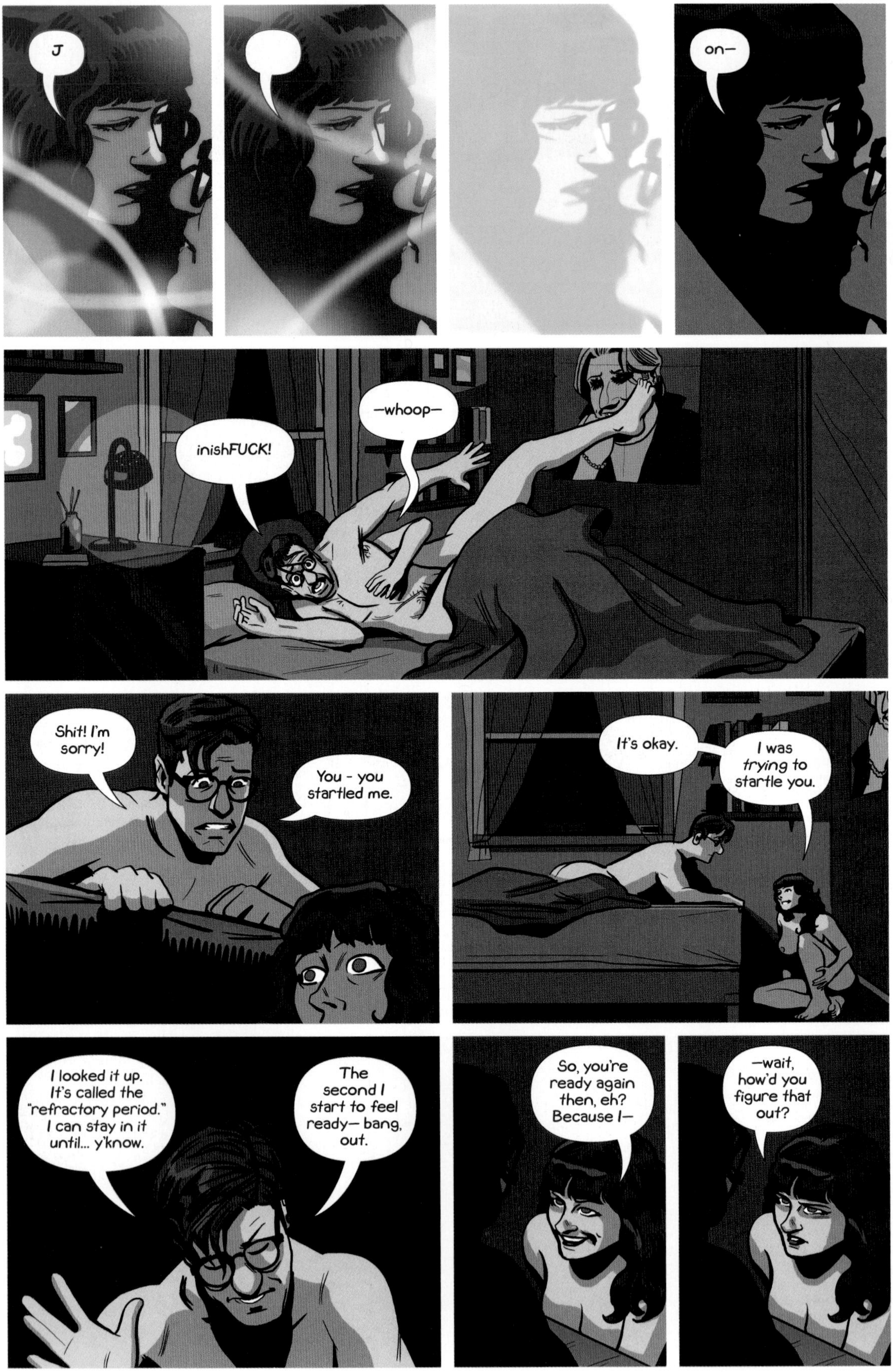
J
on—
inishFUCK!
—whoop—
Shit! I'm sorry!
You - you startled me.
It's okay.
I was *trying* to startle you.
I looked it up. It's called the "refractory period." I can stay in it until... y'know.
The second I start to feel ready— bang, out.
So, you're ready again then, eh? Because I—
—wait, how'd you figure that out?

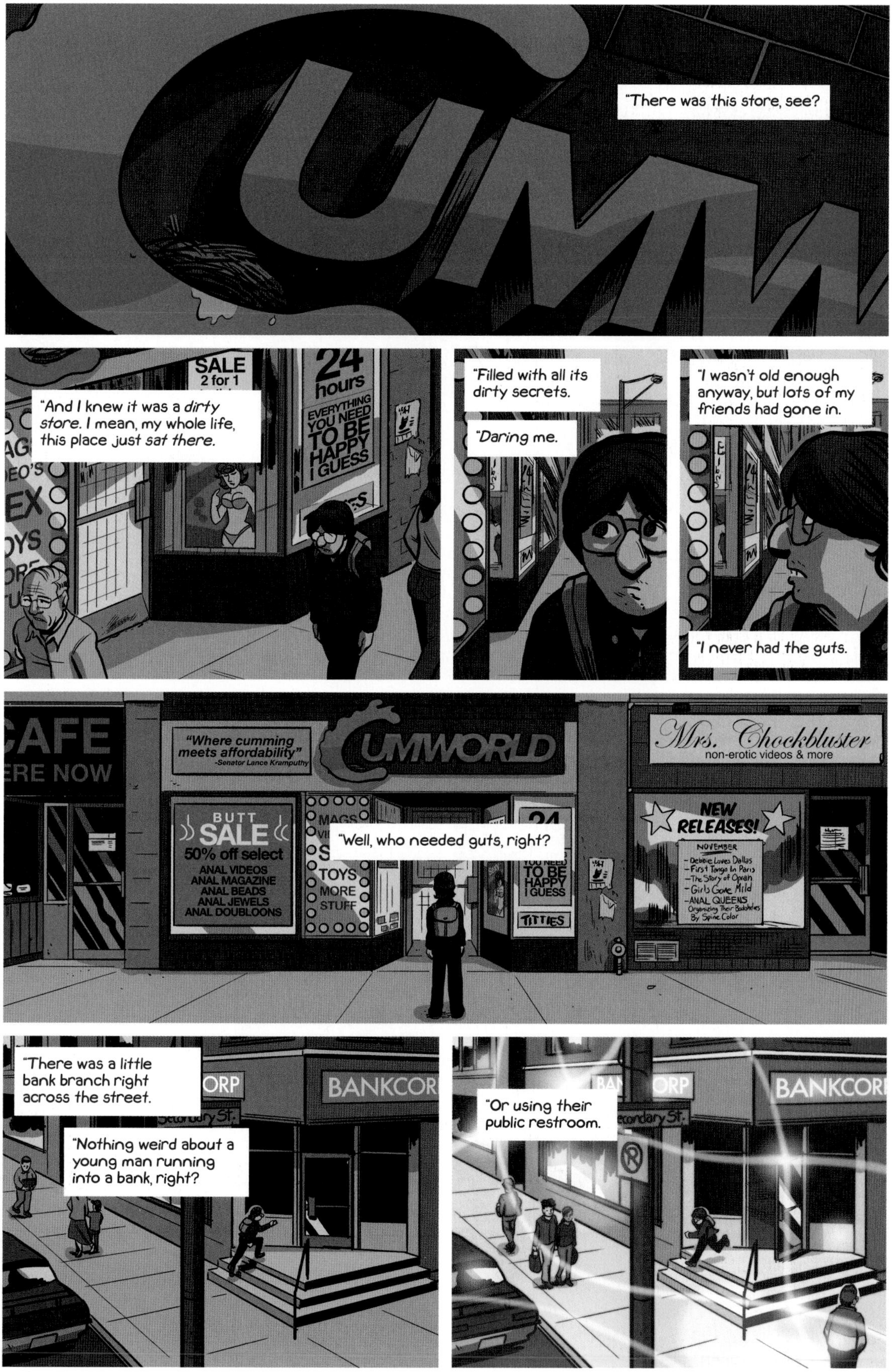
"There was this store, see?
SALE 2 for 1
24 hours EVERYTHING YOU NEED TO BE HAPPY I GUESS
"And I knew it was a *dirty store*. I mean, my whole life, this place just *sat there.*
"Filled with all its dirty secrets.
"*Daring* me.
"I wasn't old enough anyway, but lots of my friends had gone in.
"I never had the guts.
CAFE
"Where cumming meets affordability" -Senator Lance Kramputhy
CUMWORLD
Mrs. Chockbluster non-erotic videos & more
BUTT SALE 50% off select ANAL VIDEOS ANAL MAGAZINE ANAL BEADS ANAL JEWELS ANAL DOUBLOONS
TOYS MORE STUFF
TITTIES
NEW RELEASES!
NOVEMBER
- Debbie Loves Dallas
- First Tango In Paris
- The Story of Oprah
- Girls Gone Mild
- ANAL QUEENS Organizing Their Bookshelves By Spine Color
"Well, who needed guts, right?
"There was a little bank branch right across the street.
BANKCORP
Secondary St.
"Nothing weird about a young man running into a bank, right?
"Or using their public restroom.

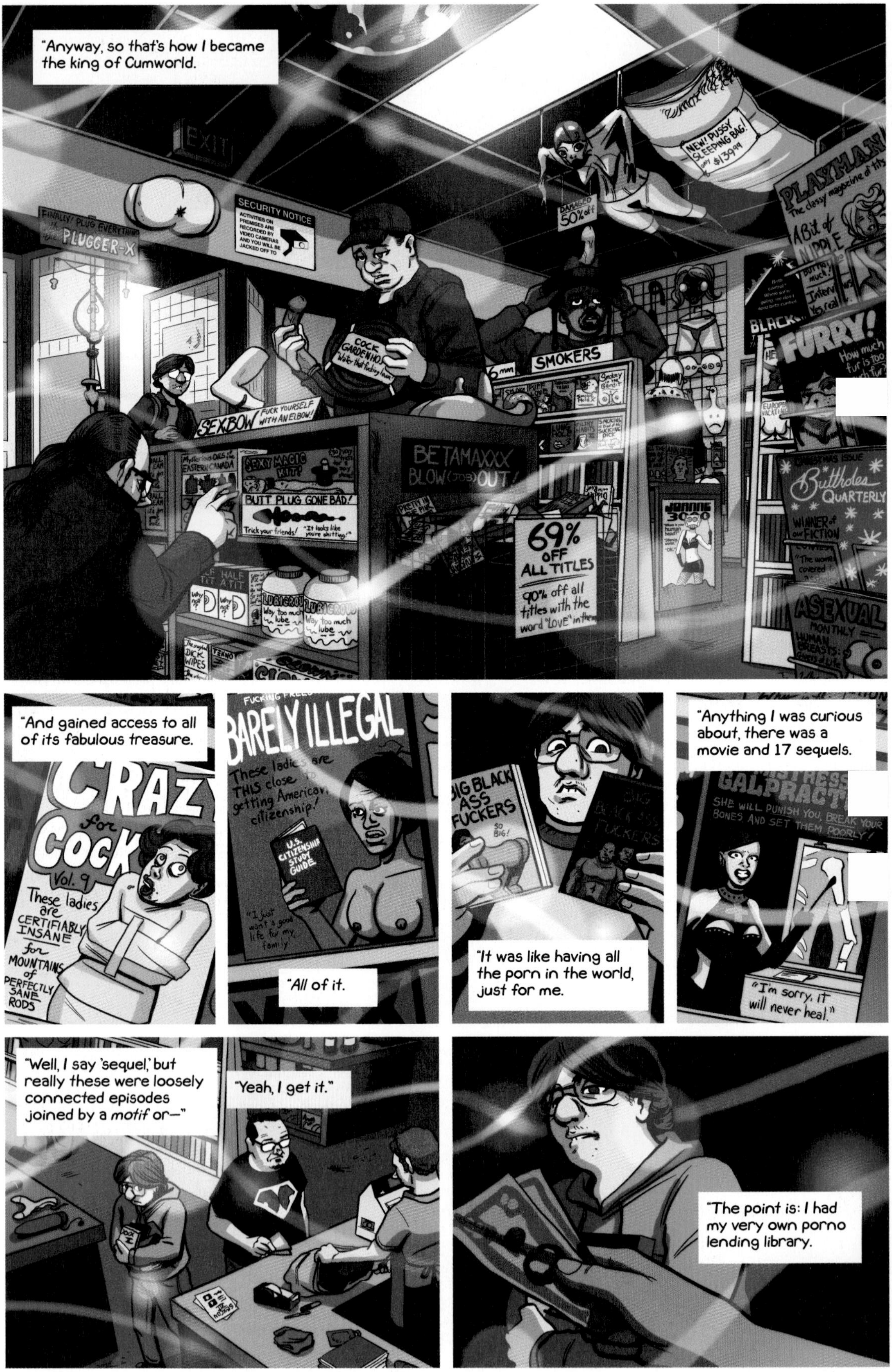
"Anyway, so that's how I became the king of Cumworld.
EXIT
NEW! PUSSY SLEEPING BAG! only $139.99
PLAXMAN The classy magazine of tits
SECURITY NOTICE
ACTIVITIES ON PREMISES ARE RECORDED BY VIDEO CAMERAS AND YOU WILL BE JACKED OFF TO
FINALLY! PLUG EVERYTHING with the PLUGGER-X
DAMAGED 50% off
COCK GARDEN HOSE "Water that fucking lawn"
SMOKERS
FURRY!
SEXBOW FUCK YOURSELF WITH AN ELBOW!
SEXY MAGIC KIT!
BUTT PLUG GONE BAD!
Trick your friends! "It looks like you're shitting!"
BETAMAXXX BLOW(JOB)OUT!
69% OFF ALL TITLES
90% off all titles with the word "LOVE" in them
Butt holes QUARTERLY
ASEXUAL MONTHLY
LUBIGROUS Way too much lube
"And gained access to all of its fabulous treasure.
CRAZY for COCK Vol. 9
These ladies are CERTIFIABLY INSANE for MOUNTAINS of PERFECTLY SANE RODS
BARELY ILLEGAL
These ladies are THIS close to getting American citizenship!
U.S. CITIZENSHIP STUDY GUIDE
"I just want a good life for my family!"
"All of it.
BIG BLACK ASS FUCKERS SO BIG!
"It was like having all the porn in the world, just for me.
"Anything I was curious about, there was a movie and 17 sequels.
MISTRESS GALPRACTICE
SHE WILL PUNISH YOU, BREAK YOUR BONES AND SET THEM POORLY!
"I'm sorry, it will never heal."
"Well, I say 'sequel,' but really these were loosely connected episodes joined by a motif or—"
"Yeah, I get it."
"The point is: I had my very own porno lending library.

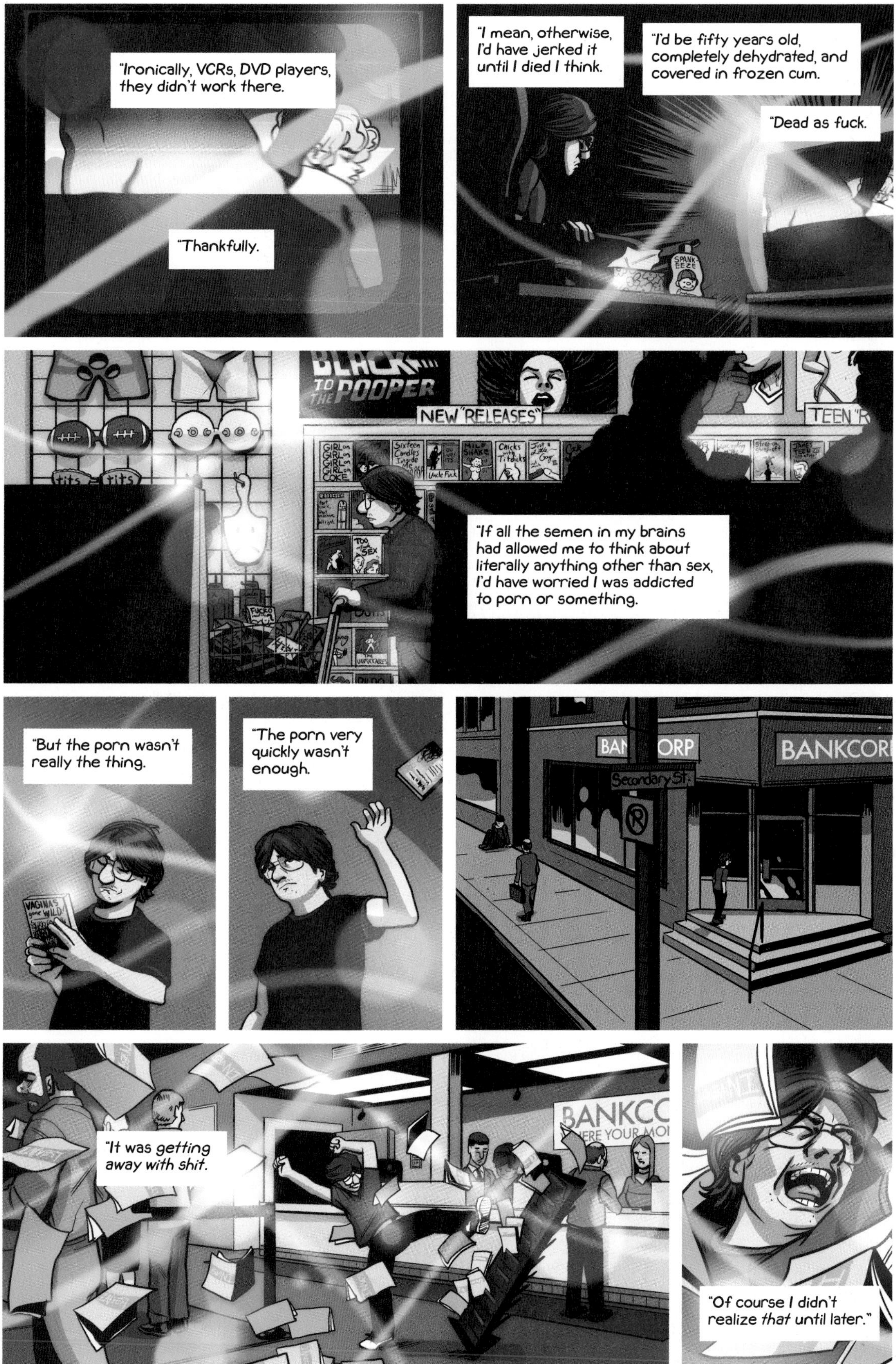
"Ironically, VCRs, DVD players, they didn't work there.
"Thankfully.
"I mean, otherwise, I'd have jerked it until I died I think.
"I'd be fifty years old, completely dehydrated, and covered in frozen cum.
"Dead as fuck.
SPANK EEZE
TO THE POOPER
NEW "RELEASES"
TEEN "R
tits tits
GIRL on GIRL on GIRL on GIRL on COKE
Sixteen Candles Inside Me
Chicks with Titdicks
Uncle Fuck
TOO SEX
THE UNFUCKABLES
"If all the semen in my brains had allowed me to think about literally anything other than sex, I'd have worried I was addicted to porn or something.
"But the porn wasn't really the thing.
VAGINAS gone WILD!
"The porn very quickly wasn't enough.
BAN ORP
BANKCOR
Secondary St.
"It was getting away with shit.
BANKCO
"Of course I didn't realize *that* until later."

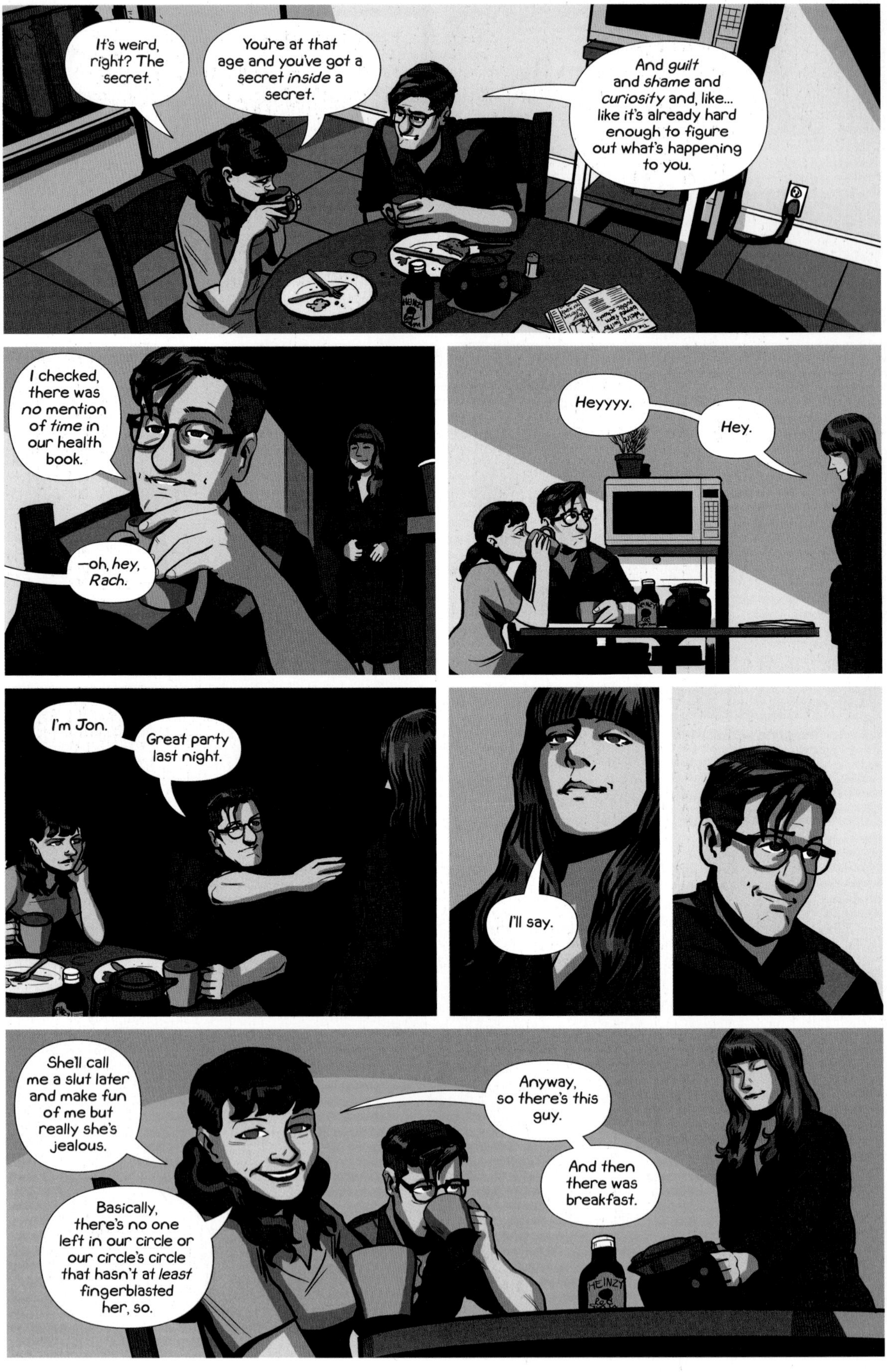
It's weird, right? The secret.
You're at that age and you've got a secret *inside* a secret.
And *guilt* and *shame* and *curiosity* and, like... like it's already hard enough to figure out what's happening to you.
I checked, there was *no* mention of *time* in our health book.
—oh, *hey*, *Rach*.
Heyyyy.
Hey.
I'm Jon.
Great party last night.
I'll say.
She'll call me a slut later and make fun of me but really she's jealous.
Basically, there's no one left in our circle or our circle's circle that hasn't at *least* fingerblasted her, so.
Anyway, so there's this guy.
And then there was breakfast.
HEINZY

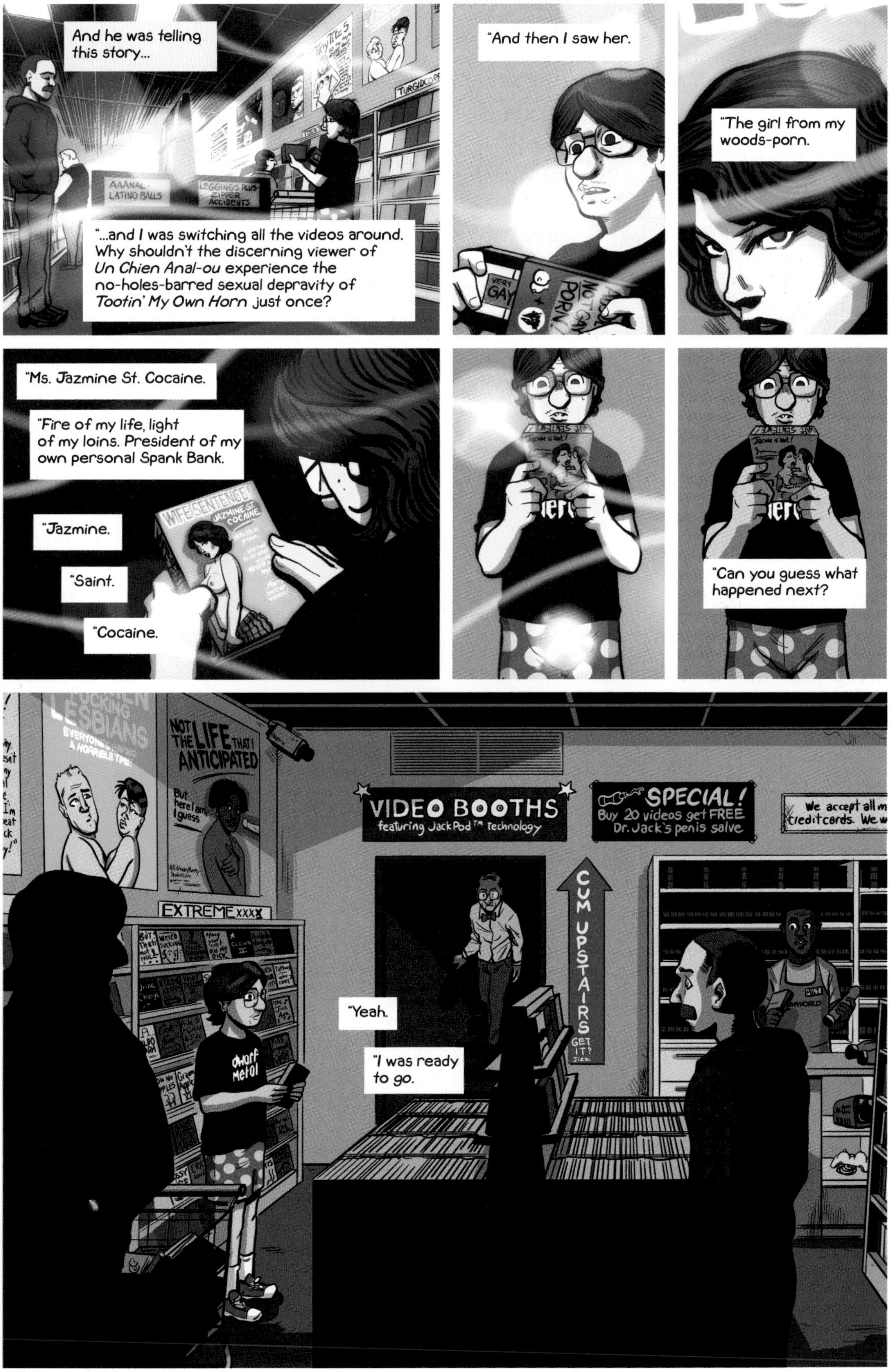
And he was telling this story...
TinyTitz
TURGIDCORP
AAANAL-LATINO BALLS
LEGGINGS PLUS ZIPPER ACCIDENTS
"...and I was switching all the videos around. Why shouldn't the discerning viewer of *Un Chien Anal-ou* experience the no-holes-barred sexual depravity of *Tootin' My Own Horn* just once?
"And then I saw her.
VERY GAY
"The girl from my woods-porn.
"Ms. Jazmine St. Cocaine.
"Fire of my life, light of my loins. President of my own personal Spank Bank.
WIFE SENTENCE! JAZMINE ST. COCAINE
"Jazmine.
"Saint.
"Cocaine.
"Can you guess what happened next?
LESBIANS
NOT THE LIFE THAT I ANTICIPATED
But here I am, I guess
EXTREME XXXX
CLOWN
VIDEO BOOTHS featuring JackPod™ technology
SPECIAL! Buy 20 videos get FREE Dr. Jack's penis salve
We accept all m credit cards. We w
CUM UPSTAIRS GET IT? Jizz
Dwarf Metal
"Yeah.
"I was ready to go.

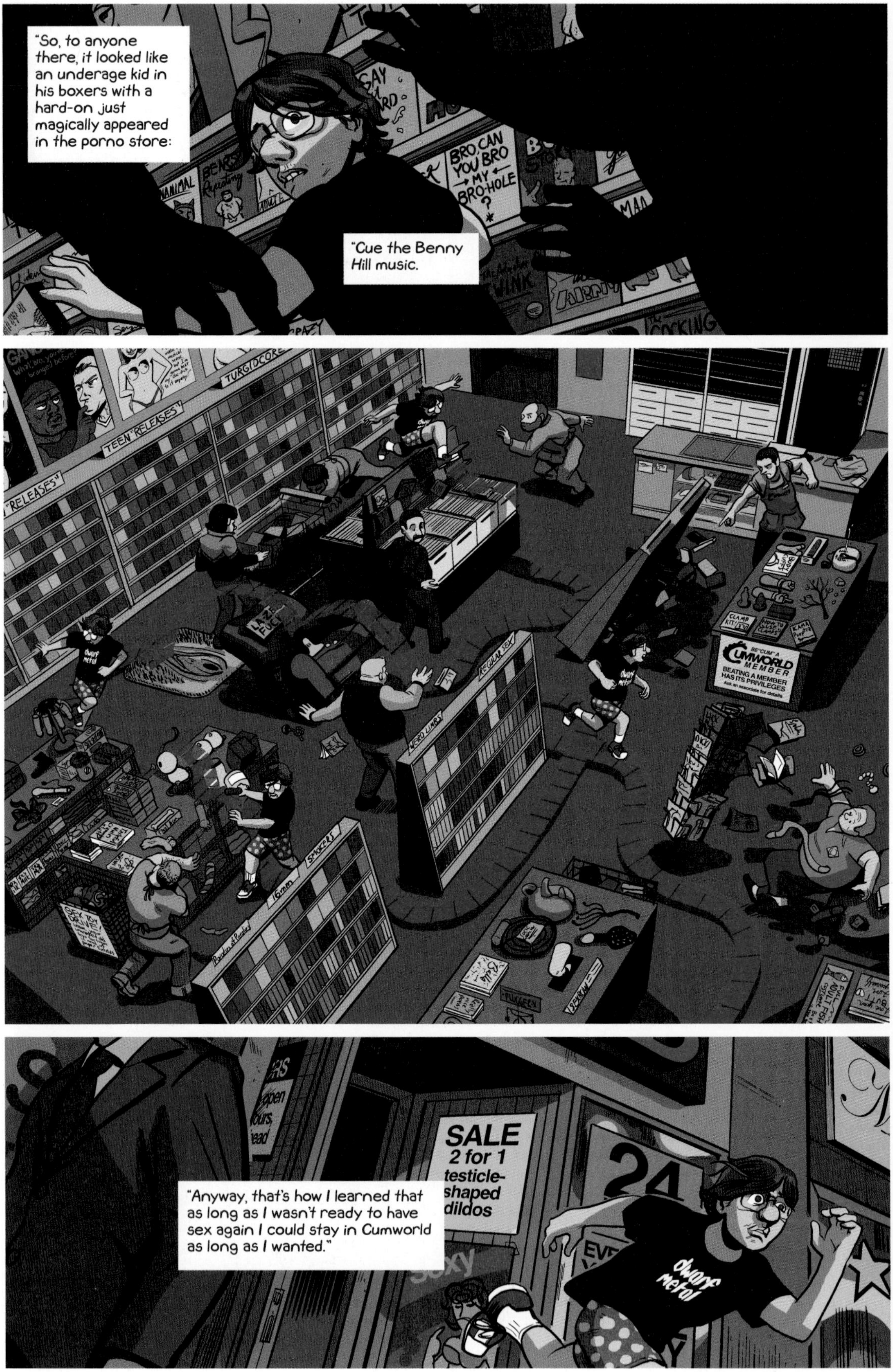
"So, to anyone there, it looked like an underage kid in his boxers with a hard-on just magically appeared in the porno store:
BRO CAN YOU BRO MY BRO-HOLE ?
"Cue the Benny Hill music.
TEEN "RELEASES"
"RELEASES"
REGULAR SEX
BE"CUM" A CUMWORLD MEMBER
BEATING A MEMBER HAS ITS PRIVILEGES
Ask an associate for details
SALE
2 for 1
testicle-shaped dildos
"Anyway, that's how I learned that as long as I wasn't ready to have sex again I could stay in Cumworld as long as I wanted."
dwarf metal

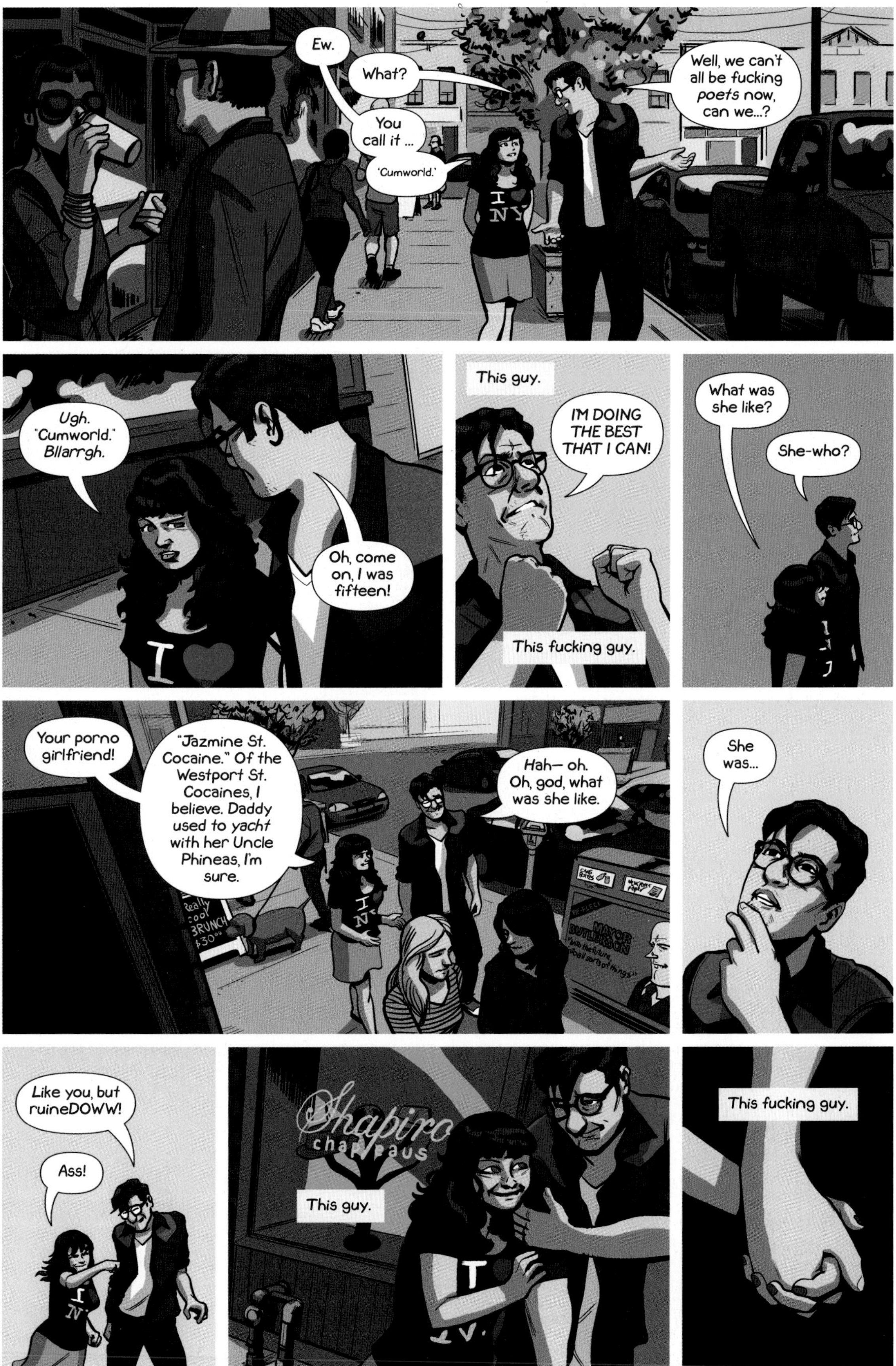
Ew.
What?
You call it ...
'Cumworld.'
Well, we can't all be fucking *poets* now, can we...?
Ugh. "Cumworld." Bllarrgh.
Oh, come on, I was fifteen!
This guy.
I'M DOING THE BEST THAT I CAN!
This fucking guy.
What was she like?
She-who?
Your porno girlfriend!
"Jazmine St. Cocaine." Of the Westport St. Cocaines, I believe. Daddy used to *yacht* with her Uncle Phineas, I'm sure.
Really cool BRUNCH $30
MAYOR BUTLERSON
Hah— oh. Oh, god, what was she like.
She was...
Like you, but ruineDOWW!
Ass!
Shapiro chapeaus
This guy.
This fucking guy.

Ah, here.
"Born in Ojai, California, 1968, adult film actress Jazmine St. Cocaine starred in over 78 features..."
I swear if I ever saw that photograph of her again I'd come so hard my heart would collapse in on itself.
shit—
Real name, real name. AH! Here.
'Rae Anne Toots.'
Jesus.
It doesn't say which of her uncles touched her, but it's Wikipedia. They have pretty high verification standards...
And, just like that, a night became a day and that day turned into another night.
It was like we were afraid to stop talking, so we didn't.
HEY!
Um.
Yes?
That's not cool. That judgmental bullshit of yours.
Jazmine S
Cocaine
I'm a real person, y'know.
And, just because I'm a sex worker, you don't get to shame me or insult me or insist I came from a background of molestation and abuse.
And even if I did—
Jesus, god, you called yourself "Jazmine St. Cocaine." Taking a little shit was inevitable—
Hiiii Jonny. It's ya girl, Suzanne DeQuaalude-Handjob.
And I want you to rrrruin me.

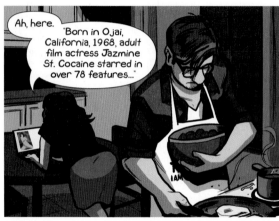

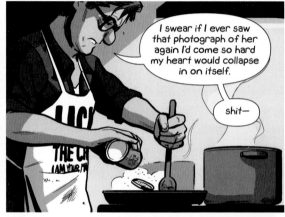

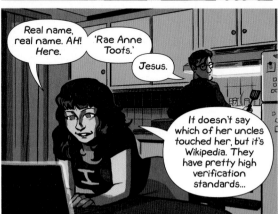

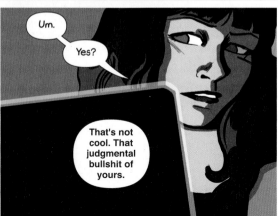

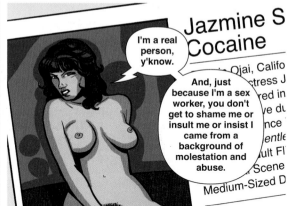

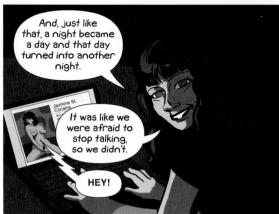

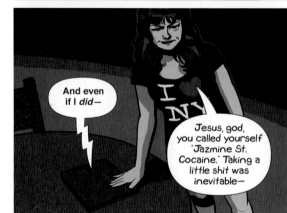

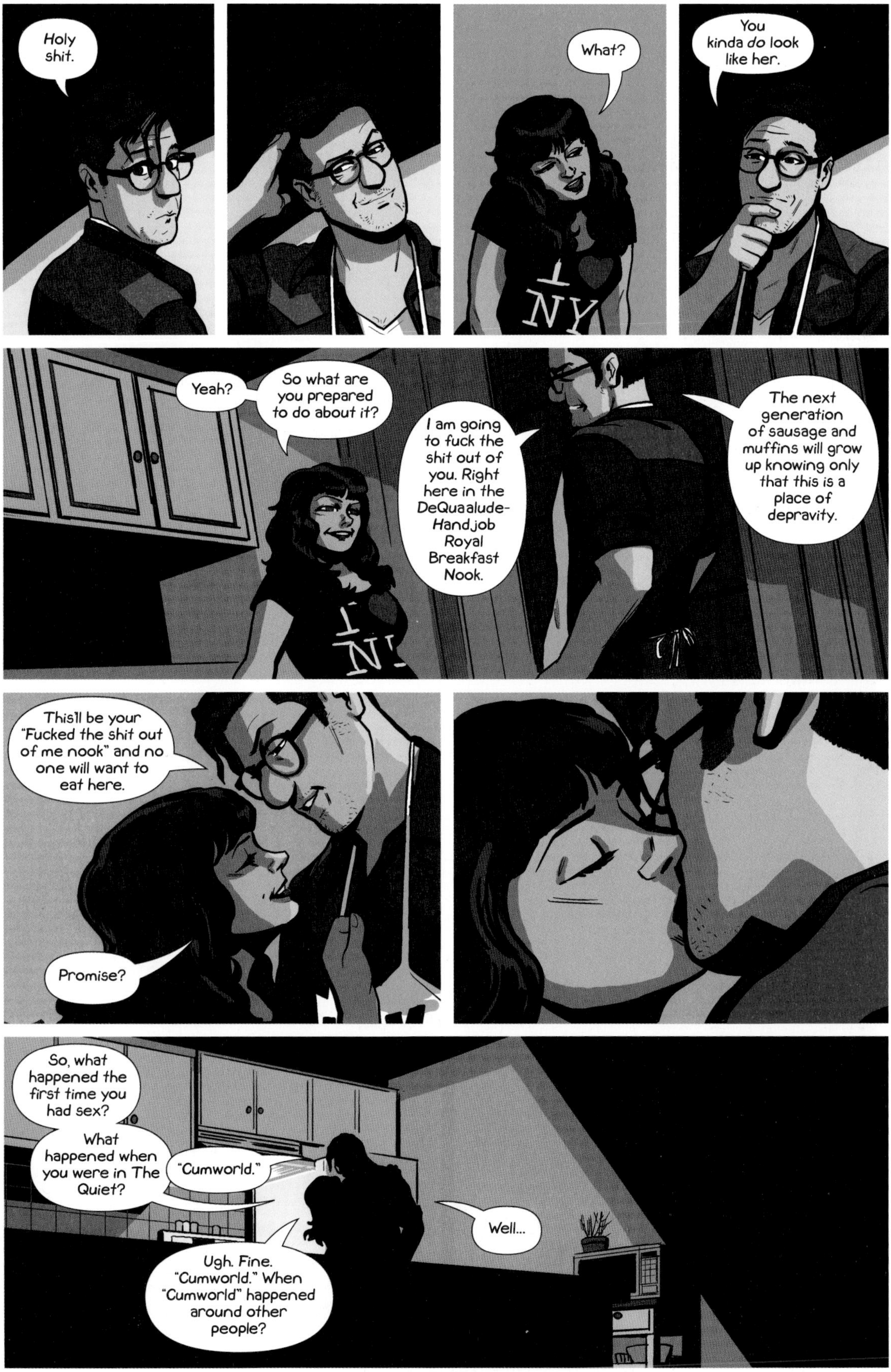
Holy shit.
What?
You kinda *do* look like her.
Yeah?
So what are you prepared to do about it?
I am going to fuck the shit out of you. Right here in the DeQuaalude-Handjob Royal Breakfast Nook.
The next generation of sausage and muffins will grow up knowing only that this is a place of depravity.
This'll be your "Fucked the shit out of me nook" and no one will want to eat here.
Promise?
So, what happened the first time you had sex?
What happened when you were in The Quiet?
"Cumworld."
Well...
Ugh. Fine. "Cumworld." When "Cumworld" happened around other people?

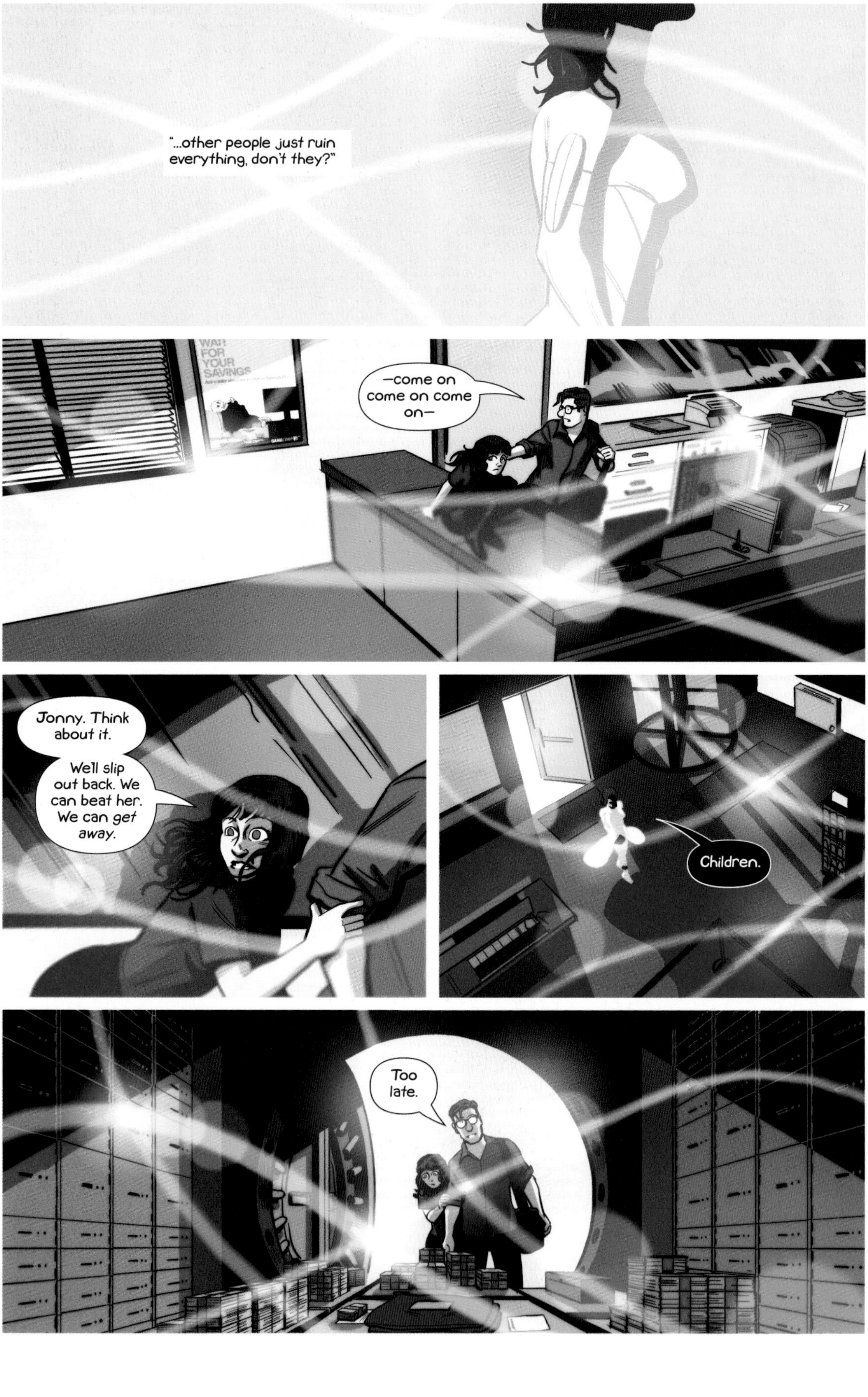

"...other people just ruin everything, don't they?"
WAIT FOR YOUR SAVINGS
—come on come on come on—
Jonny. Think about it.
We'll slip out back. We can beat her. We can *get* away.
Children.
Too late.

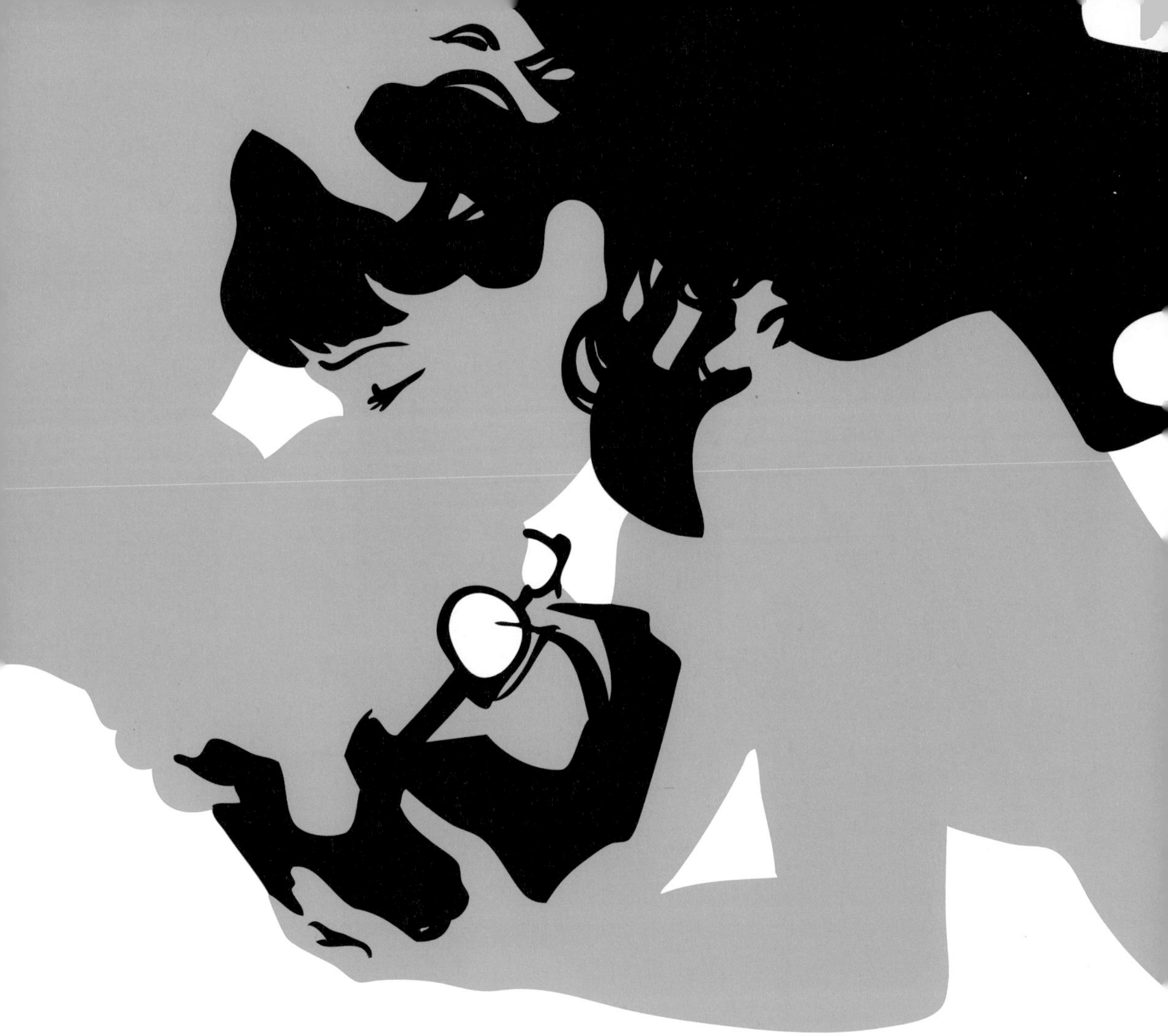

3

MY SEXUAL ERRORS & MISFORTUNES (2001-PRESENT)

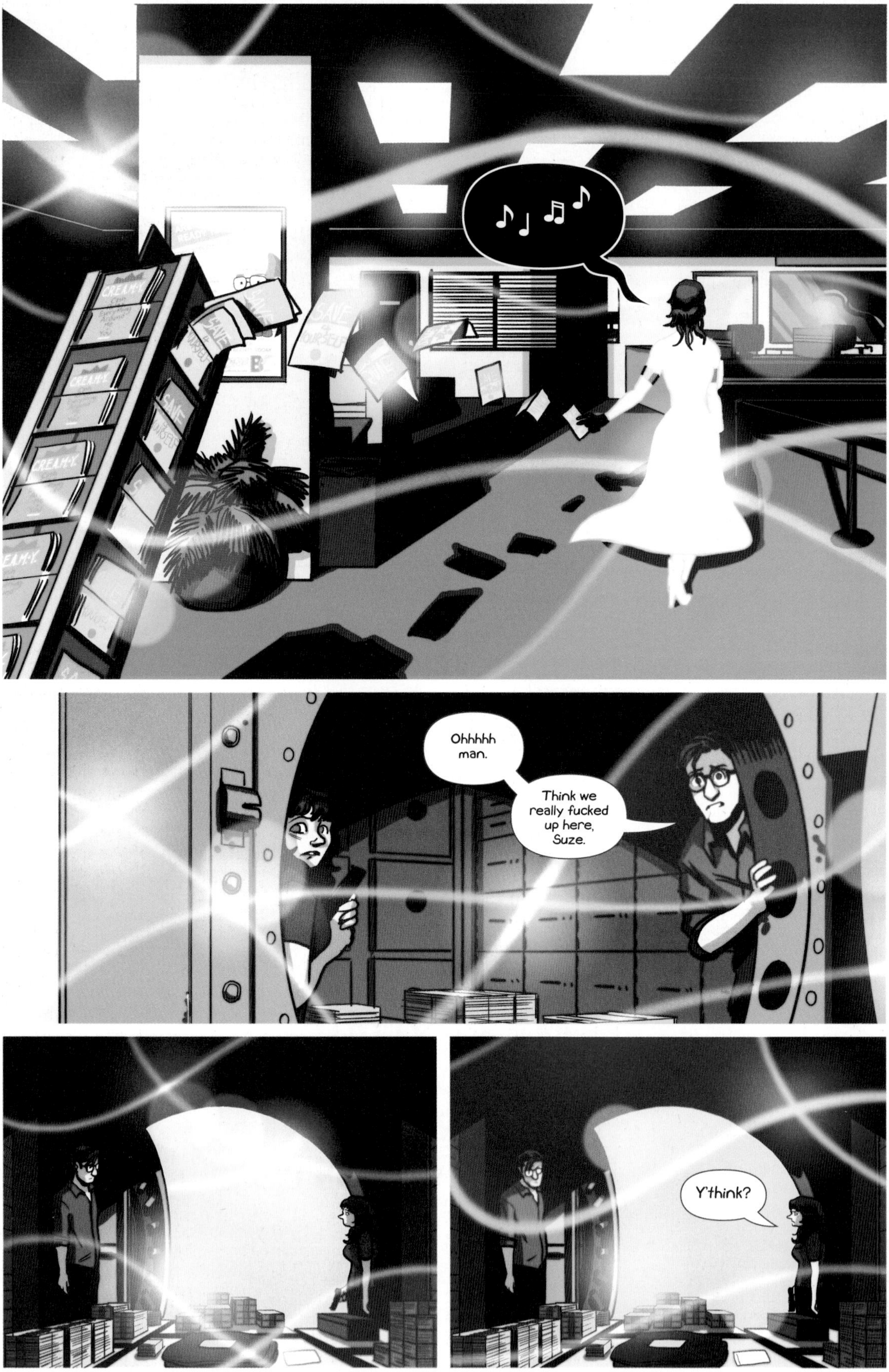
Ohhhhh man.
Think we really fucked up here, Suze.
Y'think?

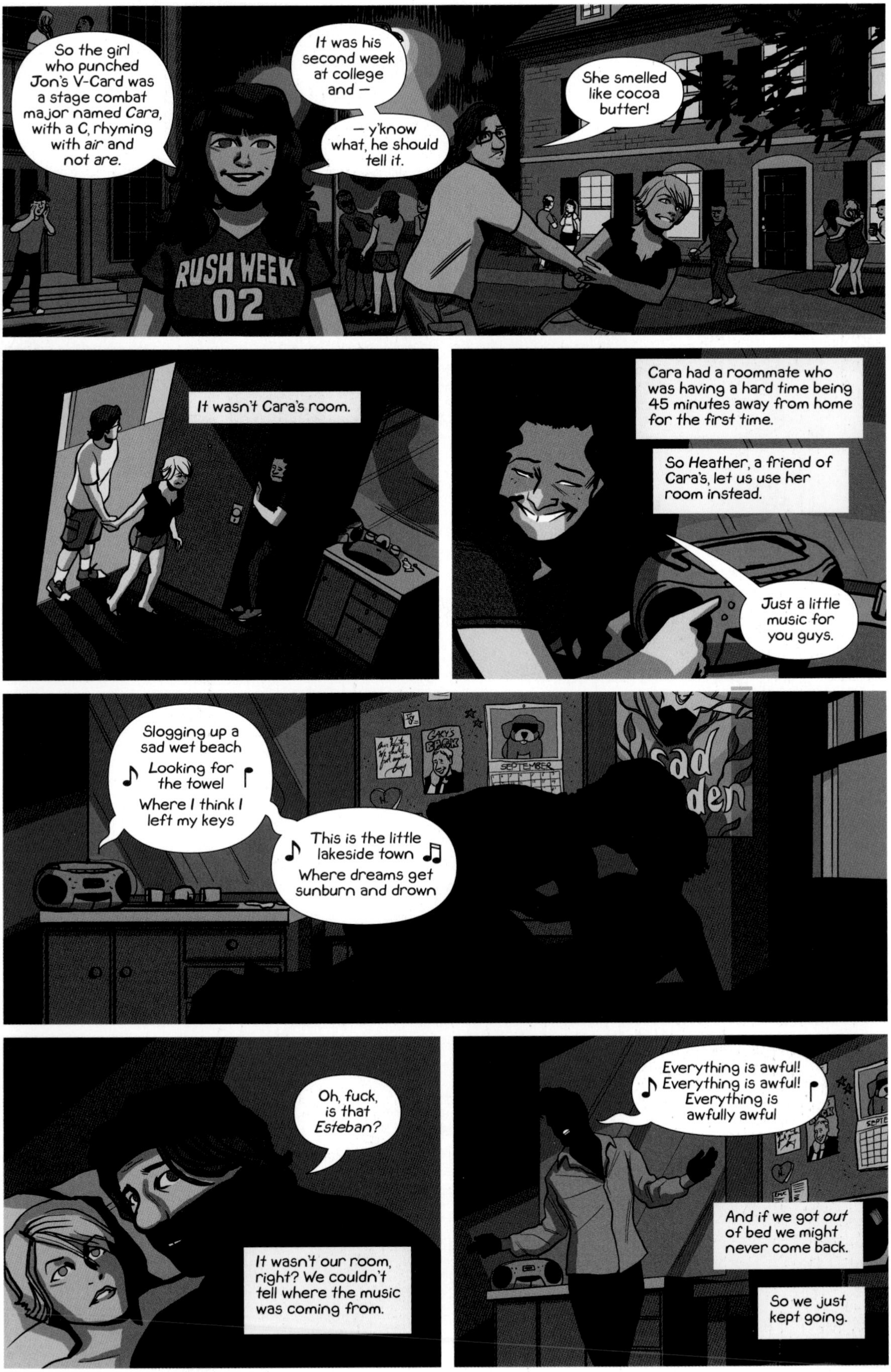

So the girl who punched Jon's V-Card was a stage combat major named *Cara*, with a C, rhyming with *air* and not *are*.
It was his second week at college and —
— y'know what, he should tell it.
She smelled like cocoa butter!
RUSH WEEK 02
It wasn't Cara's room.
Cara had a roommate who was having a hard time being 45 minutes away from home for the first time.
So Heather, a friend of Cara's, let us use her room instead.
Just a little music for you guys.
Slogging up a sad wet beach Looking for the towel Where I think I left my keys
This is the little lakeside town Where dreams get sunburn and drown
SEPTEMBER
Oh, fuck, is that *Esteban?*
It wasn't our room, right? We couldn't tell where the music was coming from.
Everything is awful! Everything is awful! Everything is awfully awful
And if we got *out* of bed we might never come back.
So we just kept going.

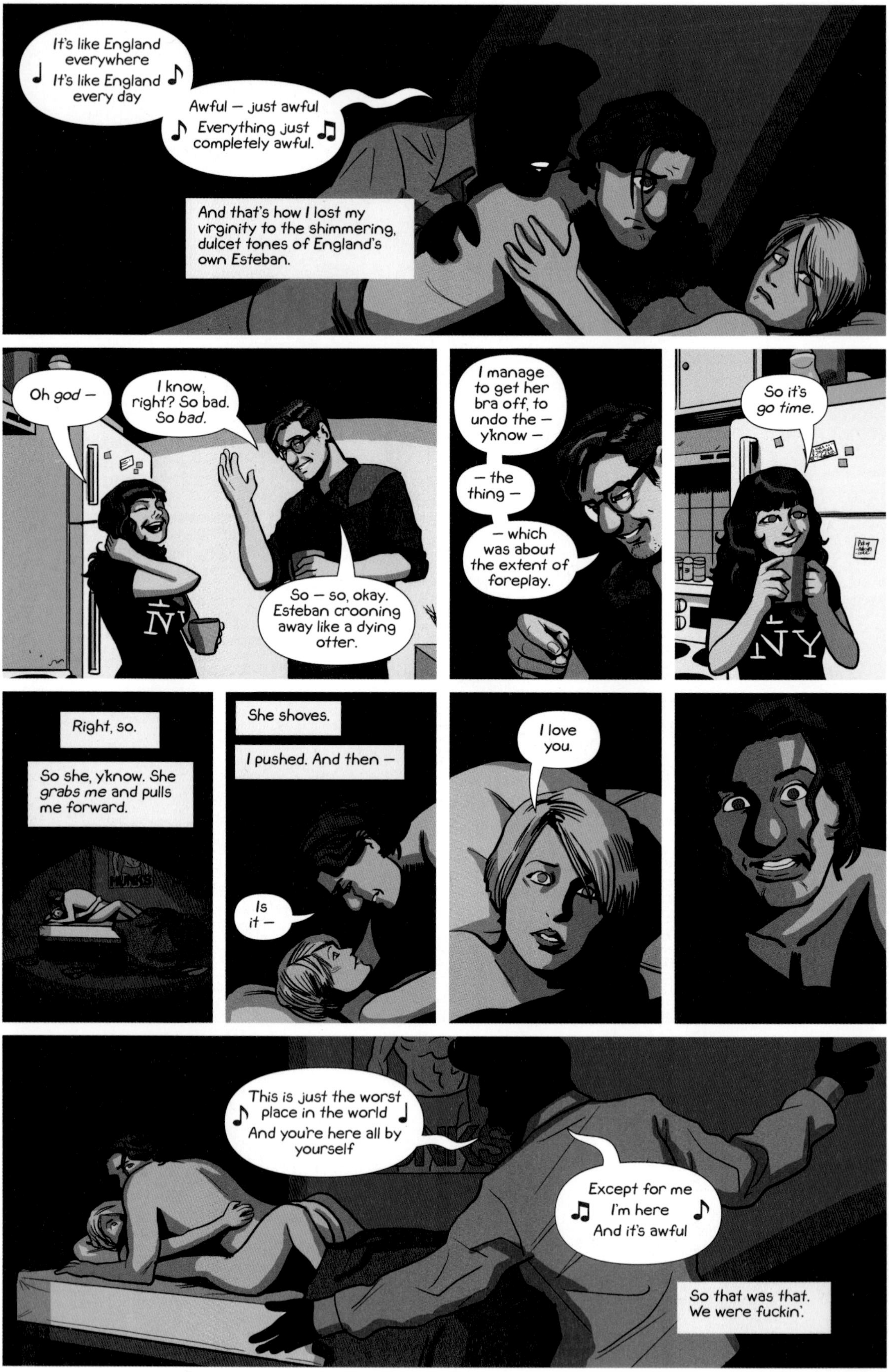

It's like England everywhere ♩ It's like England ♪ every day
Awful — just awful ♪ Everything just ♫ completely awful.
And that's how I lost my virginity to the shimmering, dulcet tones of England's own Esteban.
Oh *god* —
I know, right? So bad. So *bad*.
So — so, okay. Esteban crooning away like a dying otter.
I manage to get her bra off, to undo the — y'know —
— the thing —
— which was about the extent of foreplay.
So it's *go time*.
Right, so.
So she, y'know. She *grabs me* and pulls me forward.
She shoves.
I pushed. And then —
Is it —
I love you.
This is just the worst ♪ place in the world ♩ And you're here all by yourself
Except for me ♫ I'm here ♪ And it's awful
So that was that. We were fuckin'.

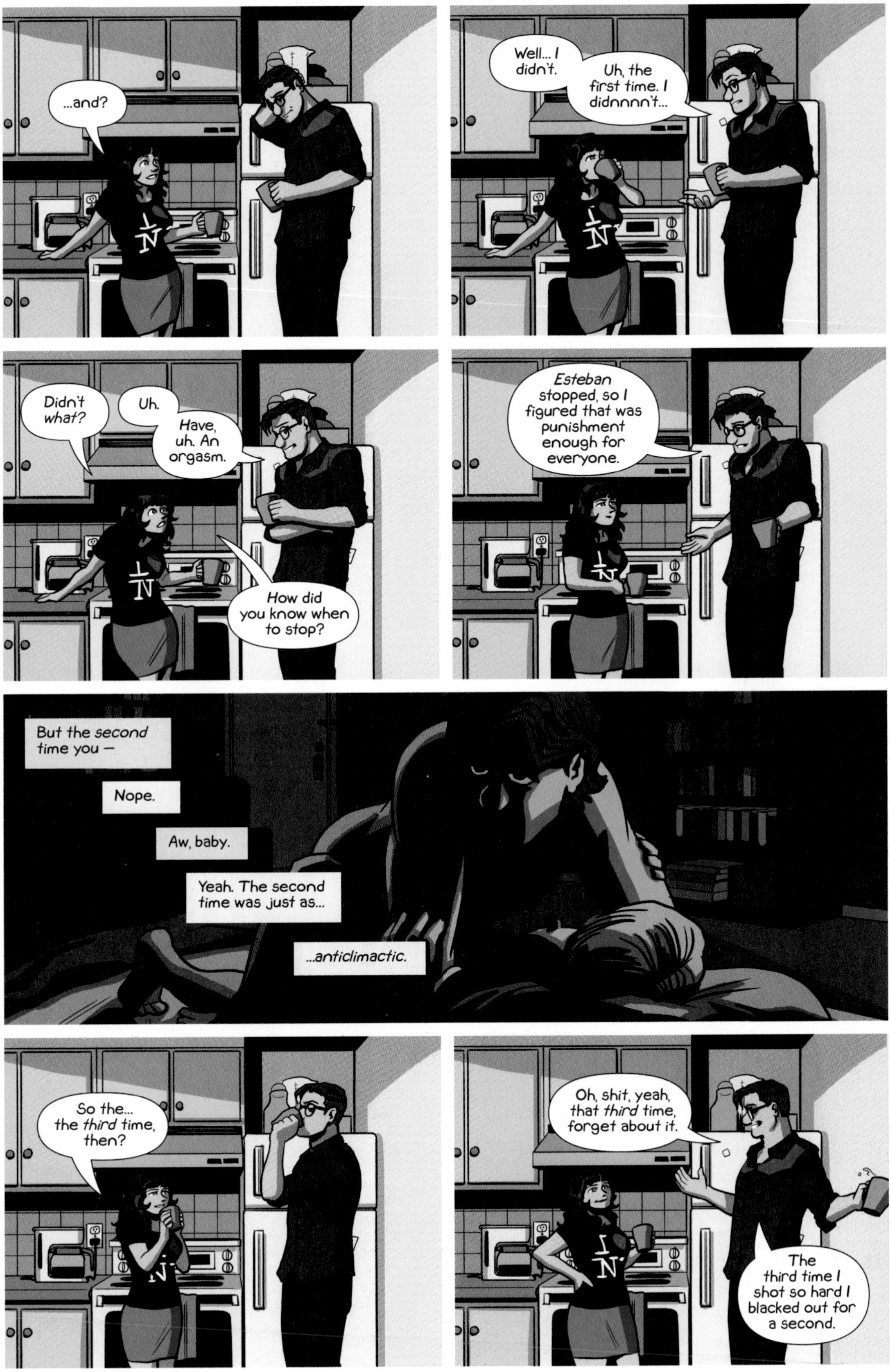
...and?
Well... I didn't.
Uh, the first time. I didnnnn't...
Didn't what?
Uh.
Have, uh. An orgasm.
How did you know when to stop?
Esteban stopped, so I figured that was punishment enough for everyone.
But the *second* time you —
Nope.
Aw, baby.
Yeah. The second time was just as...
...anticlimactic.
So the... the *third* time, then?
Oh, shit, yeah, that *third* time, forget about it.
The third time I shot so hard I blacked out for a second.

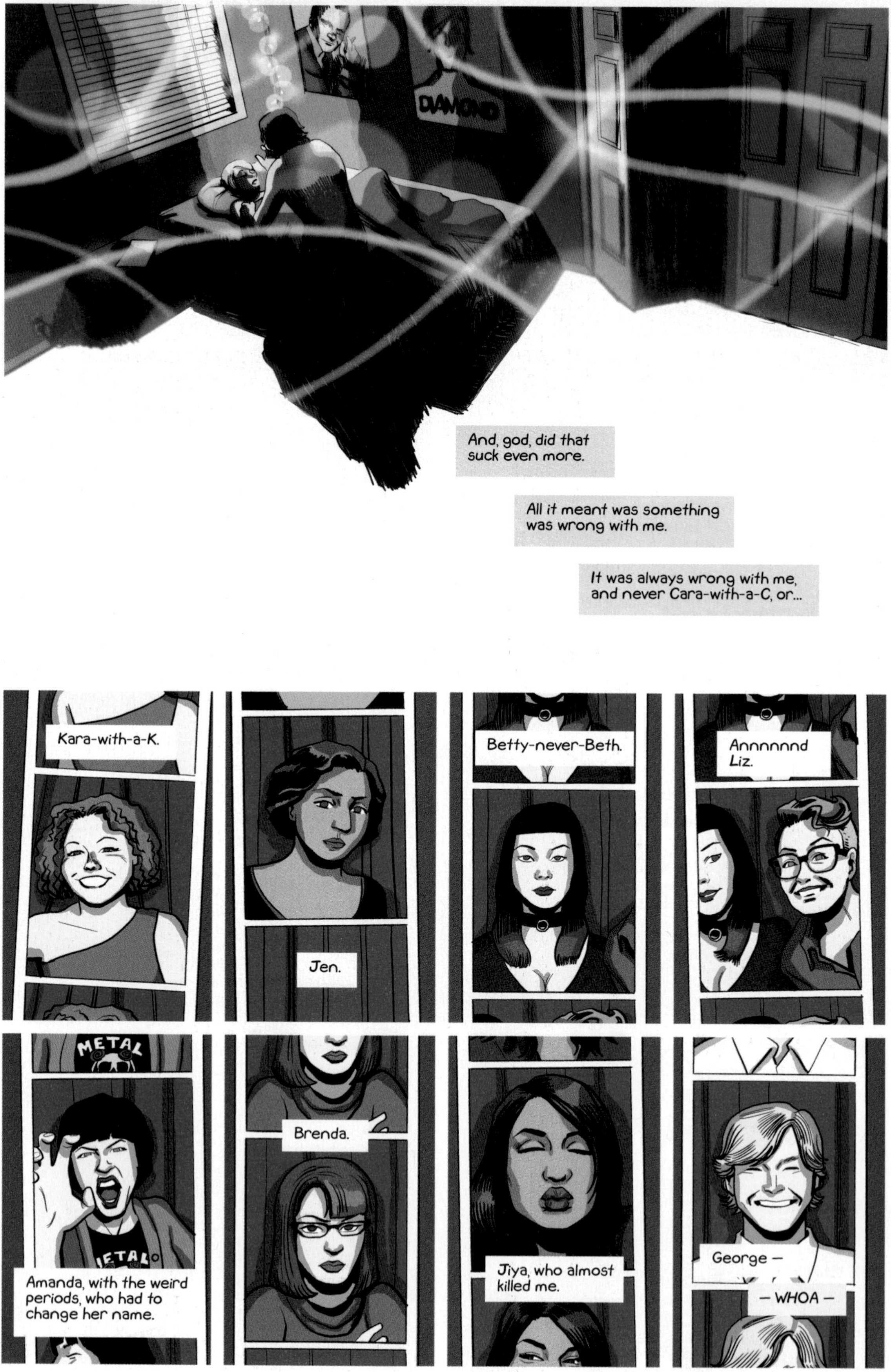
DIAMOND
And, god, did that suck even more.
All it meant was something was wrong with me.
It was always wrong with me, and never Cara-with-a-C, or...
Kara-with-a-K.
Jen.
Betty-never-Beth.
Annnnnnd Liz.
METAL
Amanda, with the weird periods, who had to change her name.
Brenda.
Jiya, who almost killed me.
George —
— WHOA —

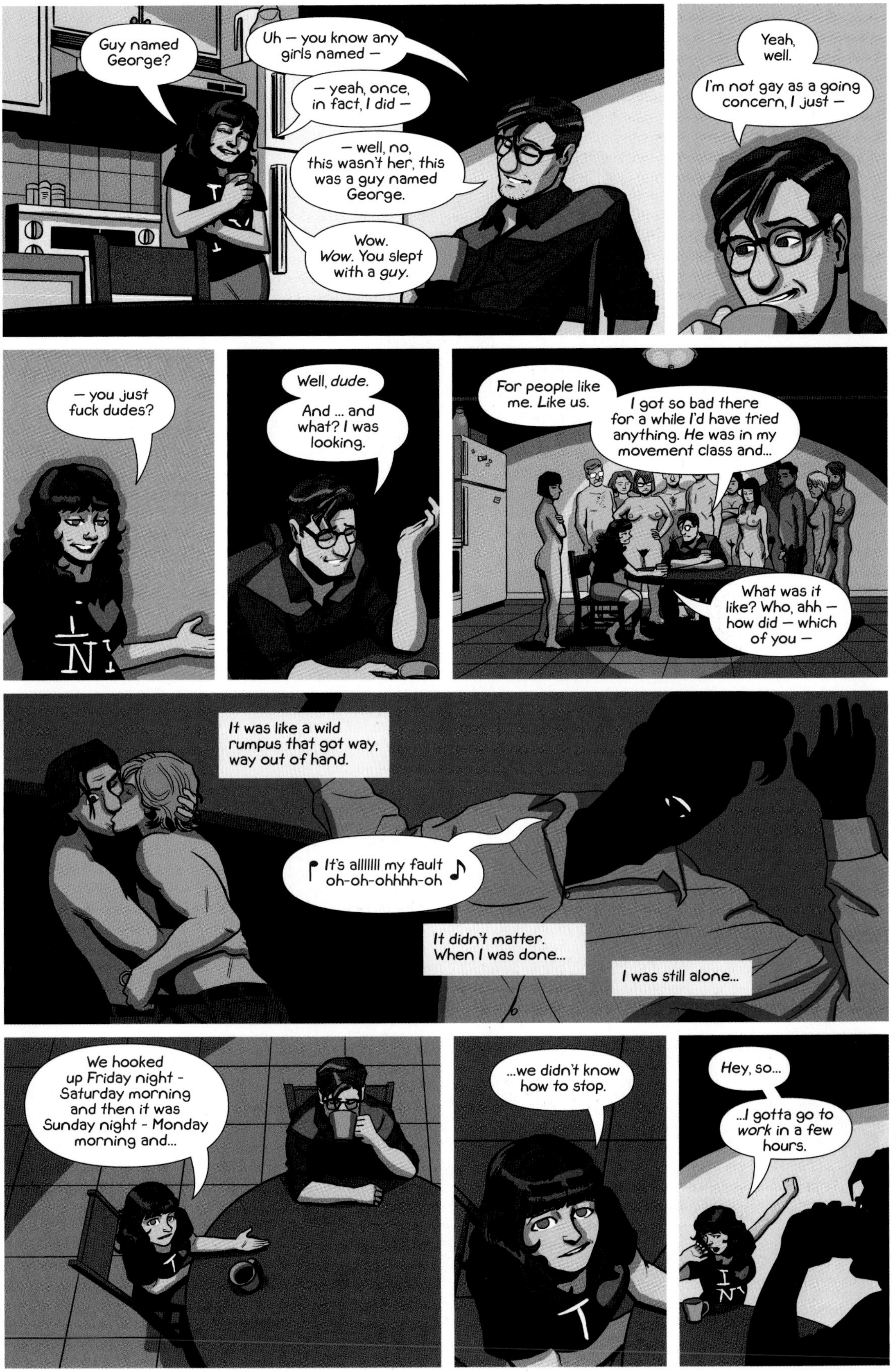
Guy named George?
Uh — you know any girls named —
— yeah, once, in fact, I did —
— well, no, this wasn't her, this was a guy named George.
Wow. *Wow.* You slept with a *guy.*
Yeah, well.
I'm not gay as a going concern, I just —
— you just fuck dudes?
Well, *dude.*
And ... and what? I was looking.
For people like me. Like us.
I got so bad there for a while I'd have tried anything. He was in my movement class and...
What was it like? Who, ahh — how did — which of you —
It was like a wild rumpus that got way, way out of hand.
It's alllllll my fault oh-oh-ohhhh-oh
It didn't matter. When I was done...
I was still alone...
We hooked up Friday night - Saturday morning and then it was Sunday night - Monday morning and...
...we didn't know how to stop.
Hey, so...
...I gotta go to *work* in a few hours.

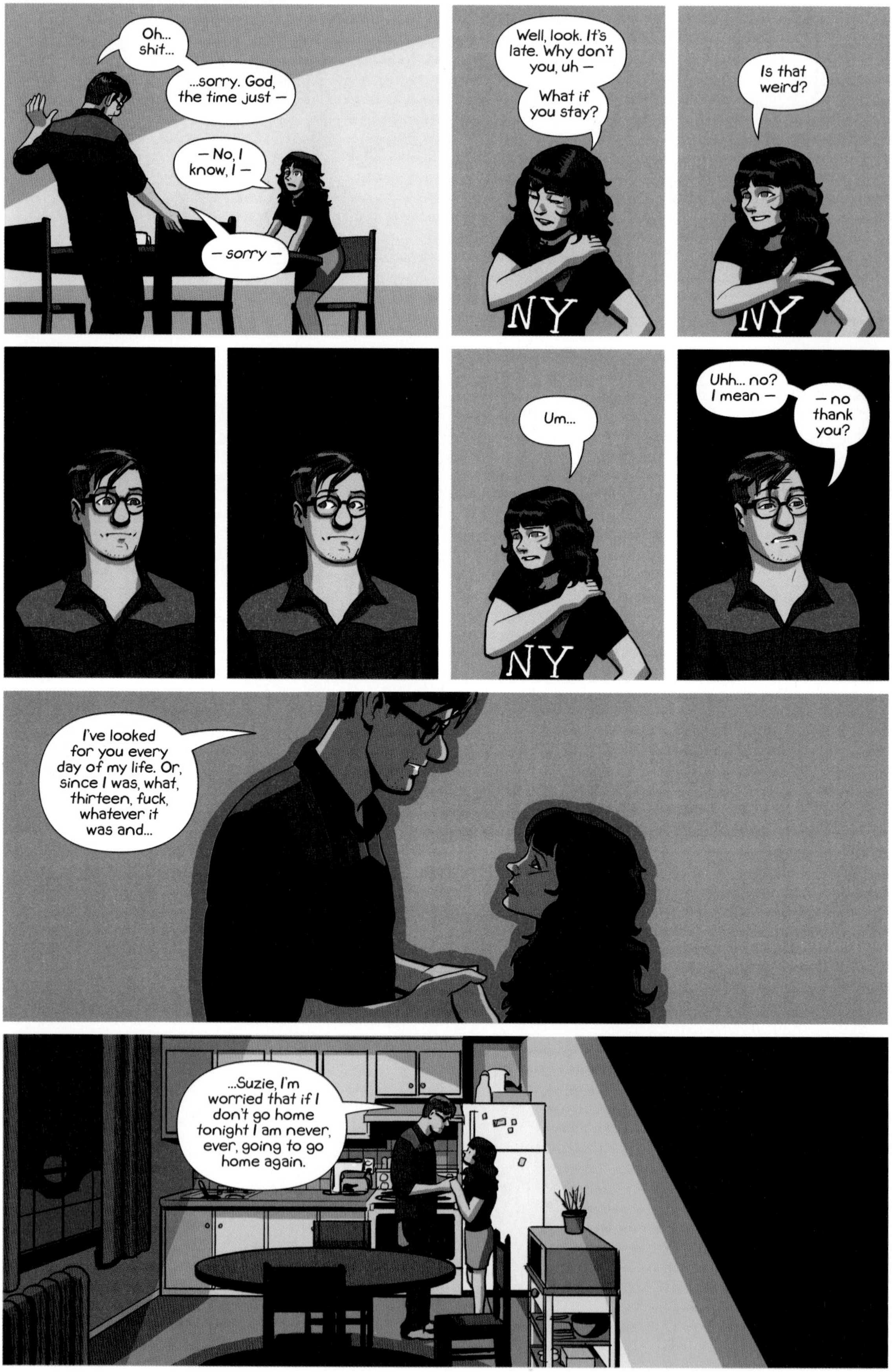
Oh... shit...
...sorry. God, the time just —
— No, I know, I —
— sorry —
Well, look. It's late. Why don't you, uh —
What if you stay?
NY
Is that weird?
NY
Um...
NY
Uhh... no? I mean —
— no thank you?
I've looked for you every day of my life. Or, since I was, what, thirteen, fuck, whatever it was and...
...Suzie, I'm worried that if I don't go home tonight I am never, ever, going to go home again.

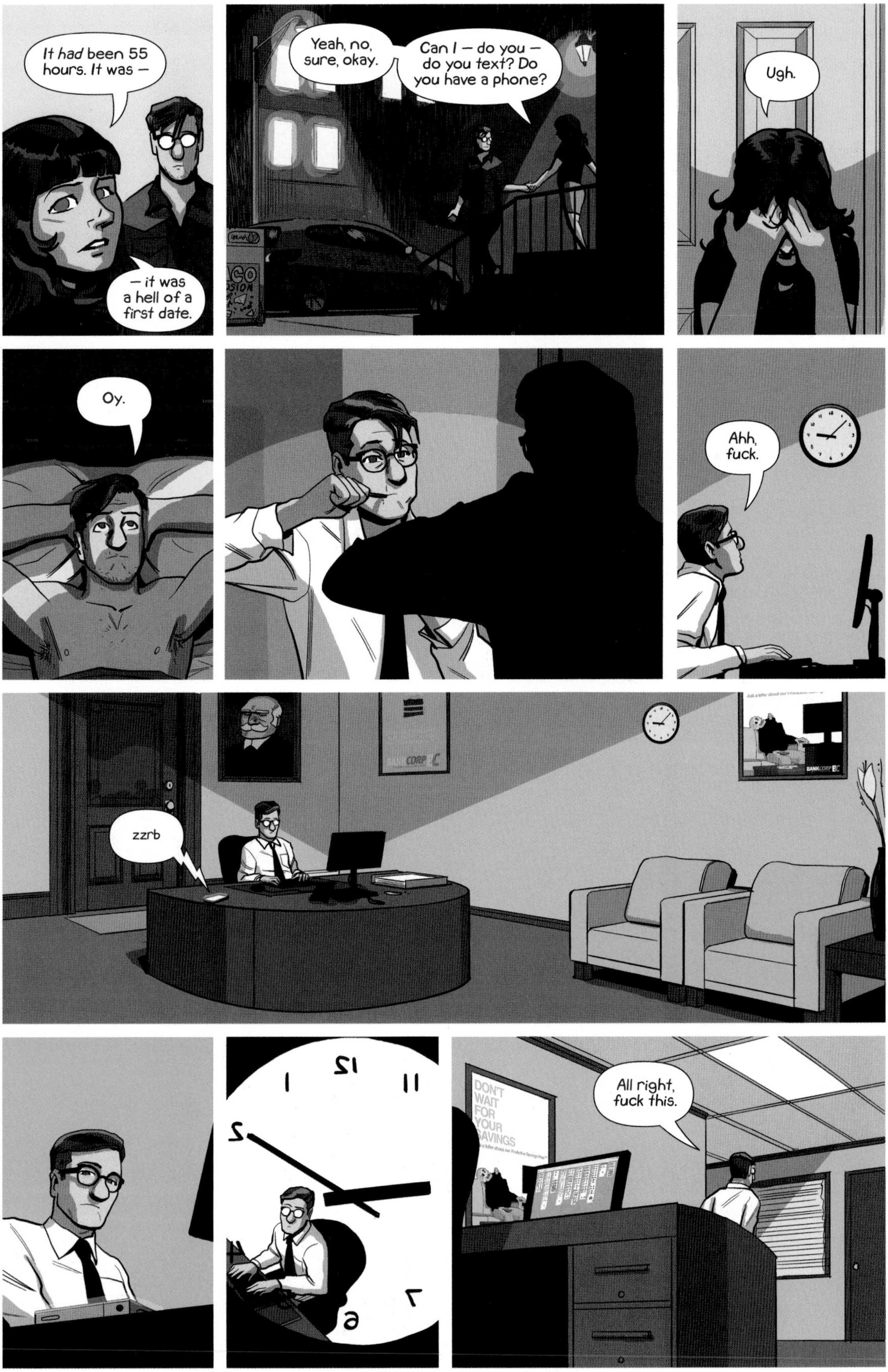
It *had* been 55 hours. It was —
— it was a hell of a first date.
Yeah, no, sure, okay.
Can I — do you — do you text? Do you have a phone?
Ugh.
Oy.
Ahh, fuck.
BANKCORP
zzrb
BANKCORP
DON'T WAIT FOR YOUR SAVINGS
All right, fuck this.

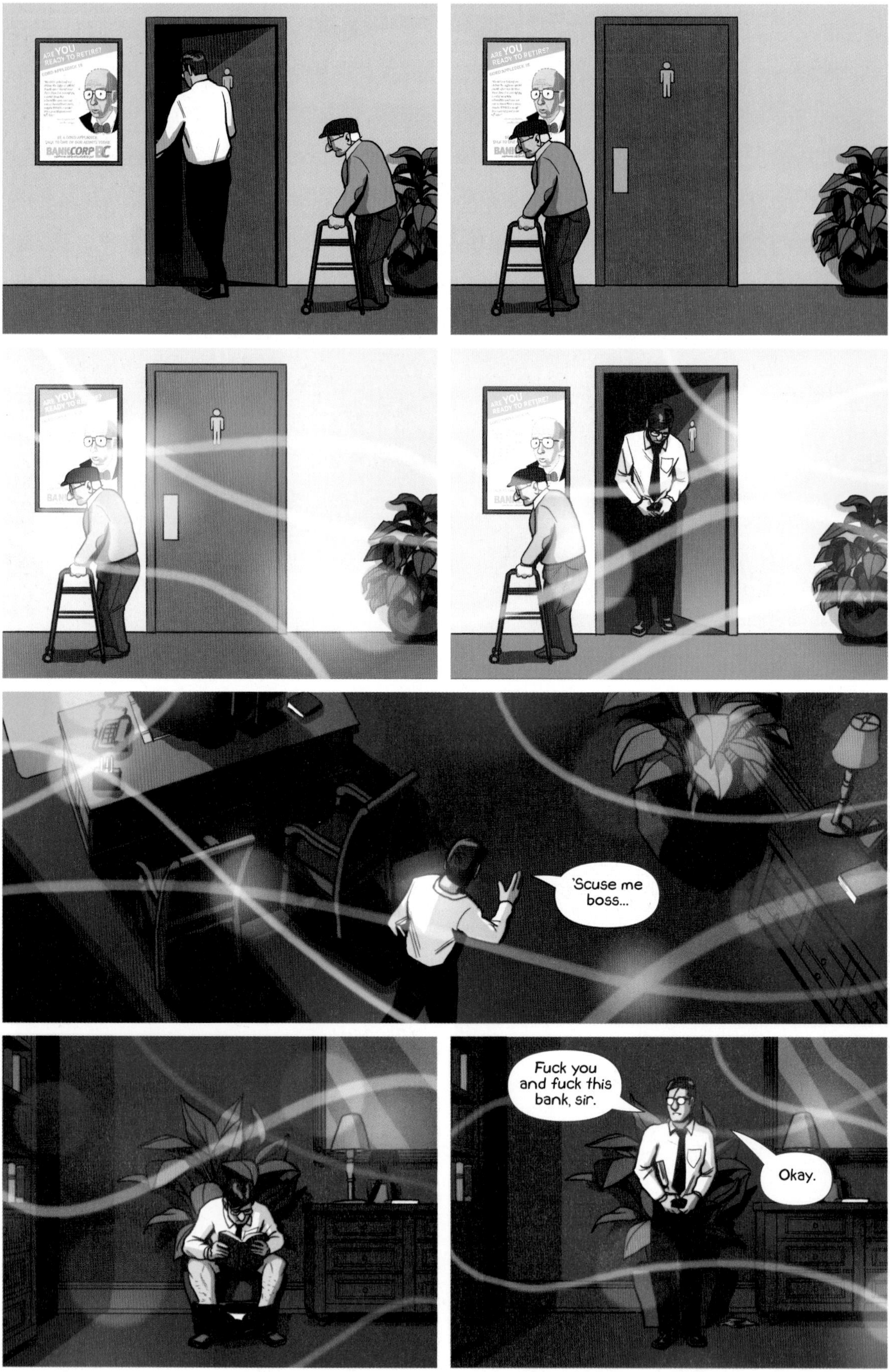
ARE YOU READY TO RETIRE?
BANKCORP
'Scuse me boss...
Fuck you and fuck this bank, sir.
Okay.

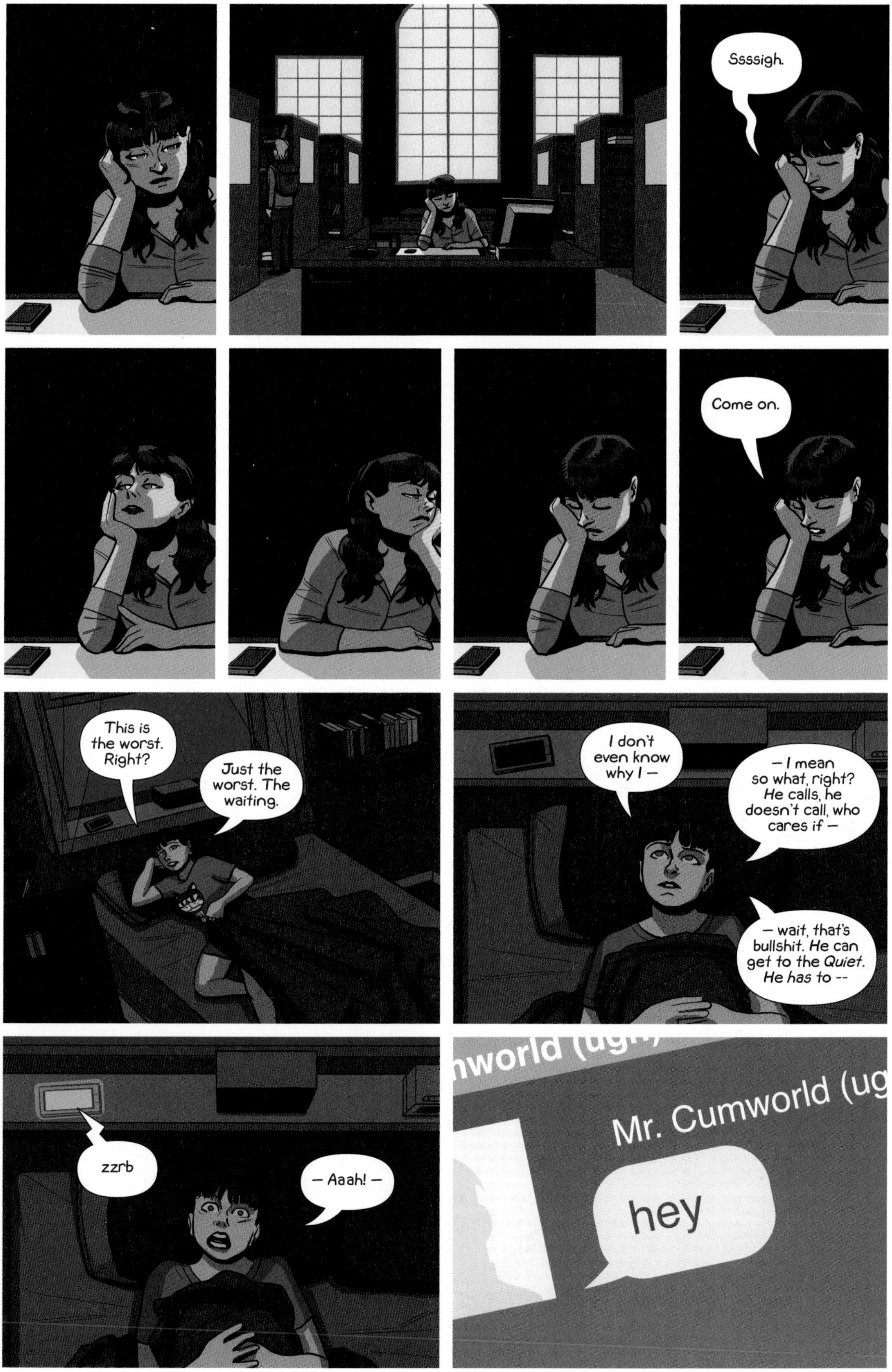
Ssssigh.
Come on.
This is the worst. Right?
Just the worst. The waiting.
I don't even know why I —
— I mean so what, right? He calls, he doesn't call, who cares if —
— wait, that's bullshit. He can get to the *Quiet*. He has to --
zzrb
— Aaah! —
Mr. Cumworld (ug
hey

Mr. Cumworld (ugh)
Mr. Cumworld (ugh)
hey
ME
HEY
I was worried you
were never calling
back
er
texting
Reply
Send
Suzie with an I & an E
HEY
I was worried you
were never calling
back
er
texting
hah. no, sorry.
work stuff.
you're kind of all
I've been
thinking about.
Send
Mr. Cumworld (ugh)
back
er
texting
Mr. Cumworld (ugh)
hah. no, sorry.
work stuff.
you're kind of all I've
been thinking about.
ME
=====> ~~~ ((
Reply
Send
Suzie with an I & an E
work stuff.
you're kind of all
I've been
thinking about.
=====> ~~~ ((
that's about right
I pack five whole
equal signs
god I hate my job
Send
Mr. Cumworld (ugh)
Mr. Cumworld (ugh)
god I hate my job
ME
I love my job. just
nobody else does.
ME
hey we've just
texted all day.
I think you like me.
take me out tonight
Reply
Send
Aww,
gentle jesus,
not again –
Suzie with an I & an E
I love my job. just
nobody else does.
hey we've just
texted all day.
I think you like me.
take me out tonight
ok
think I want to
take you
to cumworld
Send

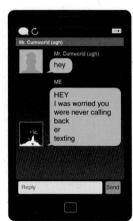

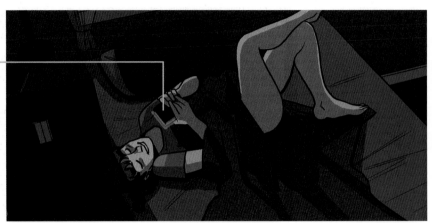

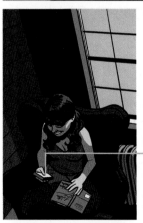

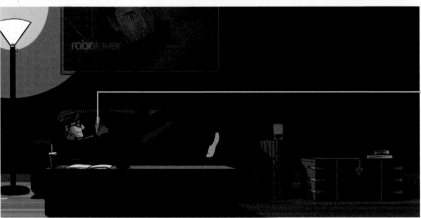

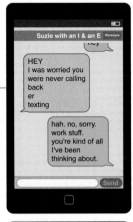

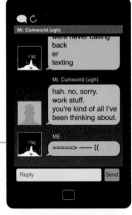

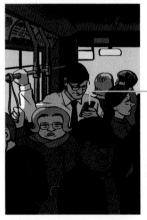

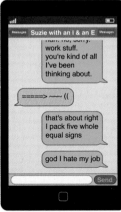

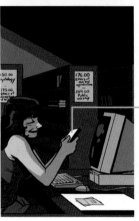

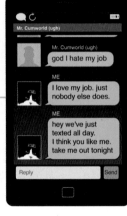

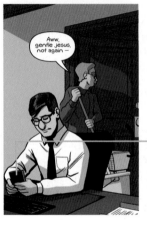

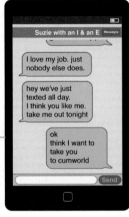

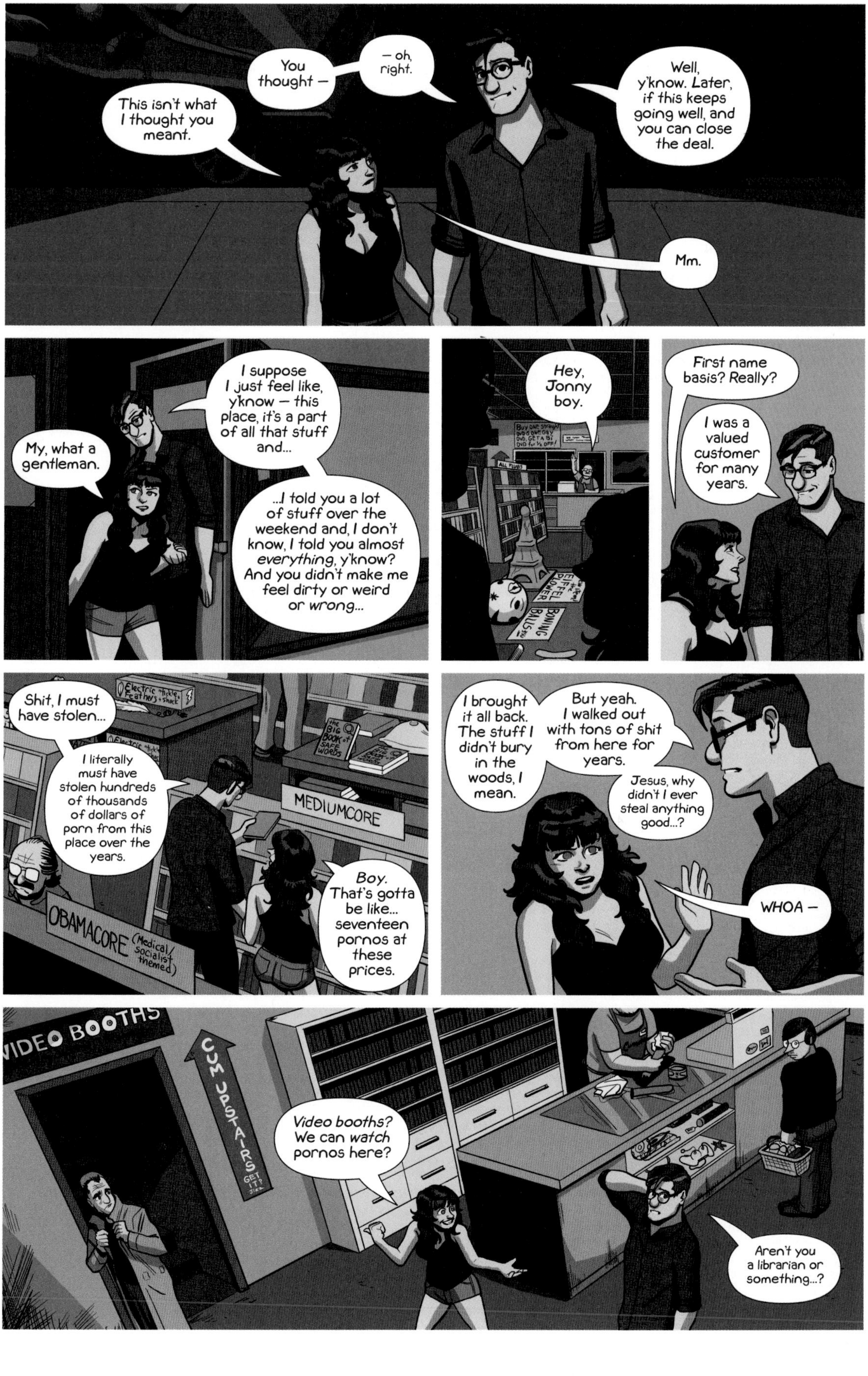
This isn't what I thought you meant.
You thought —
— oh, right.
Well, y'know. Later, if this keeps going well, and you can close the deal.
Mm.
My, what a gentleman.
I suppose I just feel like, y'know — this place, it's a part of all that stuff and...
...I told you a lot of stuff over the weekend and, I don't know, I told you almost *everything*, y'know? And you didn't make me feel dirty or weird or *wrong*...
Hey, Jonny boy.
ALL PLUGS
EIFFEL TOWER
BONING BALLS
First name basis? Really?
I was a valued customer for many years.
Shit, I must have stolen...
I literally must have stolen hundreds of thousands of dollars of porn from this place over the years.
Boy. That's gotta be like... seventeen pornos at these prices.
Electric tickle Feathers + shock
THE BIG BOOK of SAFE WORDS
MEDIUMCORE
OBAMACORE (Medical/socialist themed)
I brought it all back. The stuff I didn't bury in the woods, I mean.
But yeah. I walked out with tons of shit from here for years.
Jesus, why didn't I ever steal anything good...?
WHOA —
VIDEO BOOTHS
CUM UPSTAIRS
GET IT?
Video booths? We can *watch* pornos here?
Aren't you a librarian or something...?

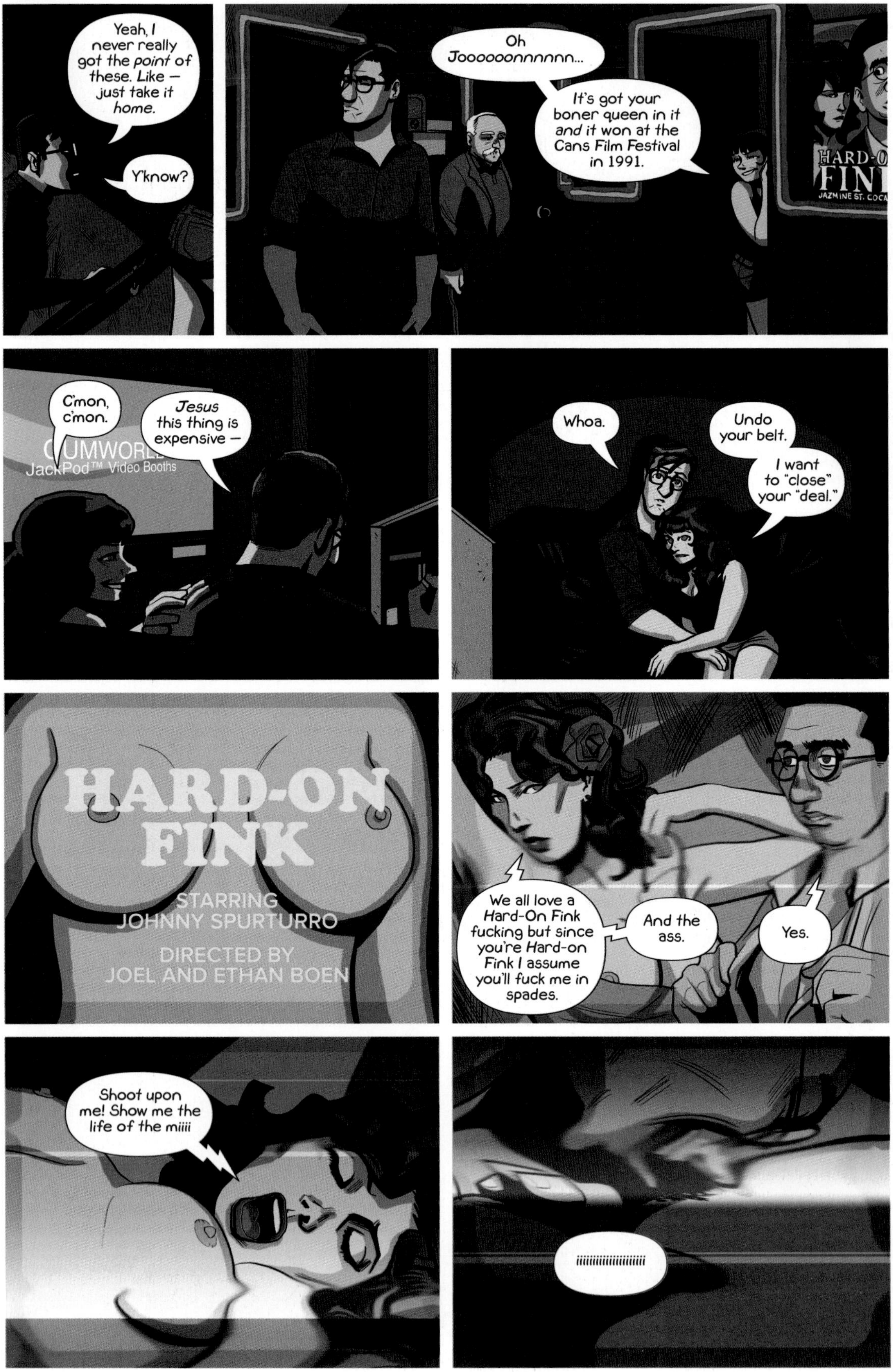
Yeah, I never really got the *point* of these. Like — just take it *home.*
Y'know?
Oh Joooooonnnnnn...
It's got your boner queen in it *and* it won at the Cans Film Festival in 1991.
JAZMINE ST. COCA
C'mon, c'mon.
Jesus this thing is expensive —
JackPod™ Video Booths
Whoa.
Undo your belt.
I want to "close" your "deal."
HARD-ON FINK
STARRING JOHNNY SPURTURRO
DIRECTED BY JOEL AND ETHAN BOEN
We all love a *Hard-On Fink* fucking but since you're *Hard-on Fink* I assume you'll fuck me in spades.
And the ass.
Yes.
Shoot upon me! Show me the life of the miiii
iiiiiiiiiiiiiiiiiiiii

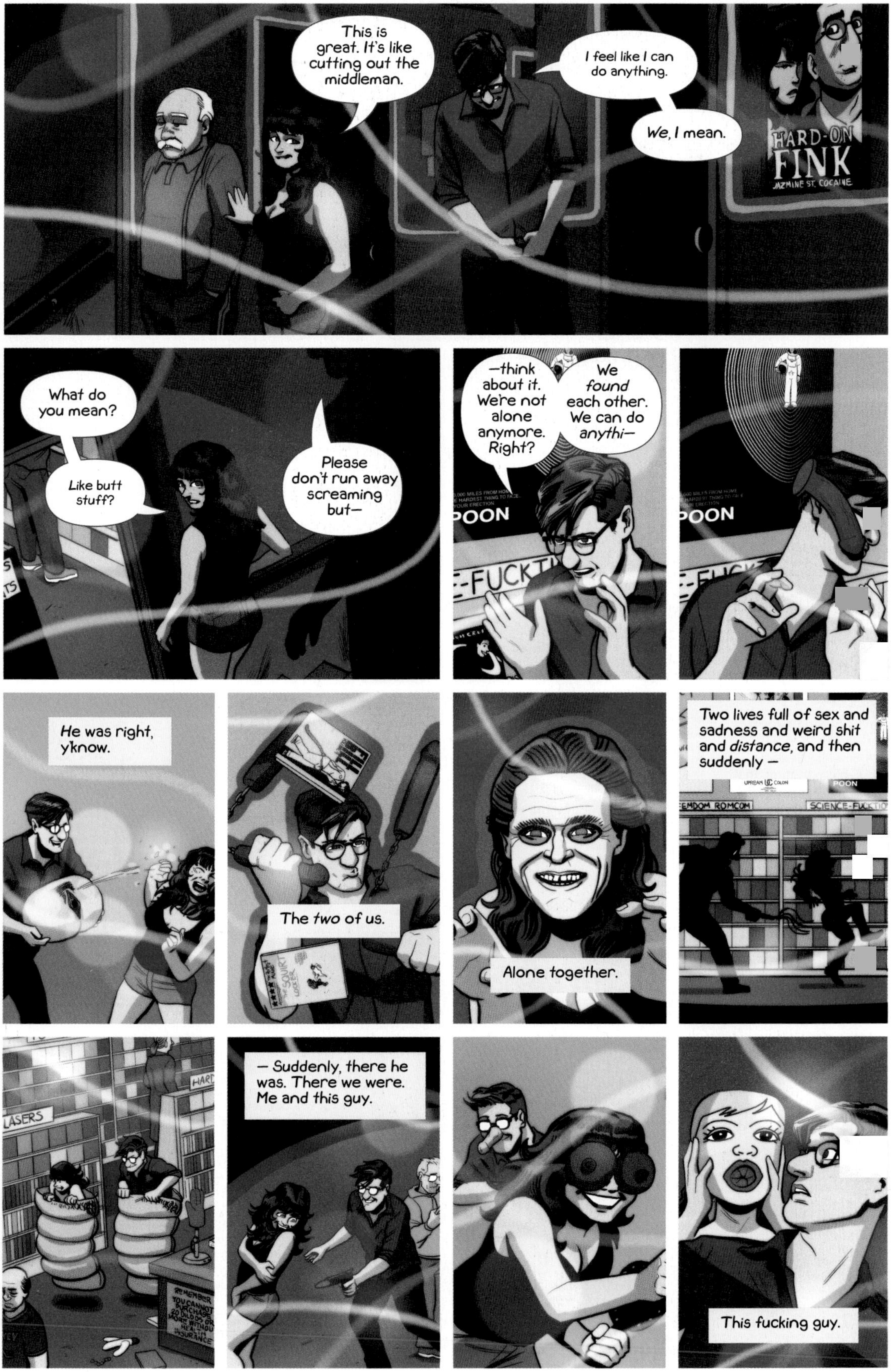
This is great. It's like cutting out the middleman.
I feel like I can do anything.
We, I mean.
HARD-ON FINK
JAZMINE ST. COCAINE
What do you mean?
Like butt stuff?
Please don't run away screaming but—
—think about it. We're not alone anymore. Right?
We *found* each other. We can do *anythi—*
POON
He was right, y'know.
The *two* of us.
Alone together.
Two lives full of sex and sadness and weird shit and *distance*, and then suddenly —
LASERS
REMEMBER YOU CANNOT PURCHASE 20 DILDOS OR MORE WITHOUT HEALTH INSURANCE
— Suddenly, there he was. There we were. Me and this guy.
This fucking guy.

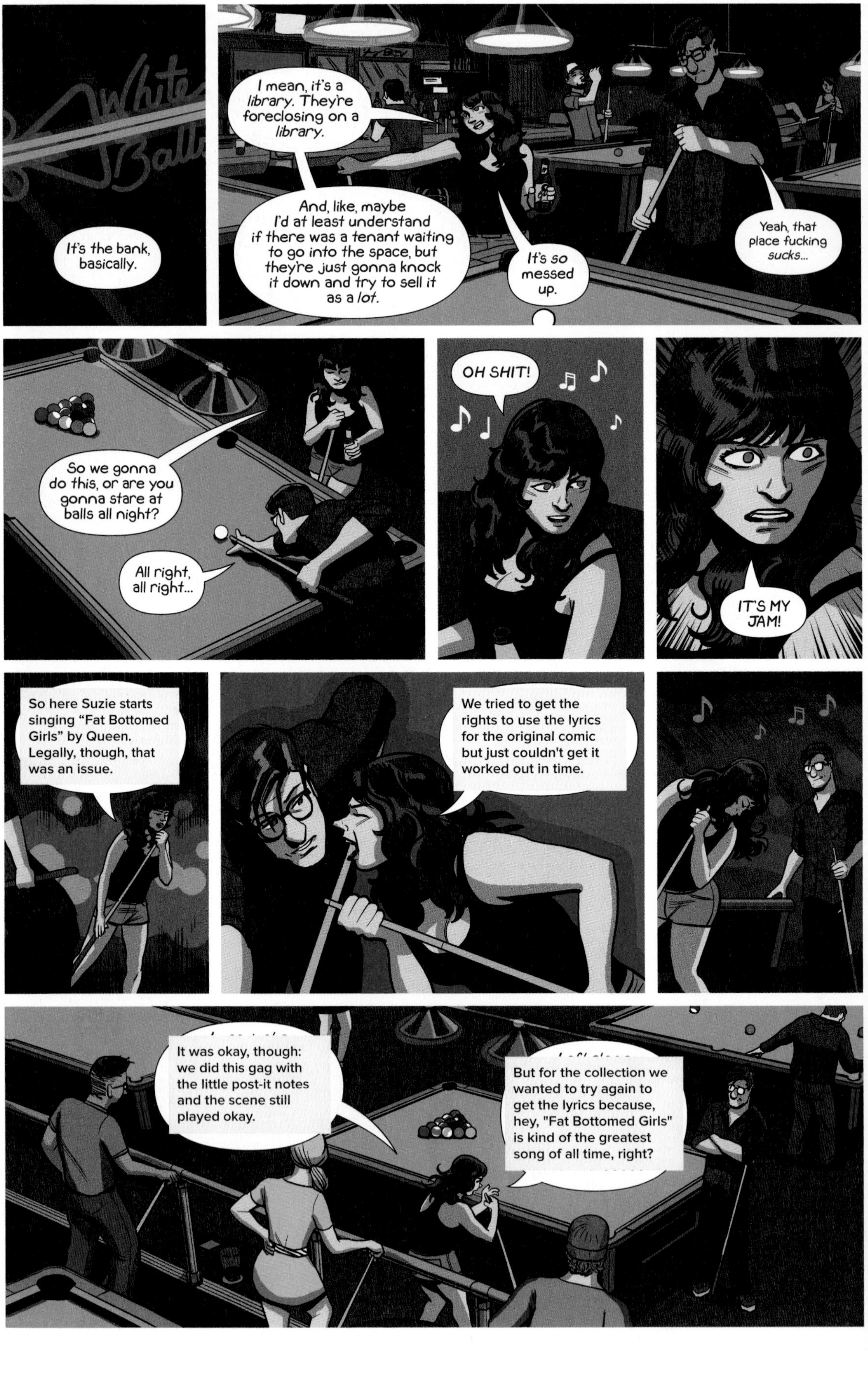
It's the bank, basically.
I mean, it's a *library*. They're foreclosing on a *library*.
And, like, maybe I'd at least understand if there was a tenant waiting to go into the space, but they're just gonna knock it down and try to sell it as a *lot*.
It's so messed up.
Yeah, that place fucking *sucks*...
So we gonna do this, or are you gonna stare at balls all night?
All right, all right...
OH SHIT!
IT'S MY JAM!
So here Suzie starts singing "Fat Bottomed Girls" by Queen. Legally, though, that was an issue.
We tried to get the rights to use the lyrics for the original comic but just couldn't get it worked out in time.
It was okay, though: we did this gag with the little post-it notes and the scene still played okay.
But for the collection we wanted to try again to get the lyrics because, hey, "Fat Bottomed Girls" is kind of the greatest song of all time, right?

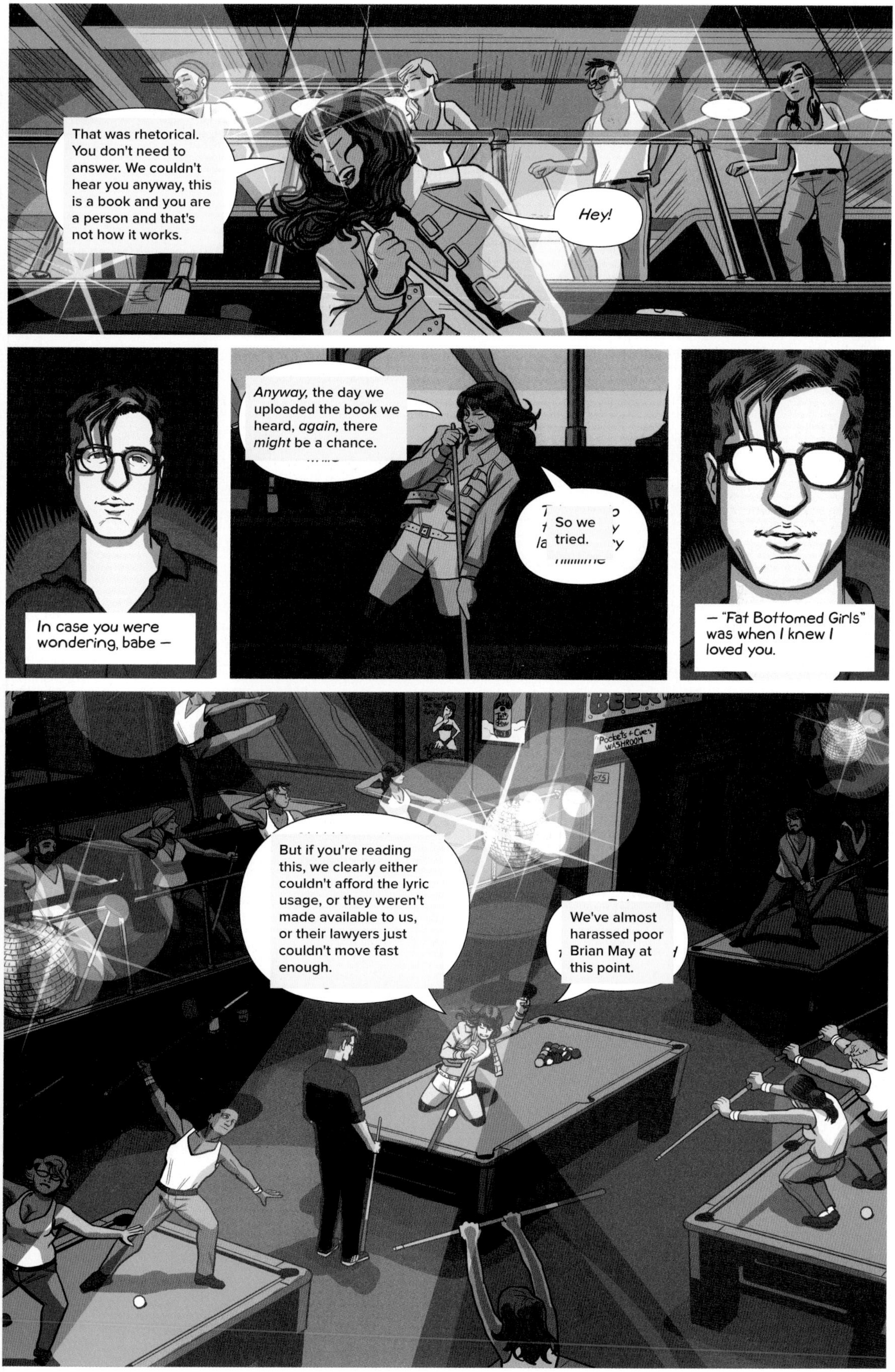
That was rhetorical. You don't need to answer. We couldn't hear you anyway, this is a book and you are a person and that's not how it works.
Hey!
In case you were wondering, babe —
Anyway, the day we uploaded the book we heard, *again,* there *might* be a chance.
So we tried.
— "Fat Bottomed Girls" was when I knew I loved you.
BEER
"Pockets + Cues" WASHROOM
But if you're reading this, we clearly either couldn't afford the lyric usage, or they weren't made available to us, or their lawyers just couldn't move fast enough.
We've almost harassed poor Brian May at this point.

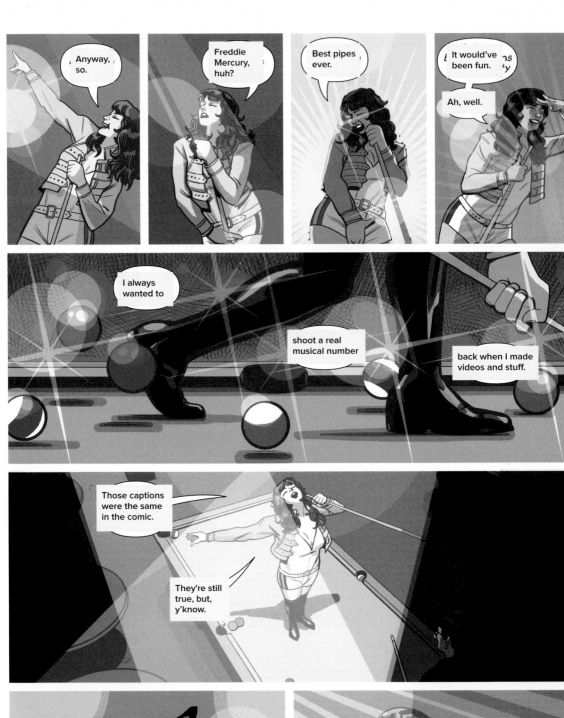

Anyway, so.

Freddie Mercury, huh?

Best pipes ever.

It would've been fun.

Ah, well.

I always wanted to

shoot a real musical number

back when I made videos and stuff.

Those captions were the same in the comic.

They're still true, but, y'know.

Ohhhhhh

I know!

I feel bad for recycling them.

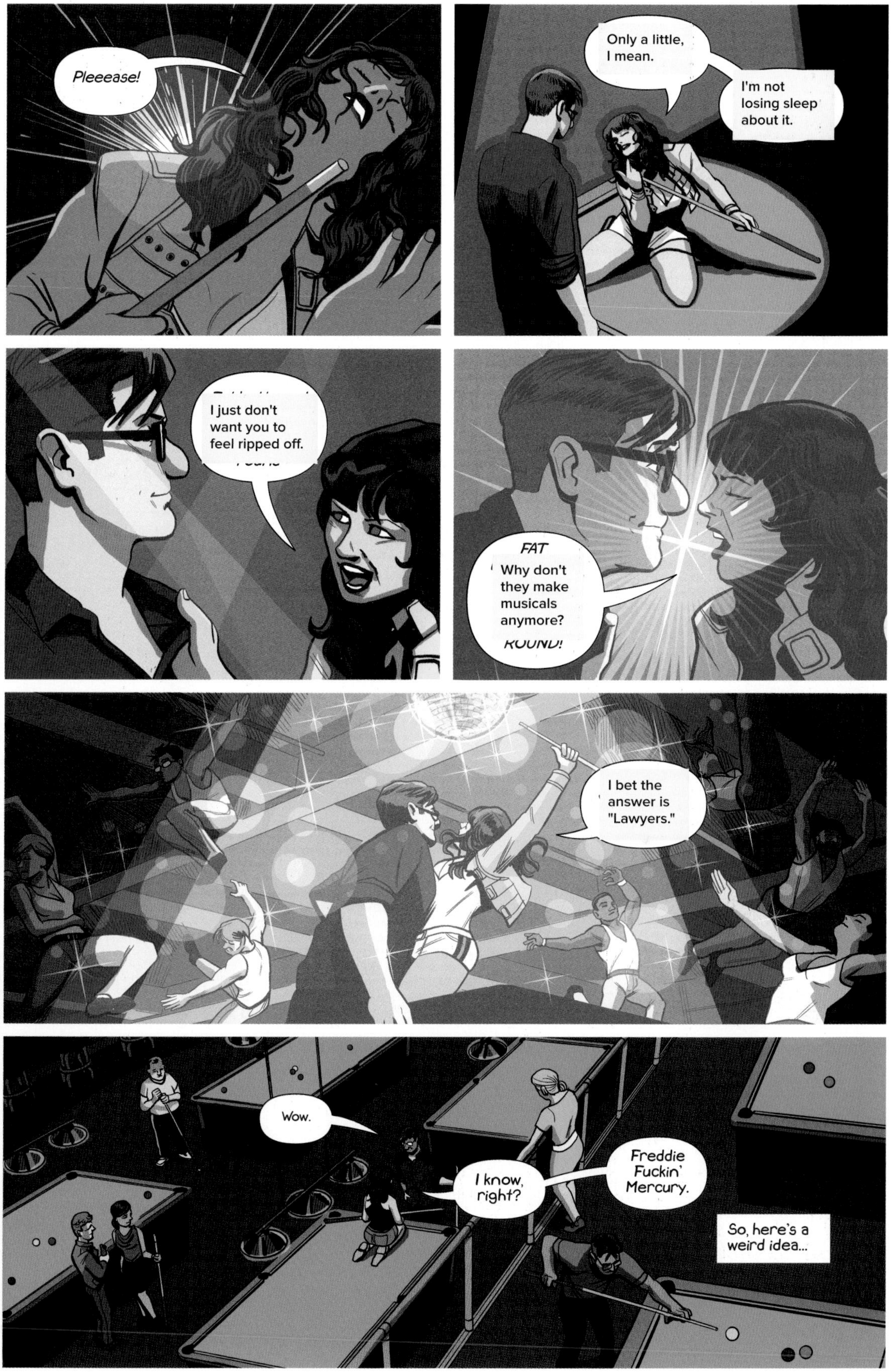

Pleeease!
Only a little, I mean.
I'm not losing sleep about it.
I just don't want you to feel ripped off.
FAT
Why don't they make musicals anymore?
I bet the answer is "Lawyers."
Wow.
I know, right?
Freddie Fuckin' Mercury.
So, here's a weird idea...

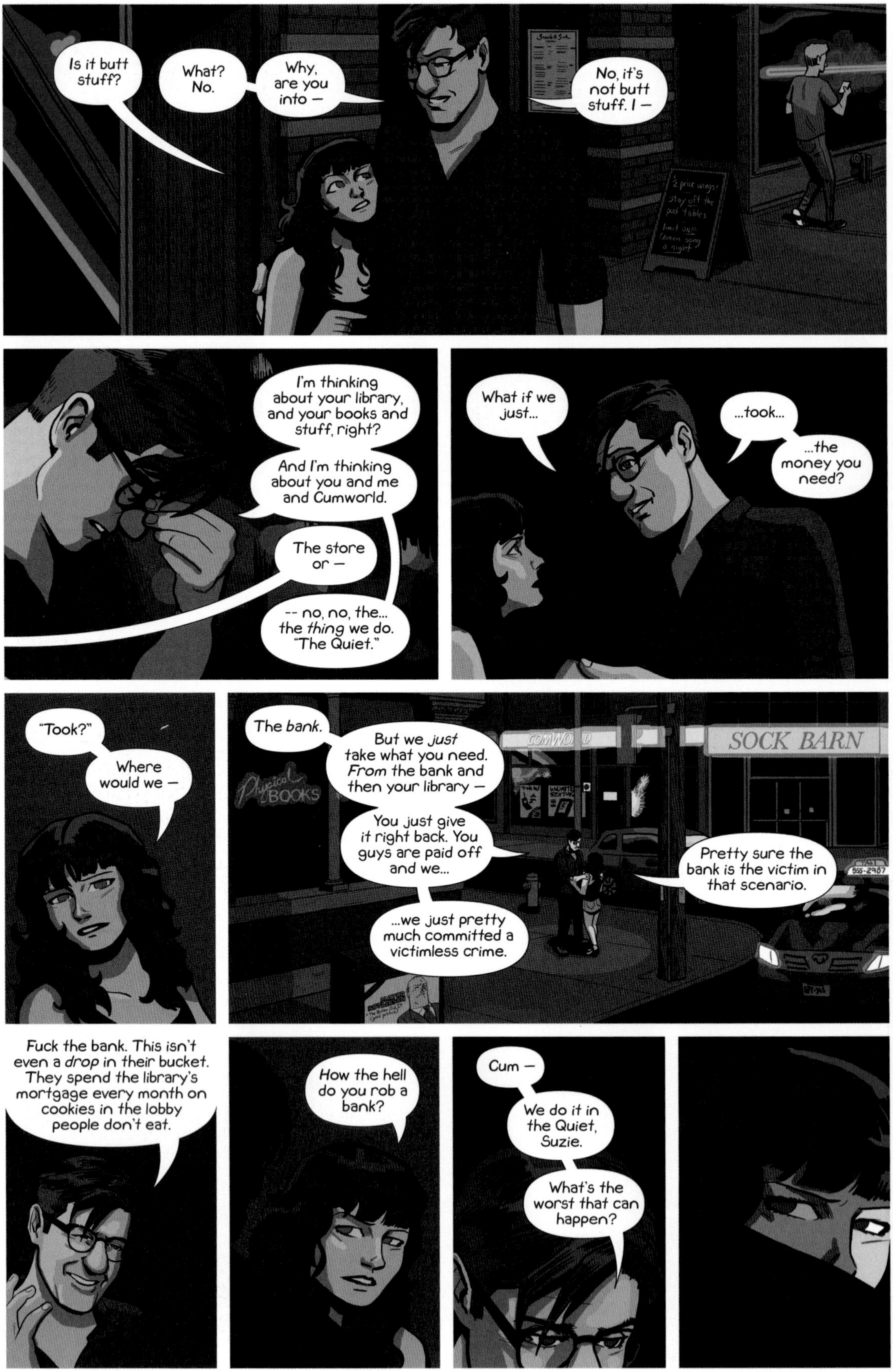
Is it butt stuff?
What? No.
Why, are you into —
No, it's not butt stuff. I —
I'm thinking about your library, and your books and stuff, right?
And I'm thinking about you and me and Cumworld.
The store or —
-- no, no, the... the *thing* we do. "The Quiet."
What if we just...
...took...
...the money you need?
"Took?"
Where would we —
The *bank.*
But we *just* take what you need. *From* the bank and then your library —
You just give it right back. You guys are paid off and we...
...we just pretty much committed a victimless crime.
Pretty sure the bank is the victim in that scenario.
SOCK BARN
Physical BOOKS
Fuck the bank. This isn't even a *drop* in their bucket. They spend the library's mortgage every month on cookies in the lobby people don't eat.
How the hell do you rob a bank?
Cum —
We do it in the Quiet, Suzie.
What's the worst that can happen?

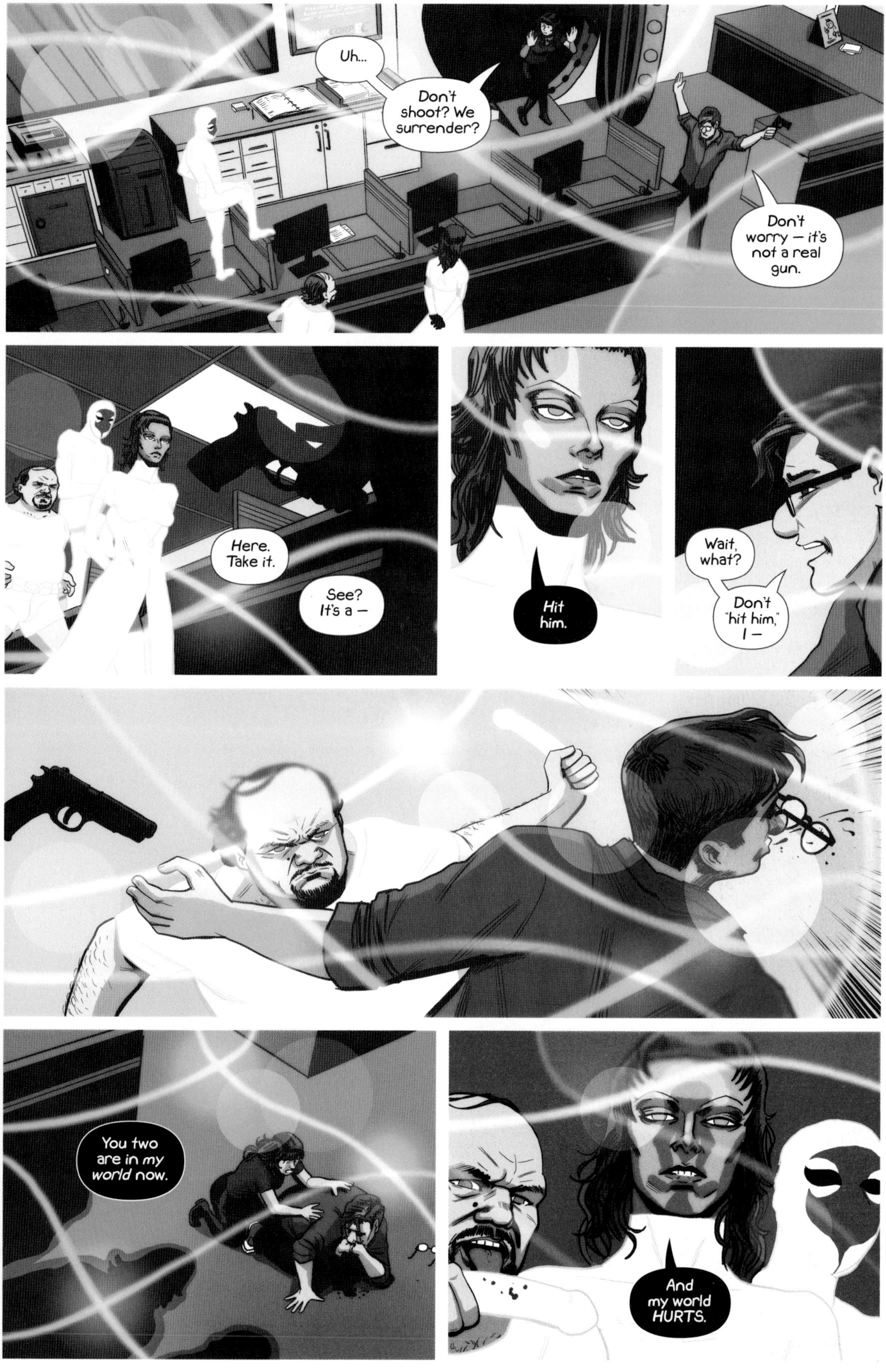
Uh...
Don't shoot? We surrender?
Don't worry — it's not a real gun.
Here. Take it.
See? It's a —
Hit him.
Wait, what?
Don't "hit him," I —
You two are in *my world* now.
And my world *HURTS.*

4
SEX
POLICE

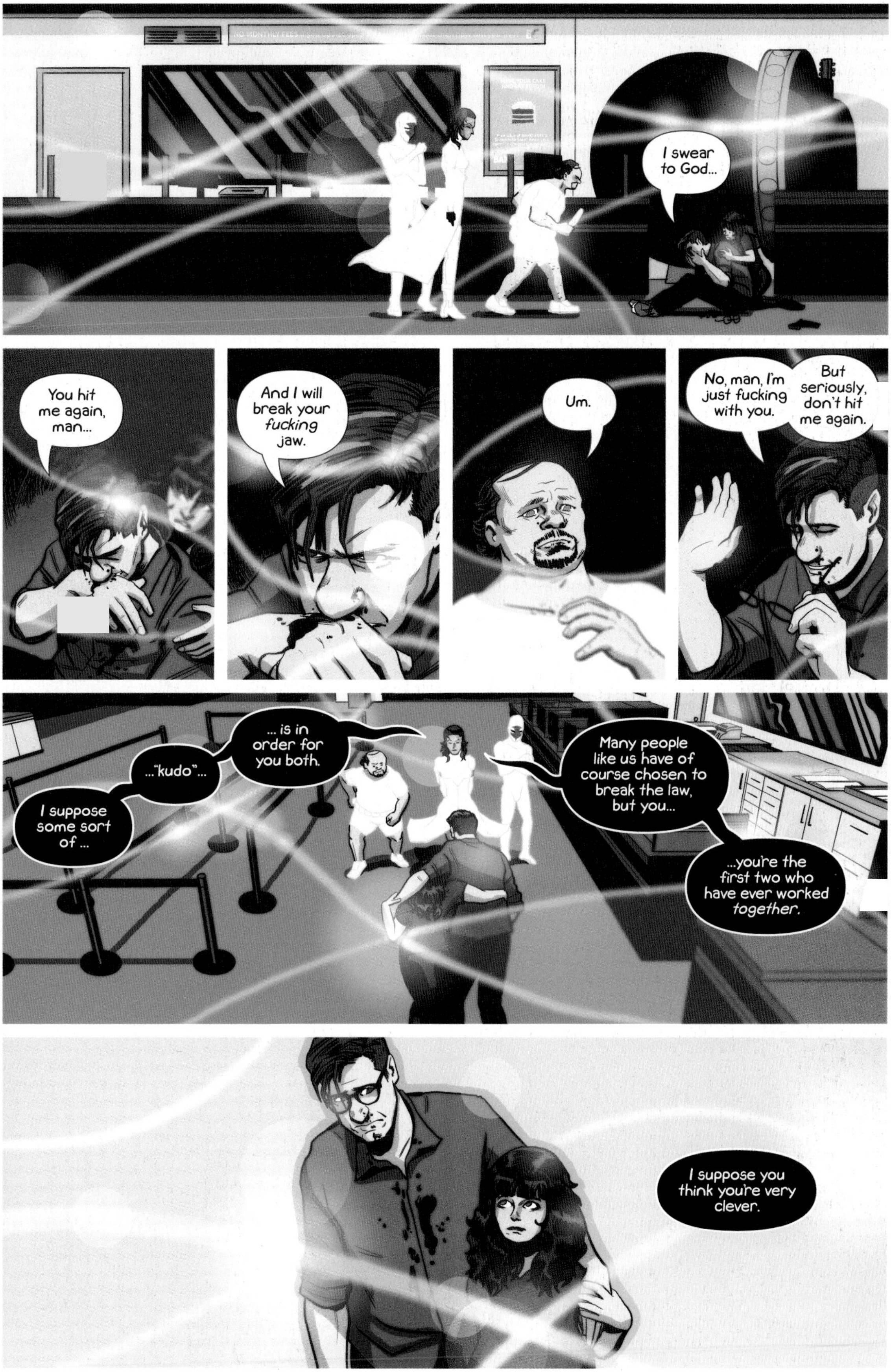
I swear to God...
You hit me again, man...
And I will break your *fucking* jaw.
Um.
No, man, I'm just fucking with you.
But seriously, don't hit me again.
I suppose some sort of ...
..."kudo"...
... is in order for you both.
Many people like us have of course chosen to break the law, but you...
...you're the first two who have ever worked *together*.
I suppose you think you're very clever.

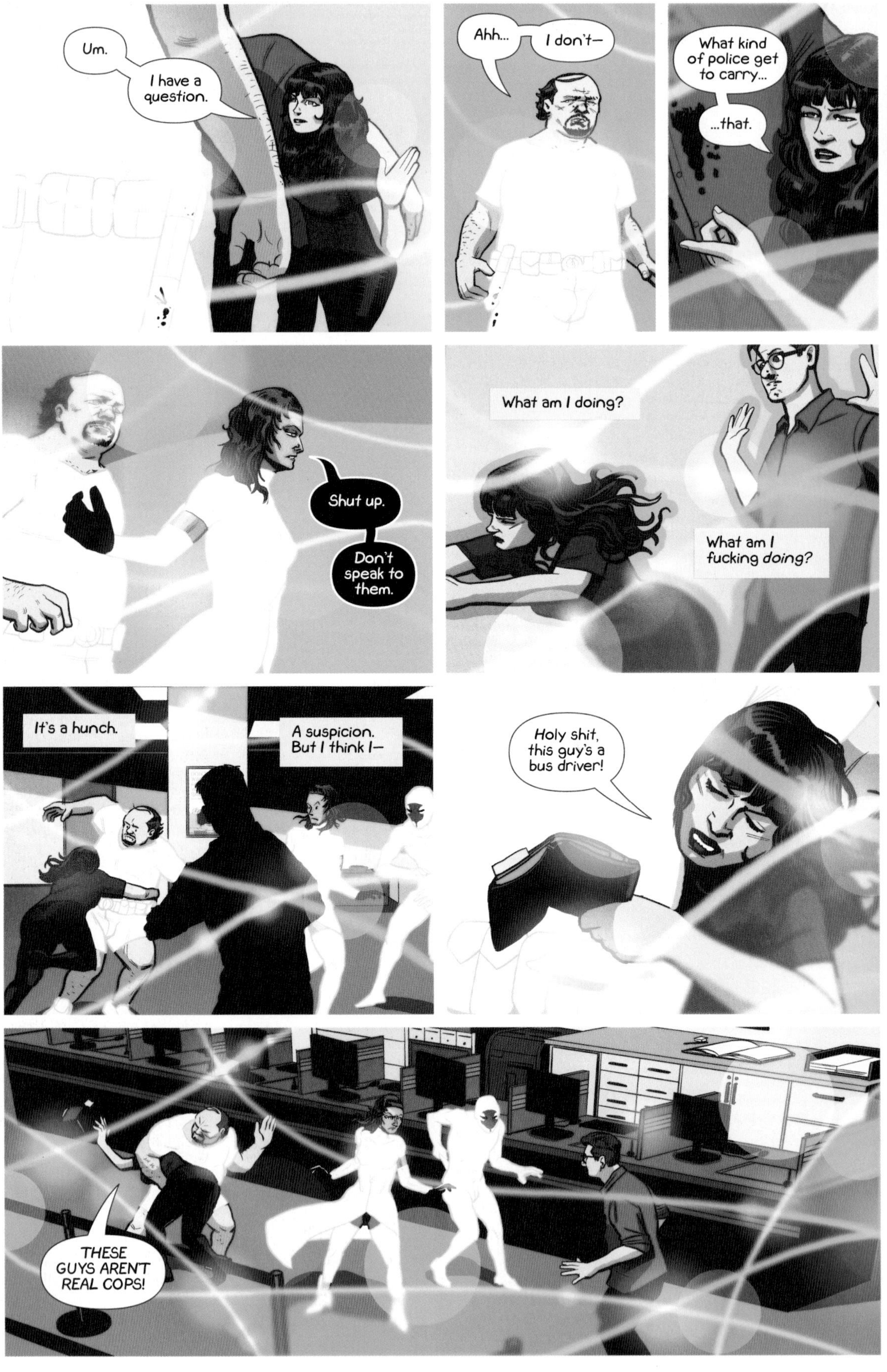
Um.
I have a question.
Ahh...
I don't—
What kind of police get to carry...
...that.
Shut up.
Don't speak to them.
What am I doing?
What am I fucking *doing*?
It's a hunch.
A suspicion. But I think I—
Holy shit, this guy's a bus driver!
THESE GUYS AREN'T REAL COPS!

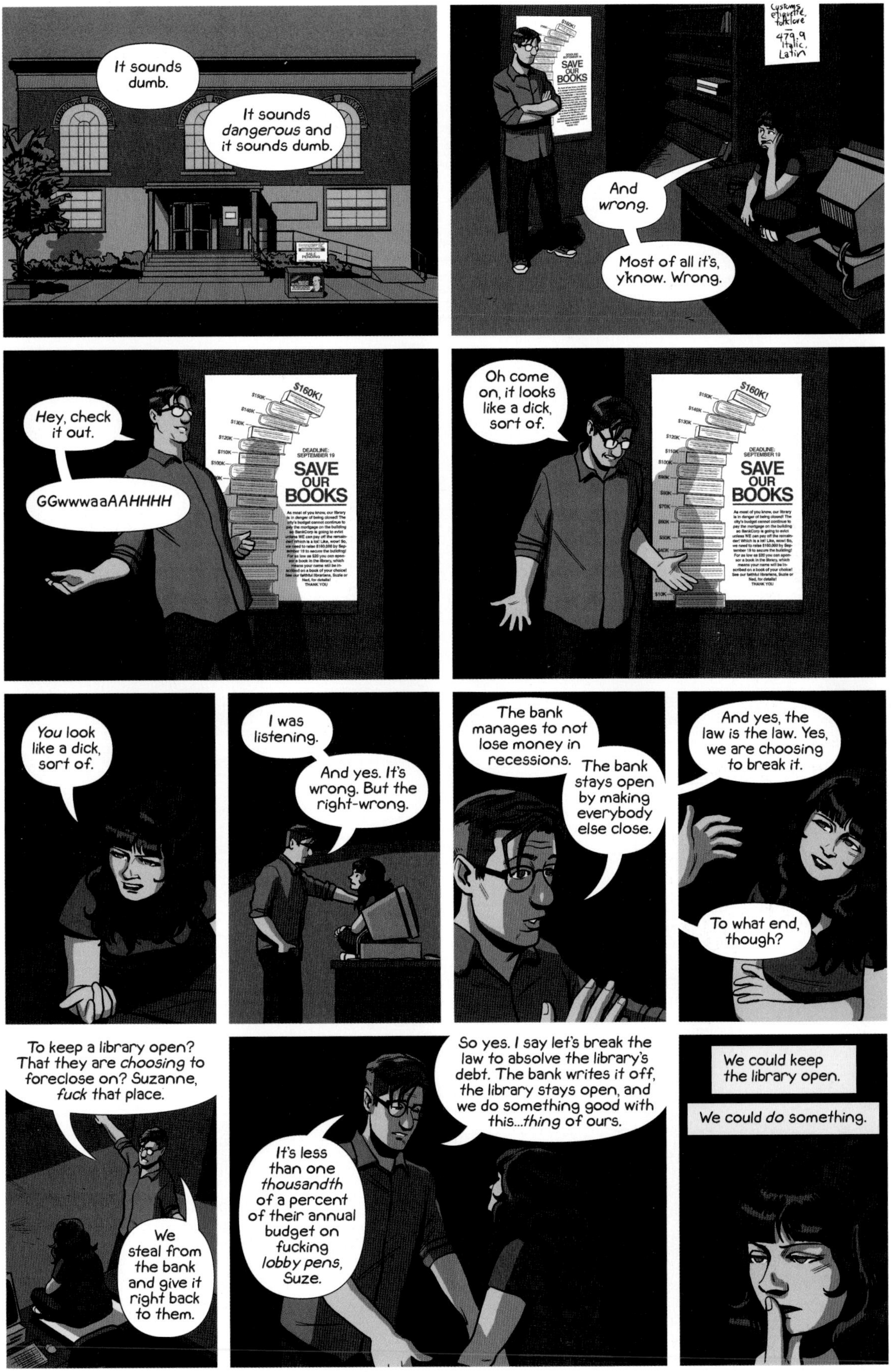

It sounds dumb.
It sounds *dangerous* and it sounds dumb.
And wrong.
Most of all it's, y'know. Wrong.
Hey, check it out.
GGwwwaaAAHHHH
$160K!
DEADLINE: SEPTEMBER 19
SAVE OUR BOOKS
Oh come on, it looks like a dick, sort of.
You look like a dick, sort of.
I was listening.
And yes. It's wrong. But the right-wrong.
The bank manages to not lose money in recessions.
The bank stays open by making everybody else close.
And yes, the law is the law. Yes, we are choosing to break it.
To what end, though?
To keep a library open? That they are *choosing* to foreclose on? Suzanne, *fuck* that place.
We steal from the bank and give it right back to them.
So yes. I say let's break the law to absolve the library's debt. The bank writes it off, the library stays open, and we do something good with this...*thing* of ours.
It's less than one *thousandth* of a percent of their annual budget on fucking *lobby pens*, Suze.
We could keep the library open.
We could *do* something.

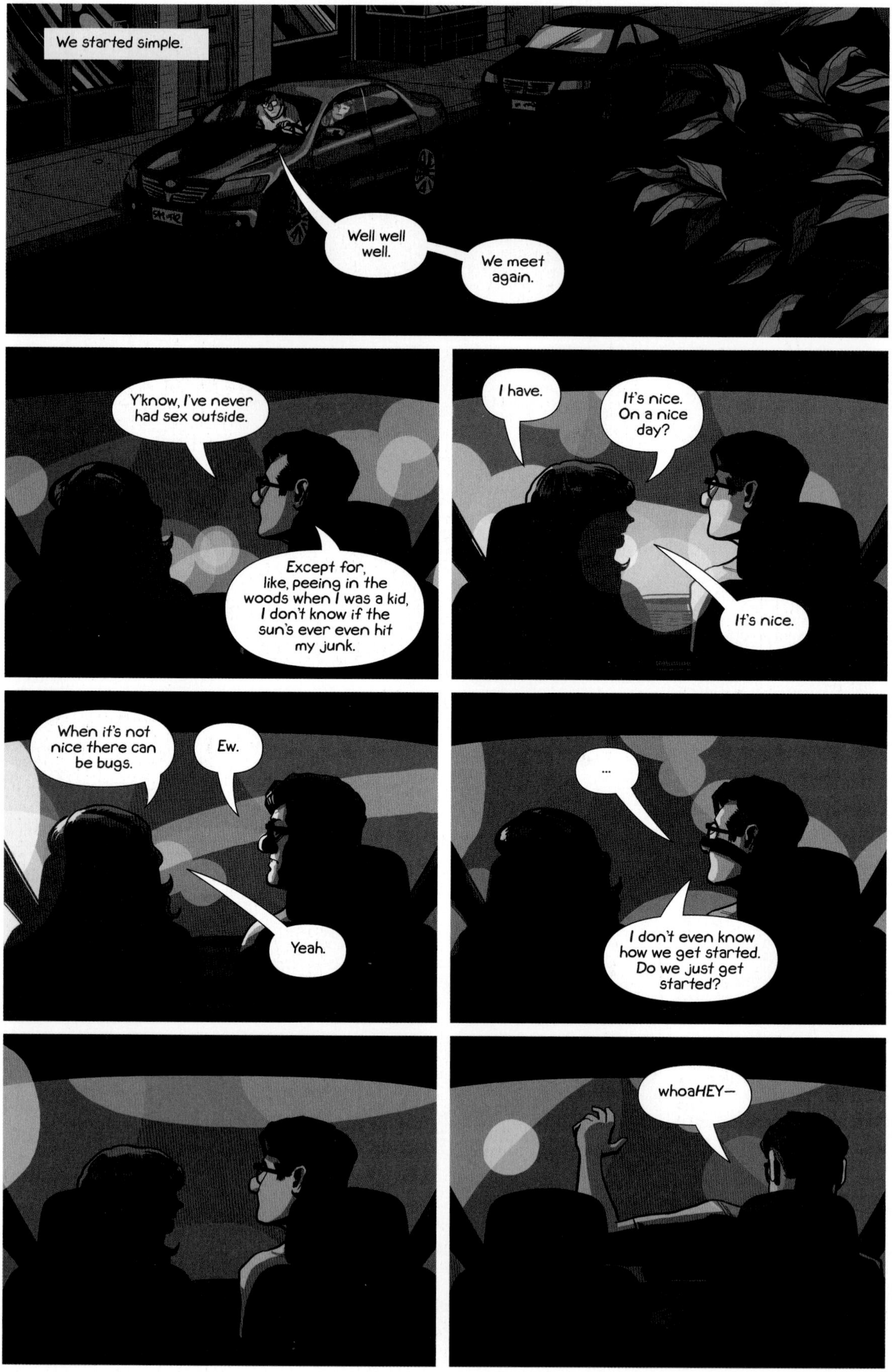
We started simple.
Well well well.
We meet again.
Y'know, I've never had sex outside.
Except for, like, peeing in the woods when I was a kid, I don't know if the sun's ever even hit my junk.
I have.
It's nice. On a nice day?
It's nice.
When it's not nice there can be bugs.
Ew.
Yeah.
...
I don't even know how we get started. Do we just get started?
whoa*HEY*—

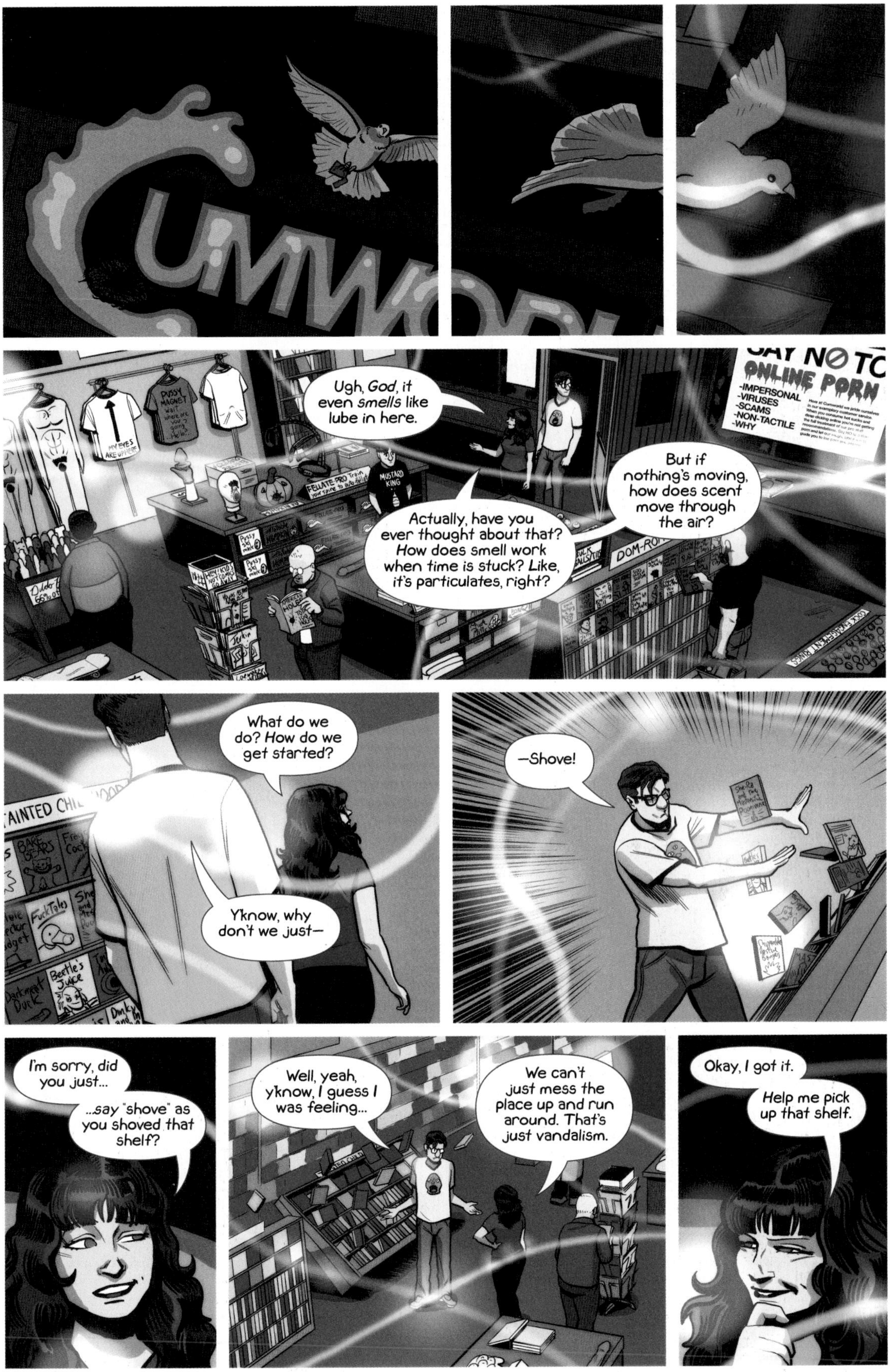

Ugh, God, it even smells like lube in here.
Actually, have you ever thought about that? How does smell work when time is stuck? Like, it's particulates, right?
But if nothing's moving, how does scent move through the air?
SAY NO TO ONLINE PORN
-IMPERSONAL
-VIRUSES
-SCAMS
-NON-TACTILE
-WHY
MY EYES ARE UP HERE
PUSSY MAGNET
MUSTARD KING
FELLATE-PRO
DOM-RO
What do we do? How do we get started?
Y'know, why don't we just—
TAINTED CHI
FuckTales
Beetle's Juice
—Shove!
I'm sorry, did you just...
...say "shove" as you shoved that shelf?
Well, yeah, y'know, I guess I was feeling...
We can't just mess the place up and run around. That's just vandalism.
Okay, I got it.
Help me pick up that shelf.

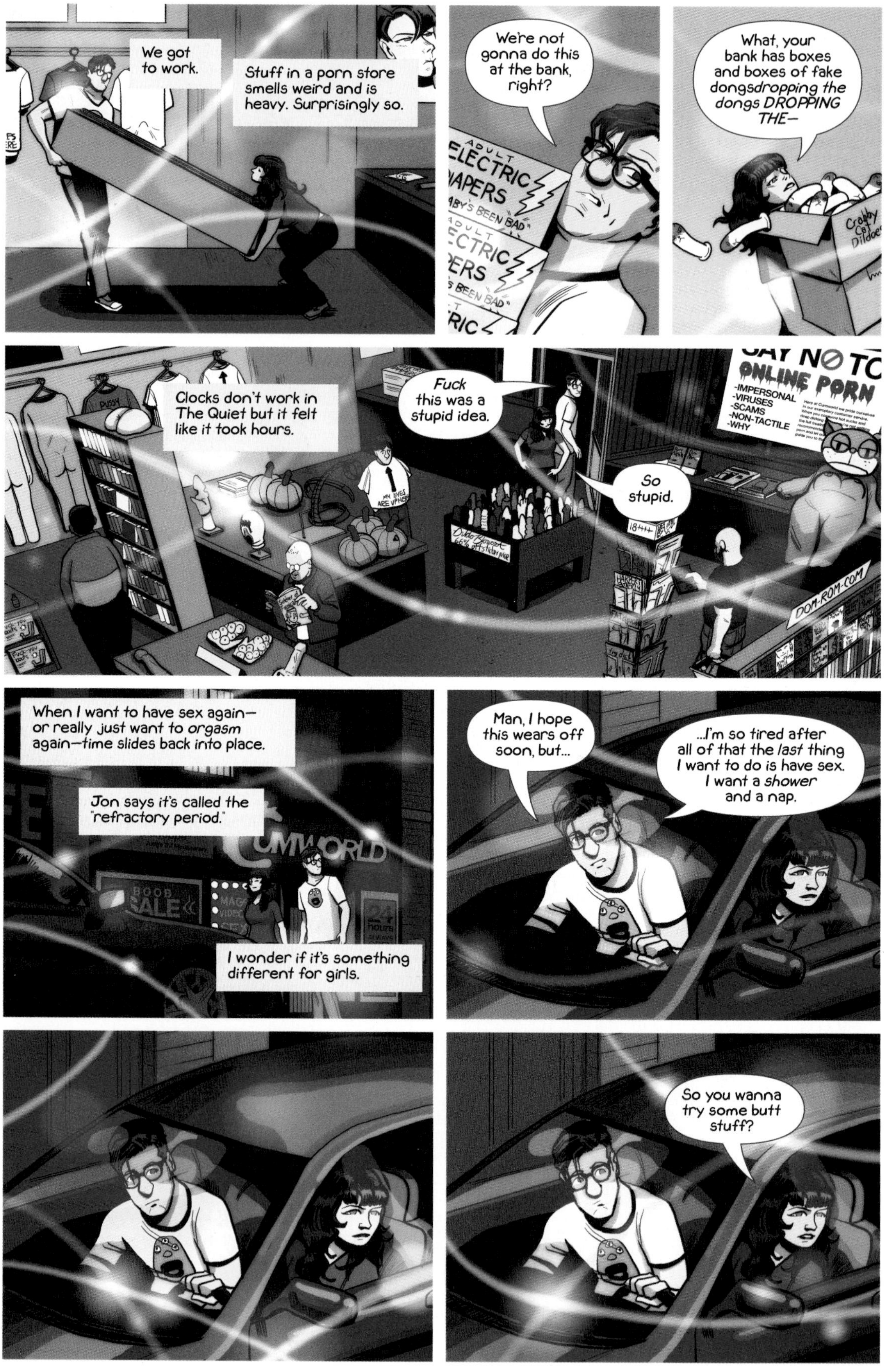
We got to work.
Stuff in a porn store smells weird and is heavy. Surprisingly so.
ADULT ELECTRIC DIAPERS "BABY'S BEEN BAD"
We're not gonna do this at the bank, right?
What, your bank has boxes and boxes of fake dongsdropping the dongs DROPPING THE–
Crabby Cat Dildoes
Clocks don't work in The Quiet but it felt like it took hours.
Fuck this was a stupid idea.
SAY NO TO ONLINE PORN
-IMPERSONAL
-VIRUSES
-SCAMS
-NON-TACTILE
-WHY
So stupid.
DOM-ROM-COM
When I want to have sex again—or really just want to *orgasm* again—time slides back into place.
Jon says it's called the "refractory period."
CUMWORLD
BOOB SALE
I wonder if it's something different for girls.
Man, I hope this wears off soon, but...
...I'm so tired after all of that the *last* thing I want to do is have sex. I want a *shower* and a nap.
So you wanna try some butt stuff?

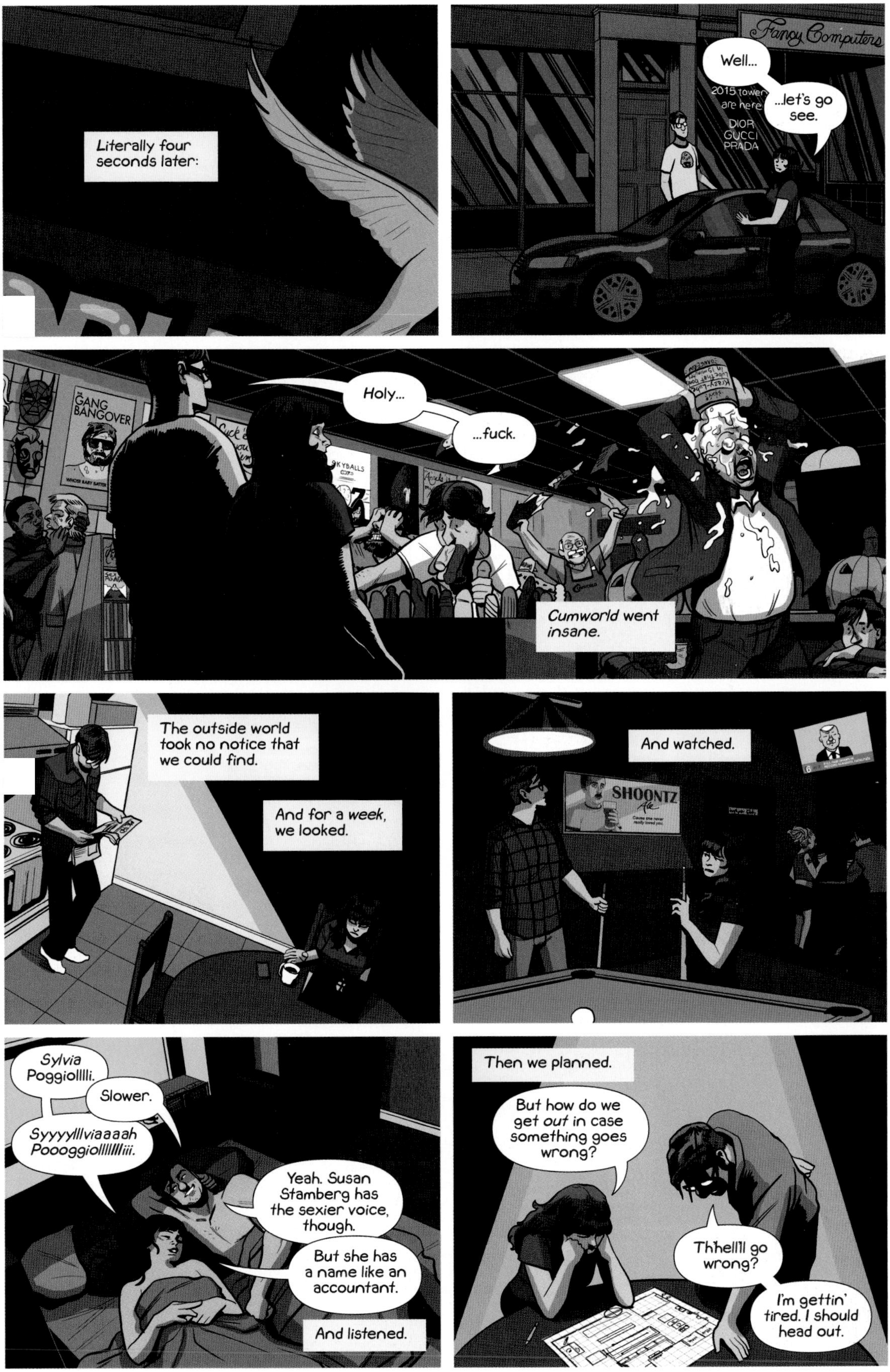
Literally four seconds later:
Fancy Computers
2015 towers are here
DIOR
GUCCI
PRADA
Well...
...let's go see.
THE GANG BANGOVER
Holy...
...fuck.
Cumworld went insane.
The outside world took no notice that we could find.
And for a week, we looked.
And watched.
SHOONTZ Ale
Sylvia Poggiollli.
Slower.
Syyyylllviaaaah Poooggiollllllliii.
Yeah. Susan Stamberg has the sexier voice, though.
But she has a name like an accountant.
And listened.
Then we planned.
But how do we get out in case something goes wrong?
Th'hell'll go wrong?
I'm gettin' tired. I should head out.

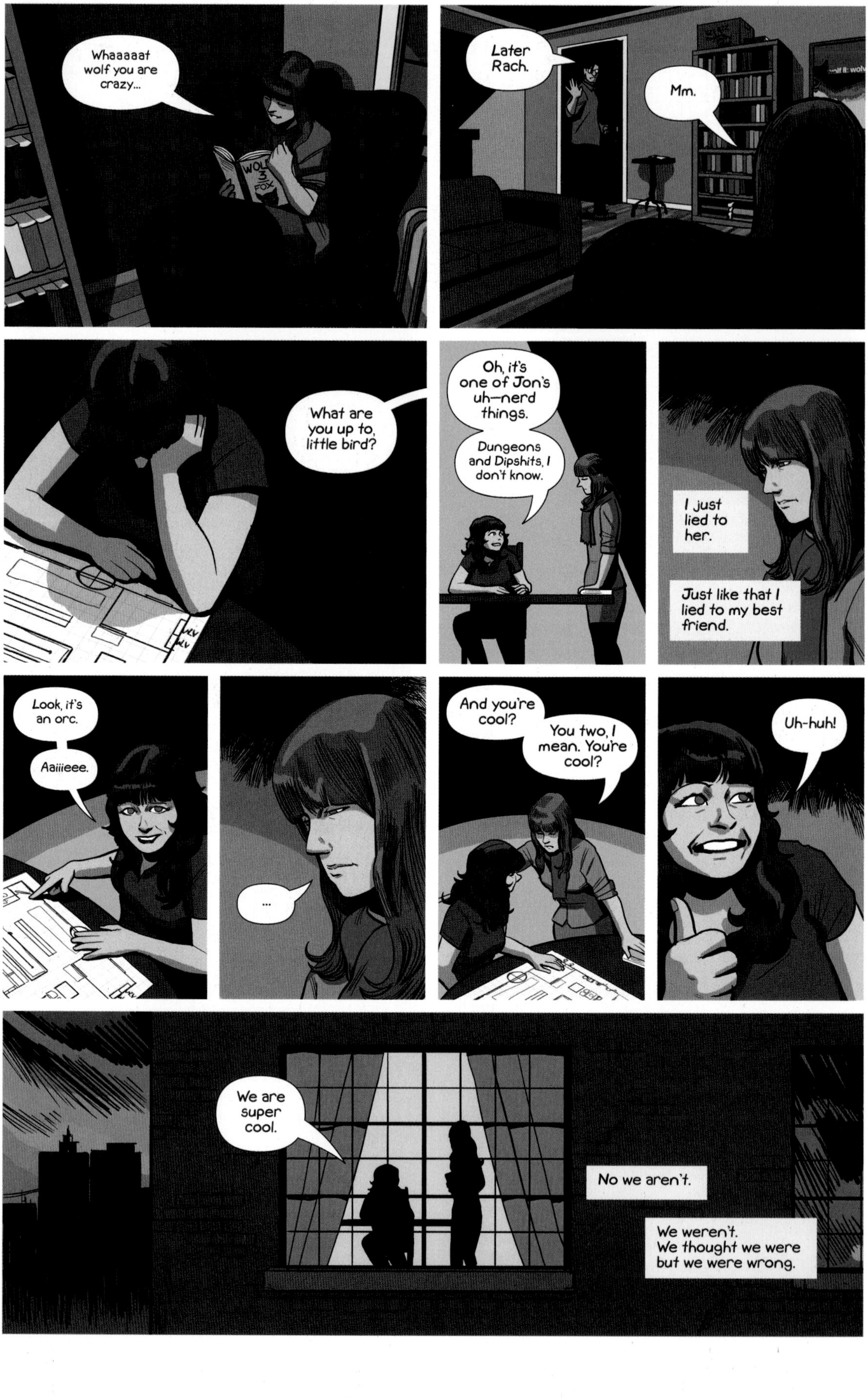
Whaaaaat wolf you are crazy...
Later Rach.
Mm.
What are you up to, little bird?
Oh, it's one of Jon's uh—nerd things.
Dungeons and Dipshits, I don't know.
I just lied to her.
Just like that I lied to my best friend.
Look, it's an orc.
Aaiiieee.
...
And you're cool?
You two, I mean. You're cool?
Uh-huh!
We are super cool.
No we aren't.
We weren't.
We thought we were but we were wrong.

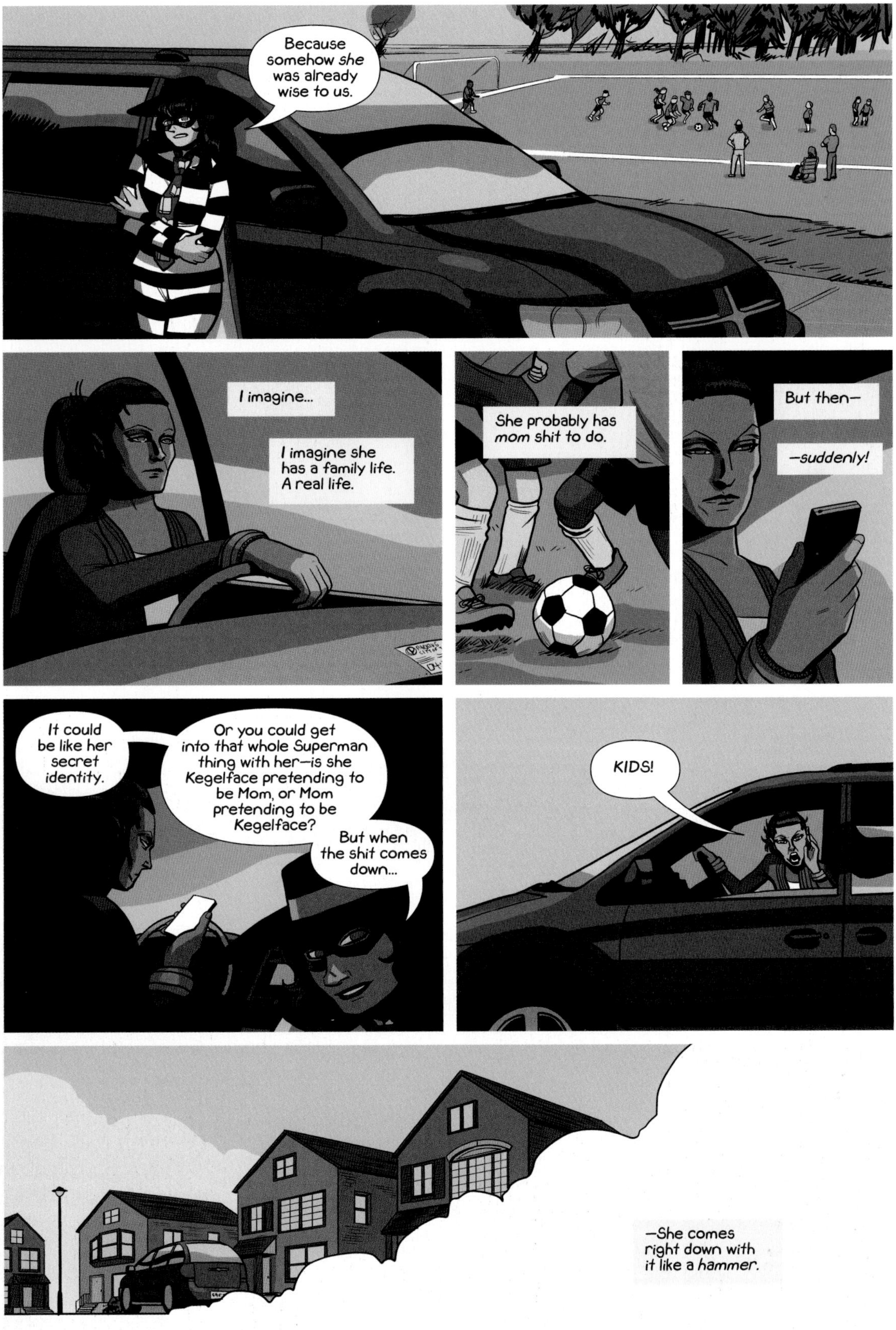
Because somehow she was already wise to us.
I imagine...
I imagine she has a family life. A real life.
She probably has mom shit to do.
But then—
—suddenly!
It could be like her secret identity.
Or you could get into that whole Superman thing with her—is she Kegelface pretending to be Mom, or Mom pretending to be Kegelface?
But when the shit comes down...
KIDS!
—She comes right down with it like a hammer.

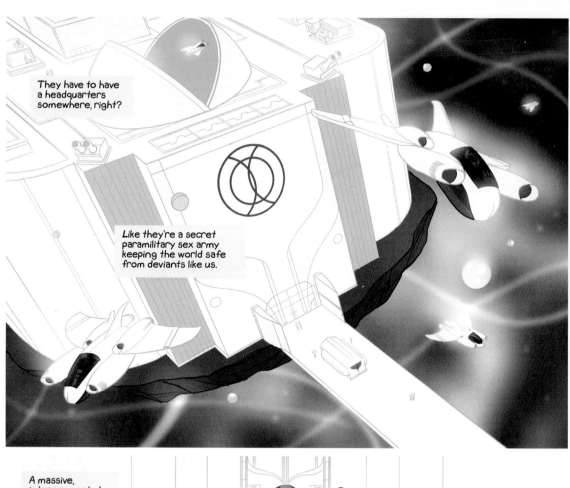

They have to have a headquarters somewhere, right?

Like they're a secret paramilitary sex army keeping the world safe from deviants like us.

A massive, interconnected network of time-freezing sex police out to destroy people like us.

With uniforms and codenames and stuff.

And she's, like, their Bruce Willis.

"ne-stop cum shoppe"
dge Bif Moulinarsky

CUMWORLD

MAGS
VIDEO'S
SEX
TOYS
MORE
STUFF

24 hours
ALWAYS OPEN GAPING & WAITING

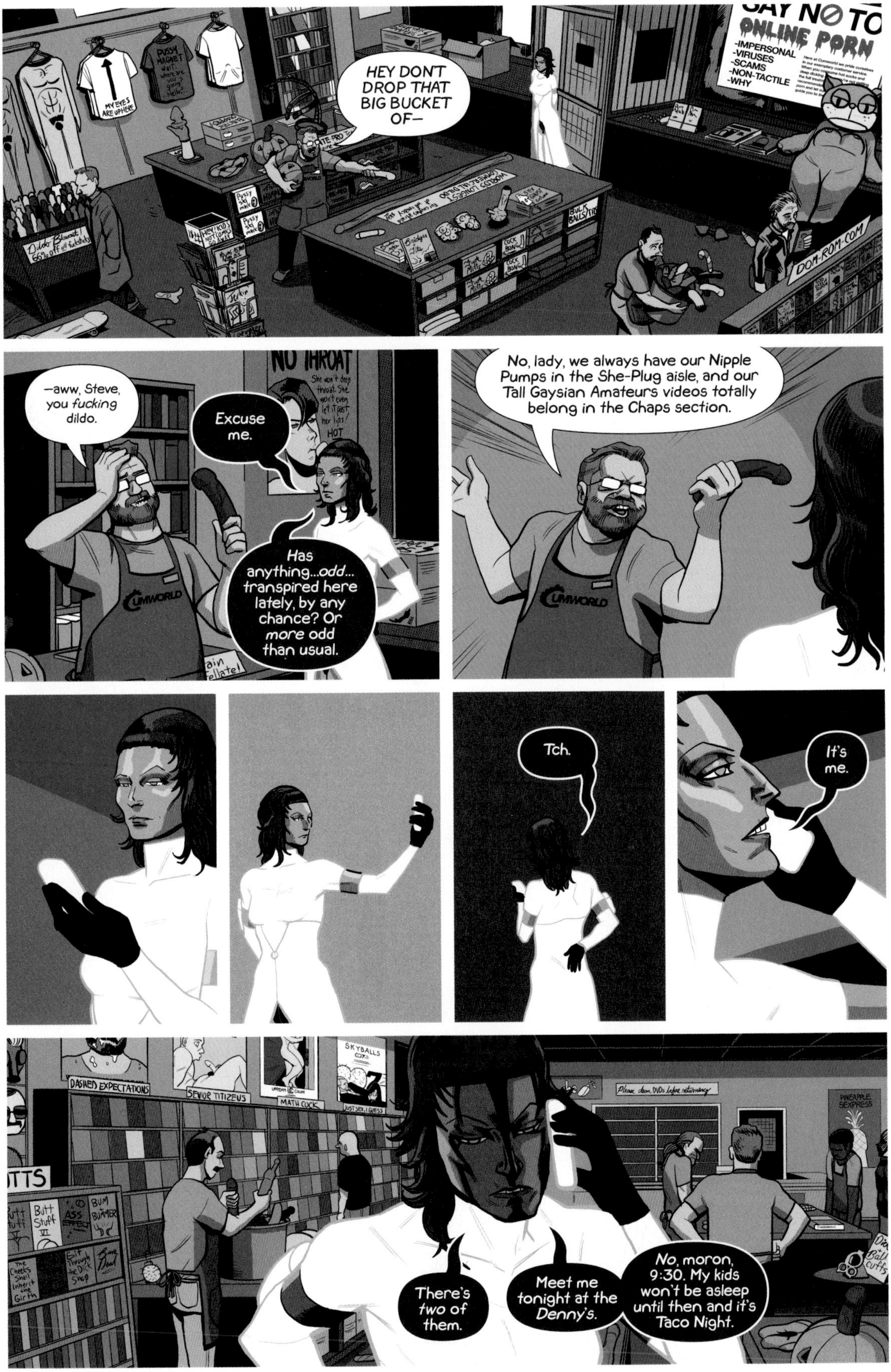
HEY DON'T DROP THAT BIG BUCKET OF—
SAY NO TO ONLINE PORN
-IMPERSONAL
-VIRUSES
-SCAMS
-NON-TACTILE
-WHY
DOM-ROM-COM
—aww, Steve, you *fucking* dildo.
Excuse me.
Has anything...*odd*... transpired here lately, by any chance? Or *more* odd than usual.
No, lady, we always have our Nipple Pumps in the She-Plug aisle, and our Tall Gaysian Amateurs videos totally belong in the Chaps section.
Tch.
It's me.
DASHED EXPECTATIONS
SENIOR TITIZENS
MATH COCK
SKYBALLS
There's *two* of them.
Meet me tonight at the *Denny's*.
No, moron, 9:30. My kids won't be asleep until then and it's Taco Night.

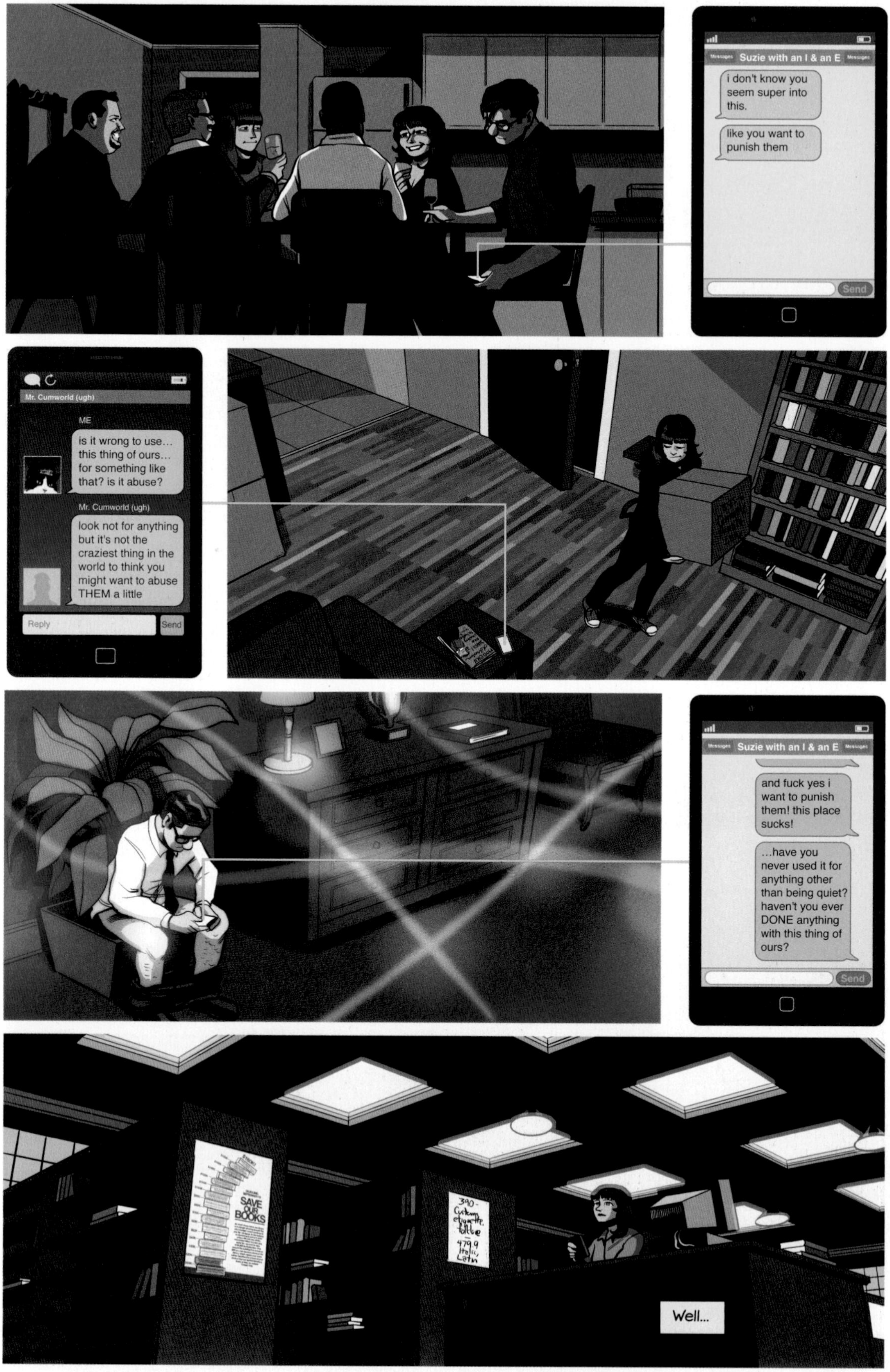
Suzie with an I & an E
i don't know you seem super into this.
like you want to punish them
Send
Mr. Cumworld (ugh)
ME
is it wrong to use… this thing of ours… for something like that? is it abuse?
Mr. Cumworld (ugh)
look not for anything but it's not the craziest thing in the world to think you might want to abuse THEM a little
Reply
Send
Suzie with an I & an E
and fuck yes i want to punish them! this place sucks!
…have you never used it for anything other than being quiet? haven't you ever DONE anything with this thing of ours?
Send
SAVE OUR BOOKS
Well…

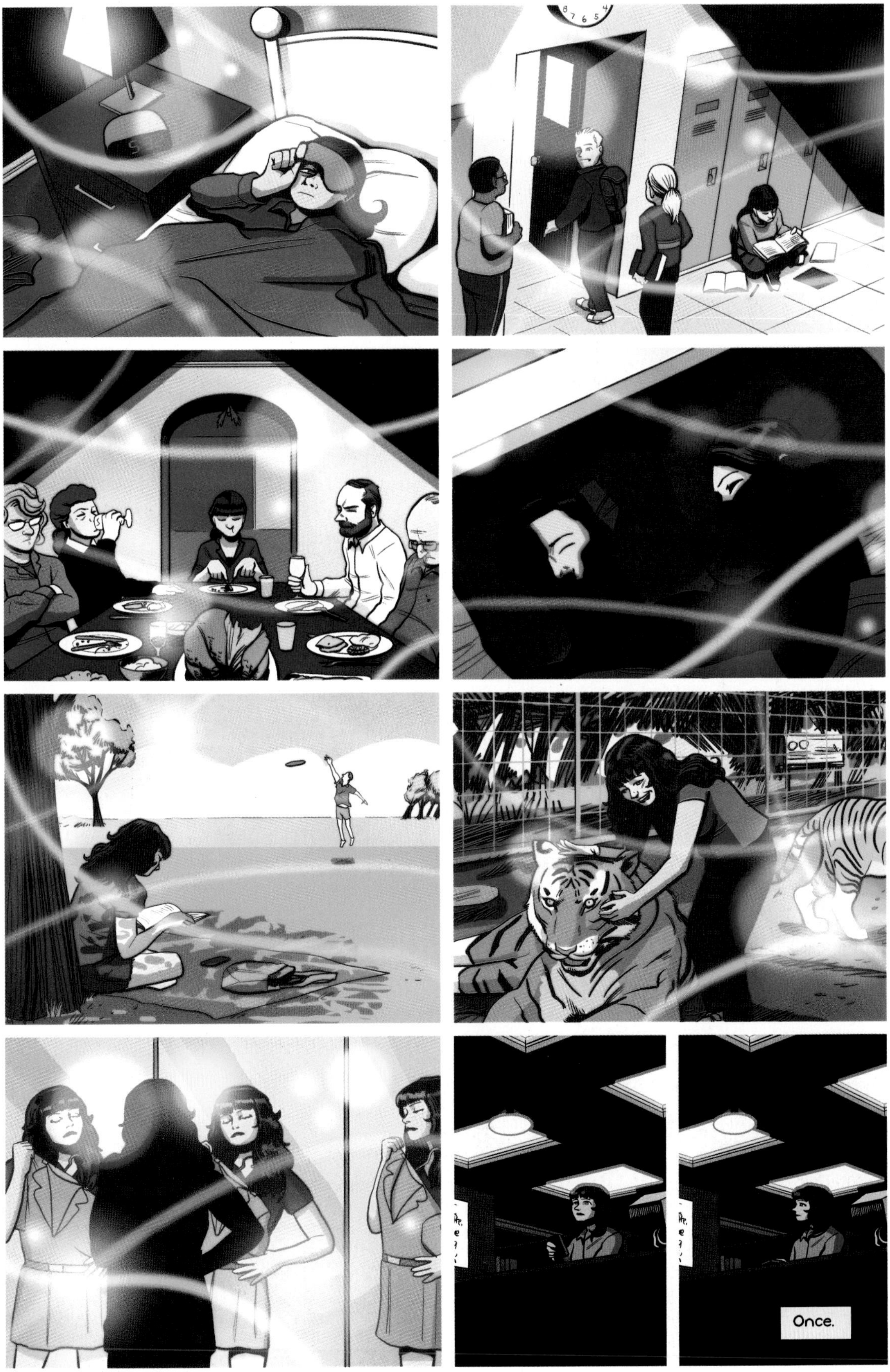
Once.

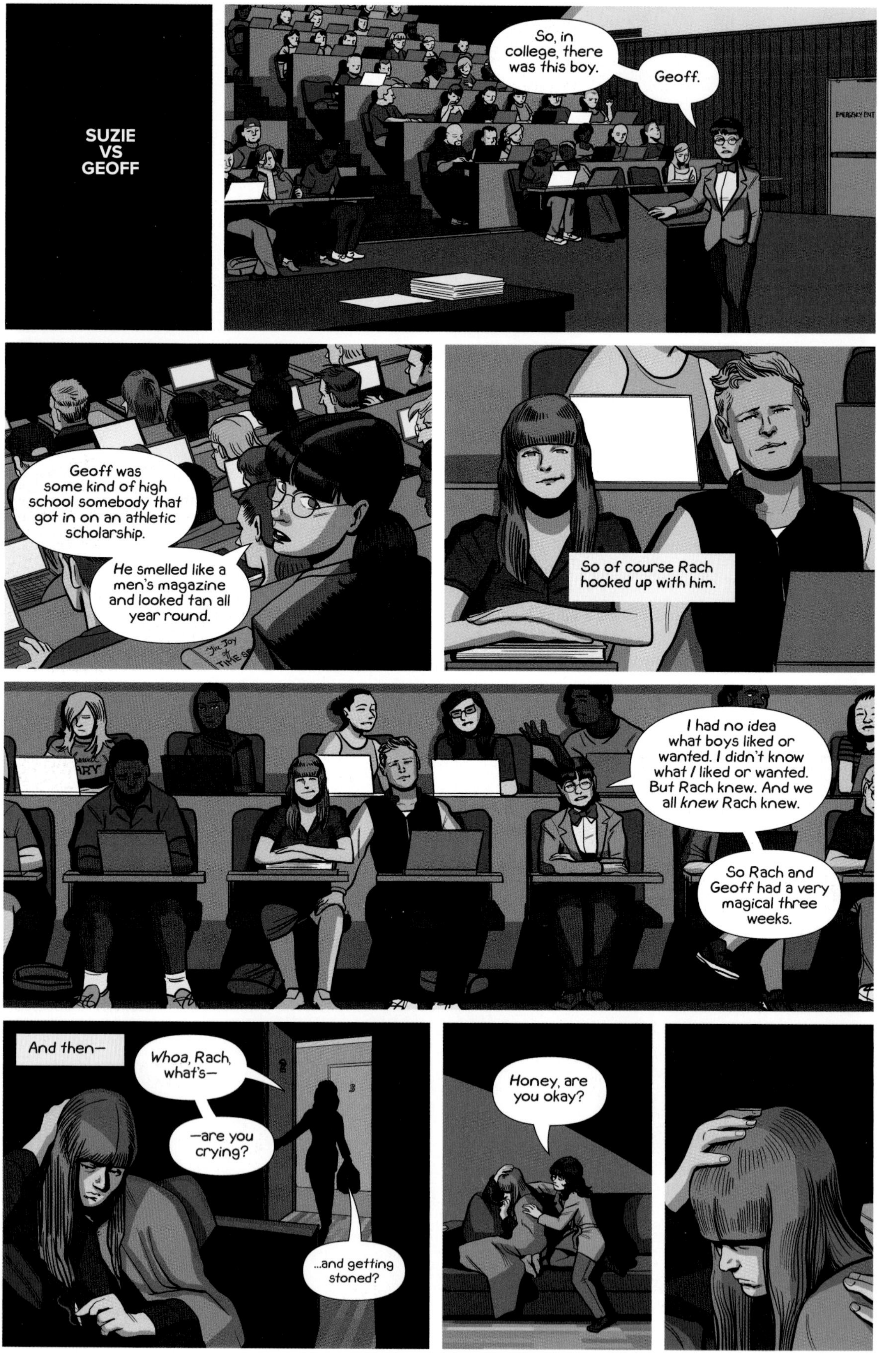
SUZIE
VS
GEOFF
So, in college, there was this boy.
Geoff.
EMERGENCY EXIT
Geoff was some kind of high school somebody that got in on an athletic scholarship.
He smelled like a men's magazine and looked tan all year round.
The Joy of TIME SE
So of course Rach hooked up with him.
I had no idea what boys liked or wanted. I didn't know what *I* liked or wanted. But Rach knew. And we all *knew* Rach knew.
So Rach and Geoff had a very magical three weeks.
And then—
Whoa, Rach, what's—
—are you crying?
...and getting stoned?
Honey, are you okay?

She said no.

Geoff said, "Shut up, slut," and did it anyway.

He was a star athlete riding free through school and life.

Nobody ever said no to him.

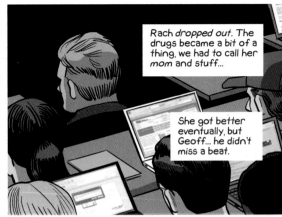

Rach *dropped out*. The drugs became a bit of a thing, we had to call her *mom* and stuff...

She got better eventually, but Geoff... he didn't miss a beat.

I called the cops, but without Rach they wouldn't do anything.

"Sounds like somebody's girlfriend doesn't like being dumped," the son of a bitch on the phone said to me.

And one day...

...one day I just kinda lost it.

I availed myself of Rach's stash.

She was so wrecked by then she didn't notice.

Hey, pointer for all you kids out there.

If rubbing one out puts you into a state of frozen time, maybe don't get high down in it.

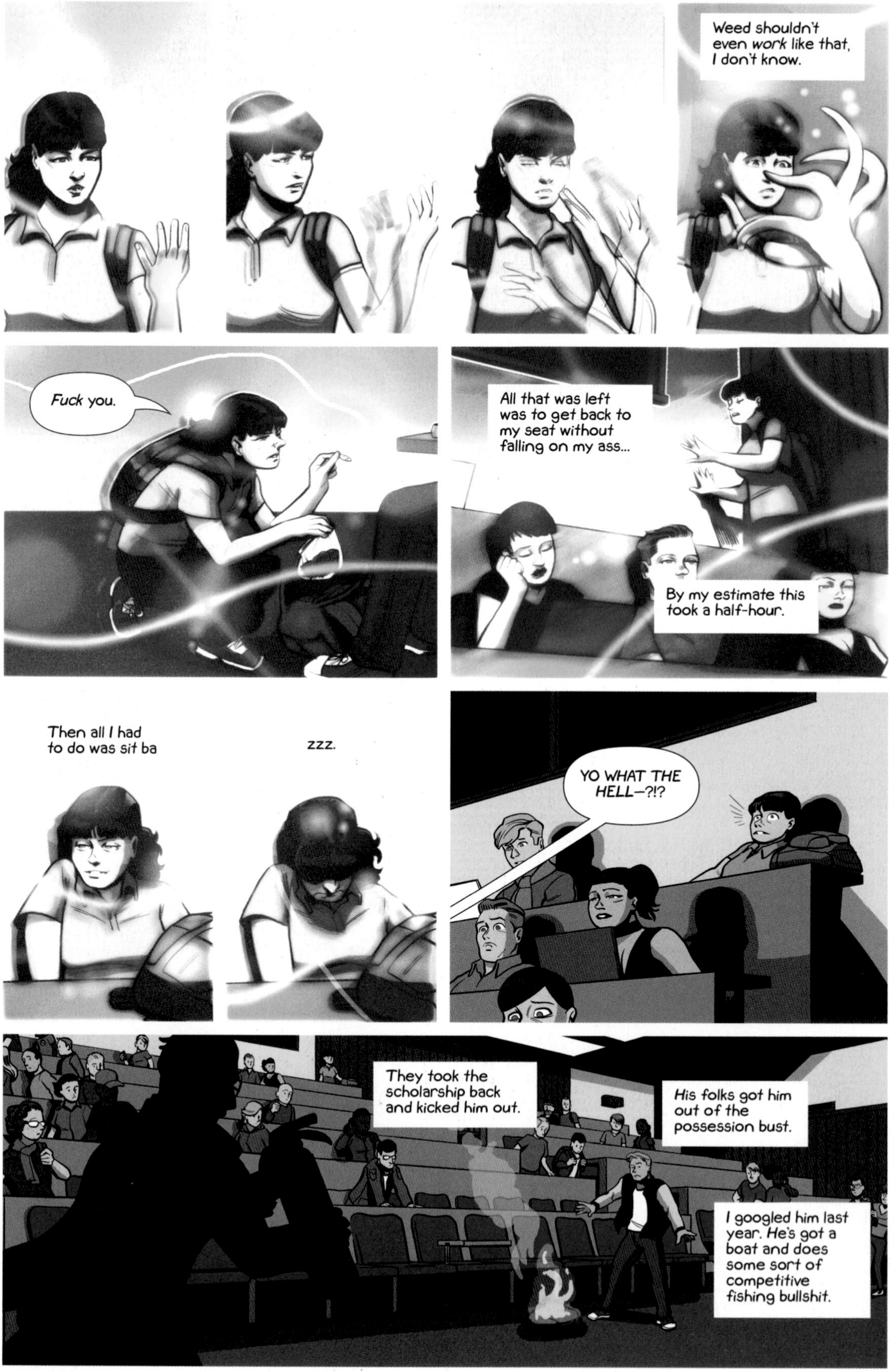

Weed shouldn't even *work* like that, I don't know.
Fuck you.
All that was left was to get back to my seat without falling on my ass...
By my estimate this took a half-hour.
Then all I had to do was sit ba
zzz.
YO WHAT THE HELL—?!?
They took the scholarship back and kicked him out.
His folks got him out of the possession bust.
I googled him last year. He's got a boat and does some sort of competitive fishing bullshit.

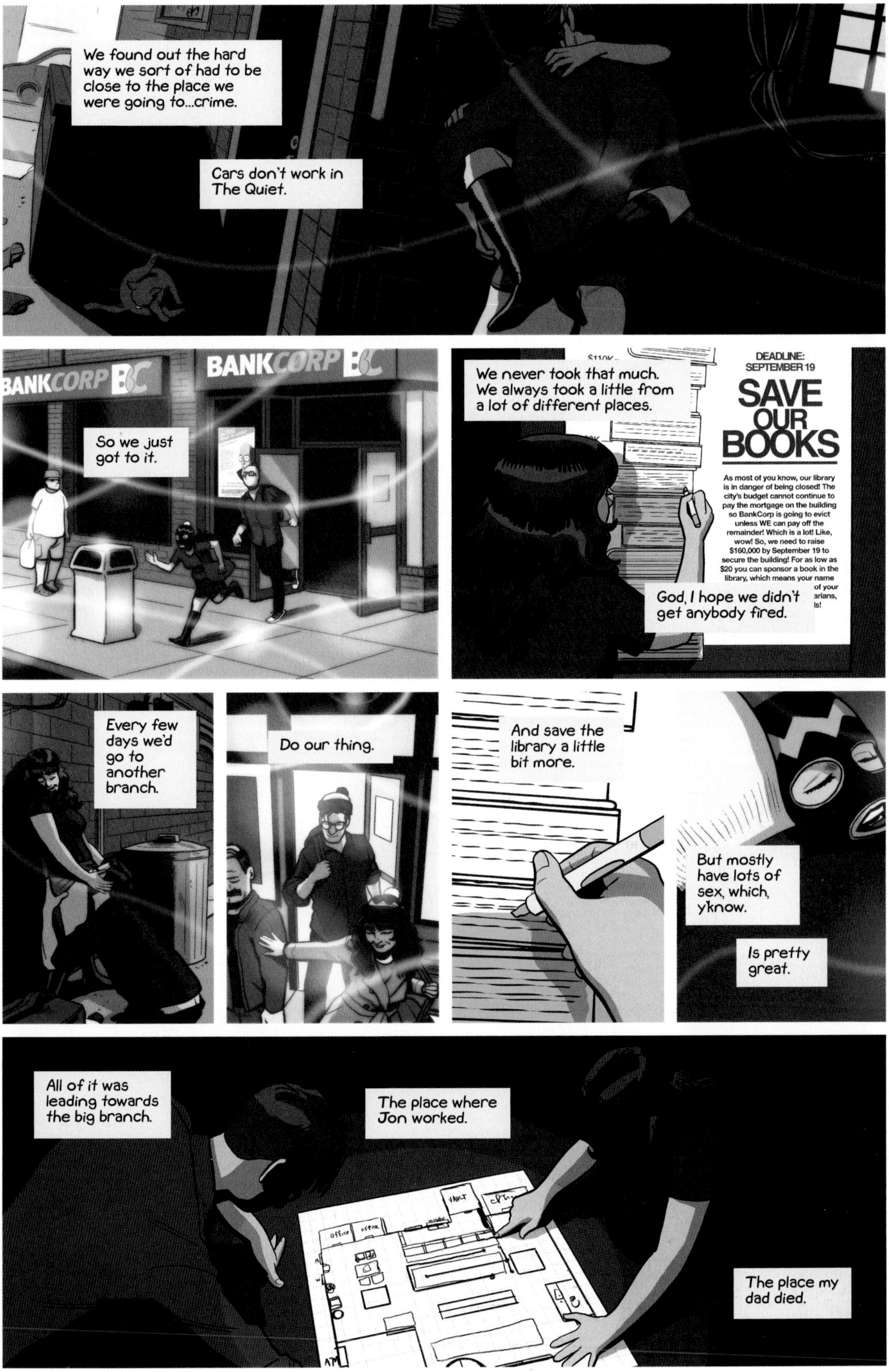

We found out the hard way we sort of had to be close to the place we were going to...crime.
Cars don't work in The Quiet.
BANKCORP BC
BANKCORP BC
So we just got to it.
We never took that much. We always took a little from a lot of different places.
DEADLINE: SEPTEMBER 19
SAVE OUR BOOKS
As most of you know, our library is in danger of being closed! The city's budget cannot continue to pay the mortgage on the building so BankCorp is going to evict unless WE can pay off the remainder! Which is a lot! Like, wow! So, we need to raise $160,000 by September 19 to secure the building! For as low as $20 you can sponsor a book in the library, which means your name
God, I hope we didn't get anybody fired.
Every few days we'd go to another branch.
Do our thing.
And save the library a little bit more.
But mostly have lots of sex, which, y'know.
Is pretty great.
All of it was leading towards the big branch.
The place where Jon worked.
VAULT
OFFICE
OFFICE
ATM
The place my dad died.

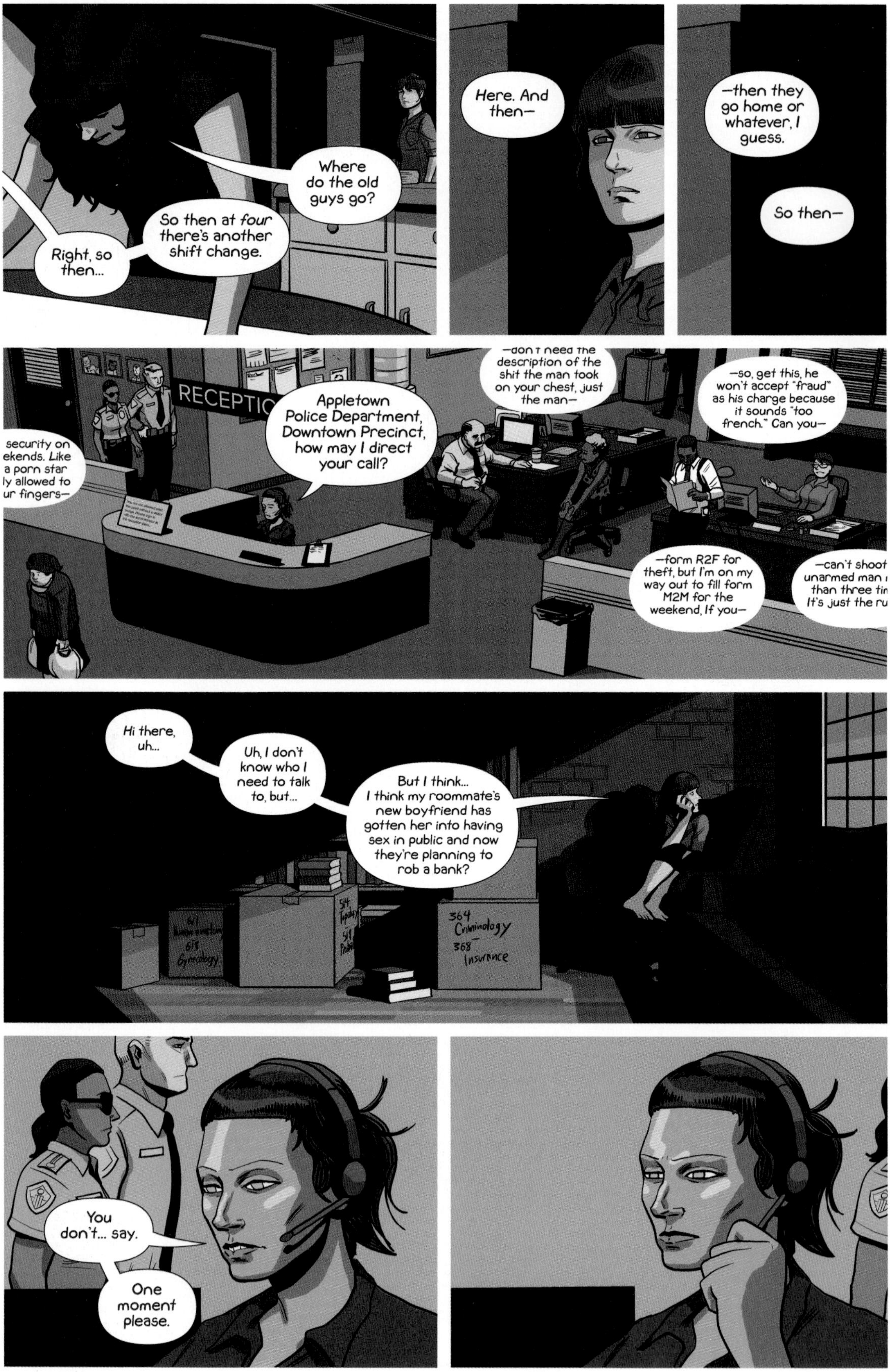

Right, so then...
So then at *four* there's another shift change.
Where do the old guys go?
Here. And then—
—then they go home or whatever, I guess.
So then—
RECEPTIO
security on
ekends. Like
a porn star
ly allowed to
ur fingers—
Appletown Police Department, Downtown Precinct, how may I direct your call?
—don't need the description of the shit the man took on your chest, just the man—
—so, get this, he won't accept "fraud" as his charge because it sounds "too french." Can you—
—form R2F for theft, but I'm on my way out to fill form M2M for the weekend, If you—
—can't shoot
unarmed man
than three tim
It's just the ru
Hi there, uh...
Uh, I don't know who I need to talk to, but...
But I think... I think my roommate's new boyfriend has gotten her into having sex in public and now they're planning to rob a bank?
618 Gynecology
364 Criminology
368 — Insurance
You don't... say.
One moment please.

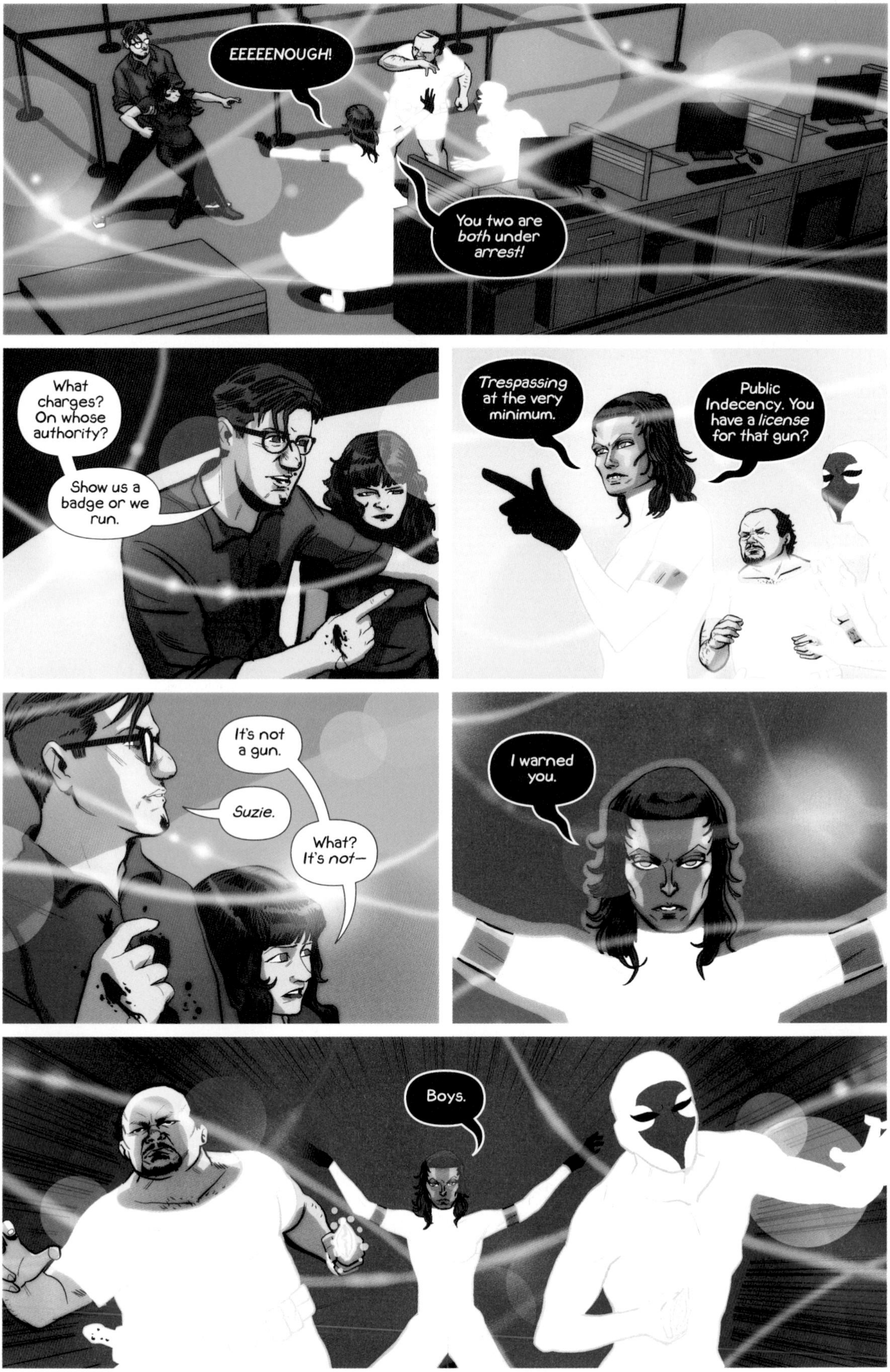
EEEEENOUGH!
You two are *both* under arrest!
What charges? On whose authority?
Show us a badge or we run.
Trespassing at the very minimum.
Public Indecency. You have a *license* for that gun?
It's not a gun.
Suzie.
What? It's *not*—
I warned you.
Boys.

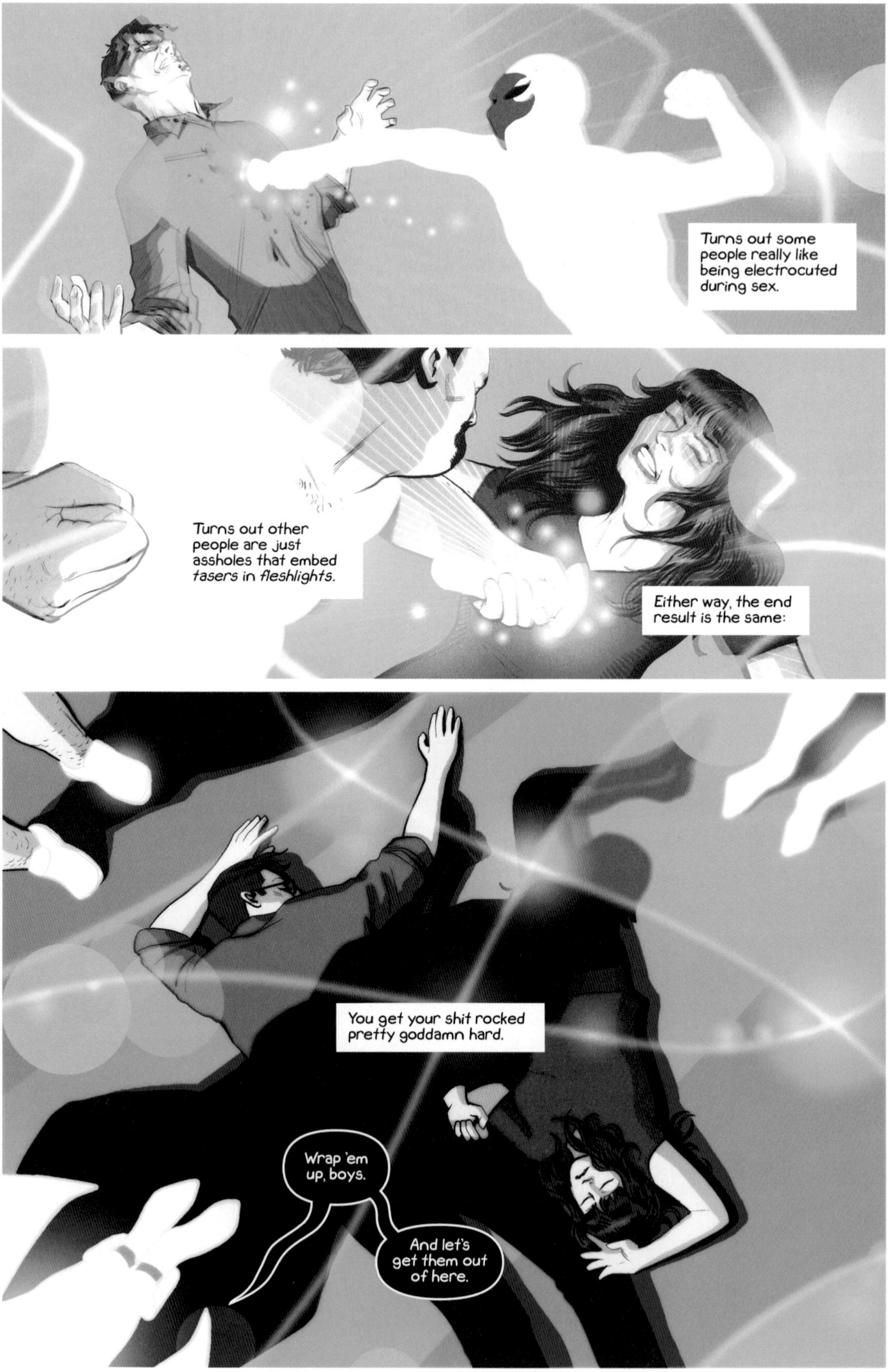
Turns out some people really like being electrocuted during sex.
Turns out other people are just assholes that embed *tasers* in *fleshlights.*
Either way, the end result is the same:
You get your shit rocked pretty goddamn hard.
Wrap 'em up, boys.
And let's get them out of here.

5
GOING DOWN

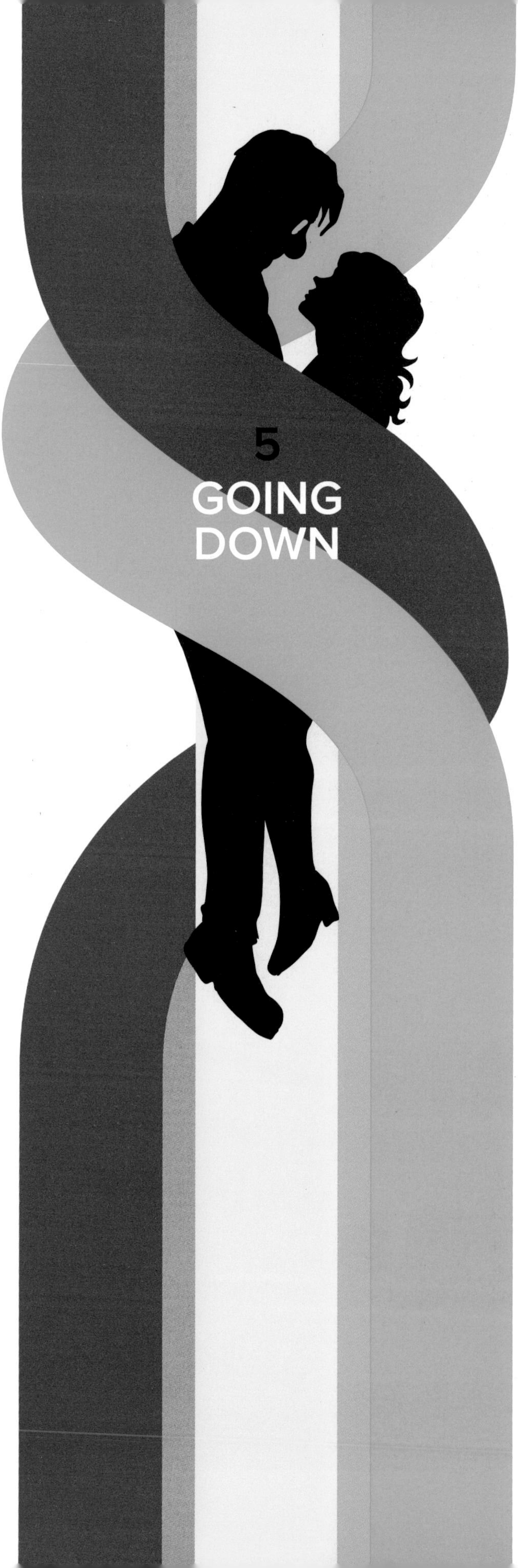

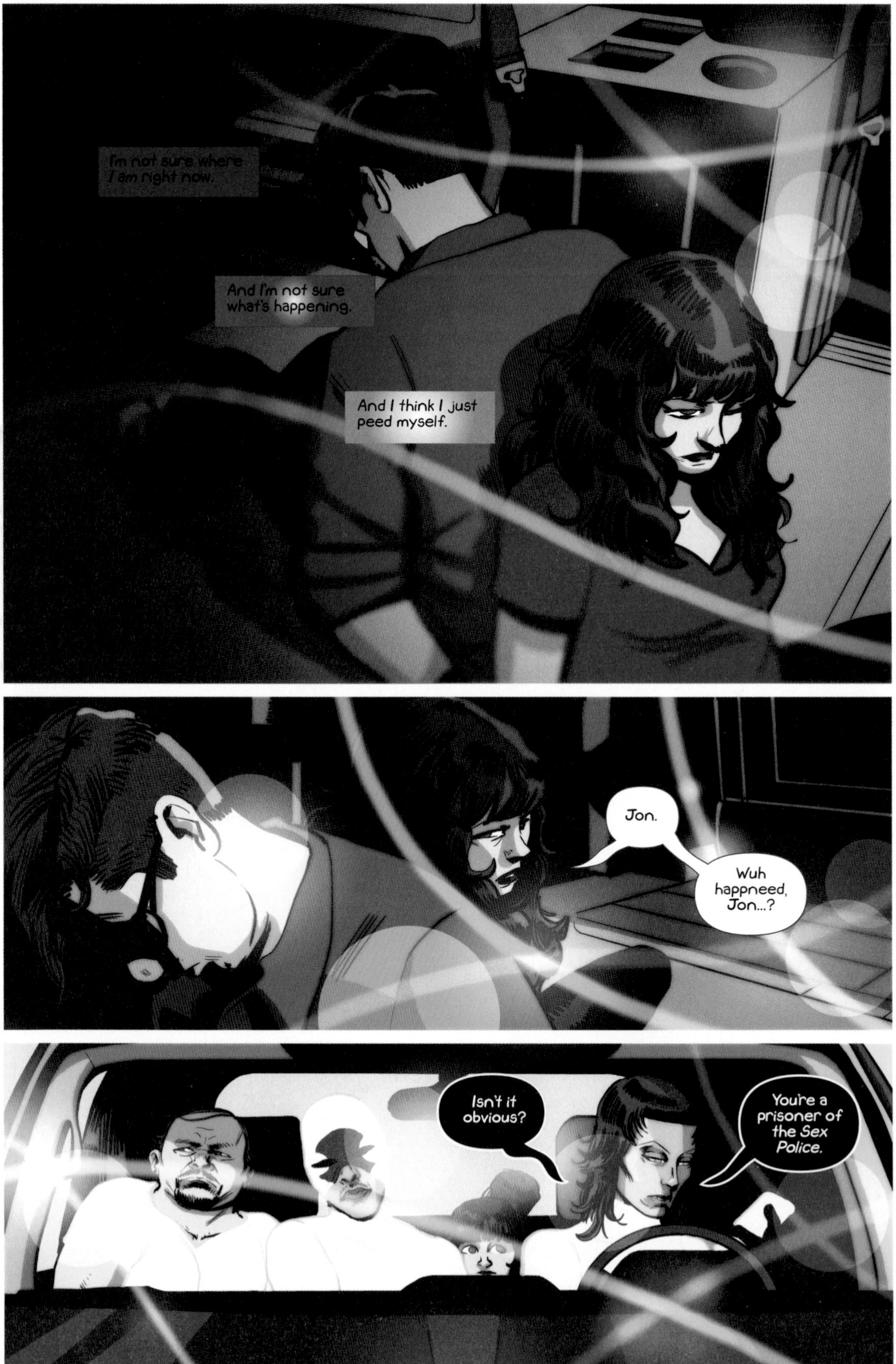
I'm not sure where I am right now.
And I'm not sure what's happening.
And I think I just peed myself.
Jon.
Wuh happneed, Jon...?
Isn't it obvious?
You're a prisoner of the *Sex Police.*

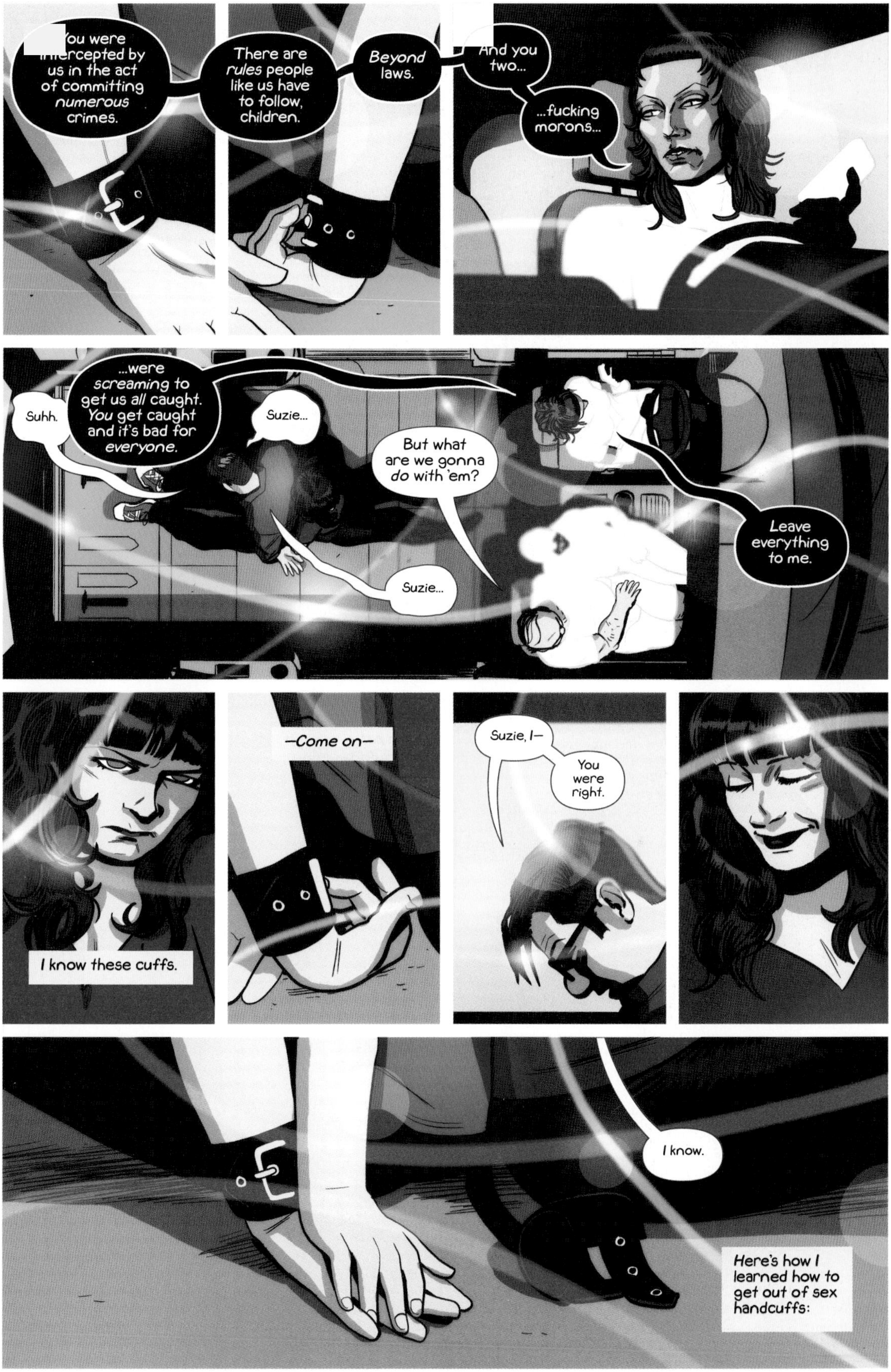
ou were ercepted by us in the act of committing *numerous* crimes.
There are *rules* people like us have to follow, children.
Beyond laws.
And you two...
...fucking morons...
...were *screaming* to get us *all* caught. *You* get caught and it's bad for *everyone.*
Suhh.
Suzie...
But what are we gonna *do* with 'em?
Suzie...
Leave everything to me.
I know these cuffs.
—Come on—
Suzie, I—
You were right.
I know.
Here's how I learned how to get out of sex handcuffs:

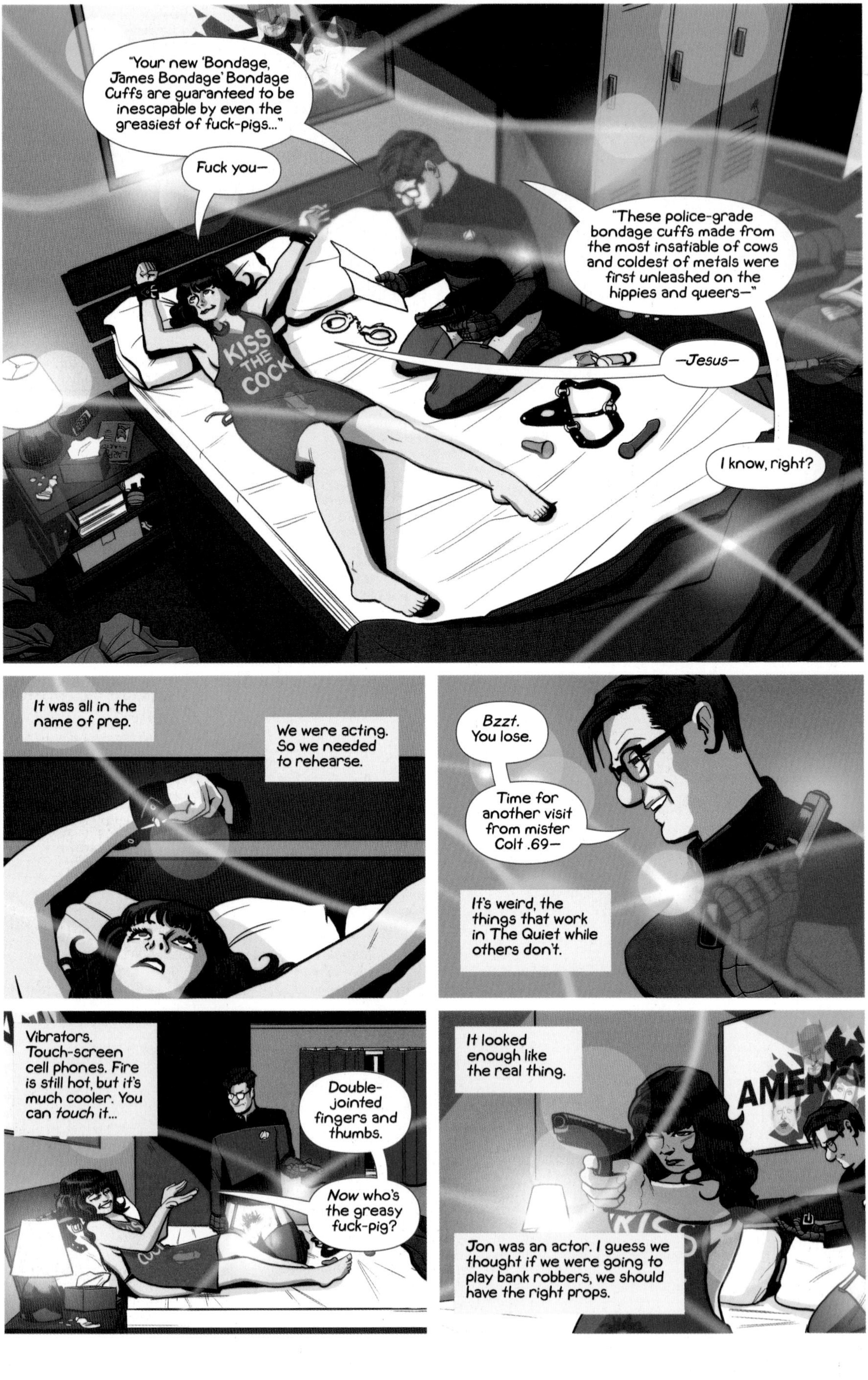
"Your new 'Bondage, James Bondage' Bondage Cuffs are guaranteed to be inescapable by even the greasiest of fuck-pigs..."
Fuck you—
KISS THE COCK
"These police-grade bondage cuffs made from the most insatiable of cows and coldest of metals were first unleashed on the hippies and queers—"
—Jesus—
I know, right?
It was all in the name of prep.
We were acting. So we needed to rehearse.
Bzzt. You lose.
Time for another visit from mister Colt .69—
It's weird, the things that work in The Quiet while others don't.
Vibrators. Touch-screen cell phones. Fire is still hot, but it's much cooler. You can *touch* it...
Double-jointed fingers and thumbs.
Now who's the greasy fuck-pig?
It looked enough like the real thing.
Jon was an actor. I guess we thought if we were going to play bank robbers, we should have the right props.

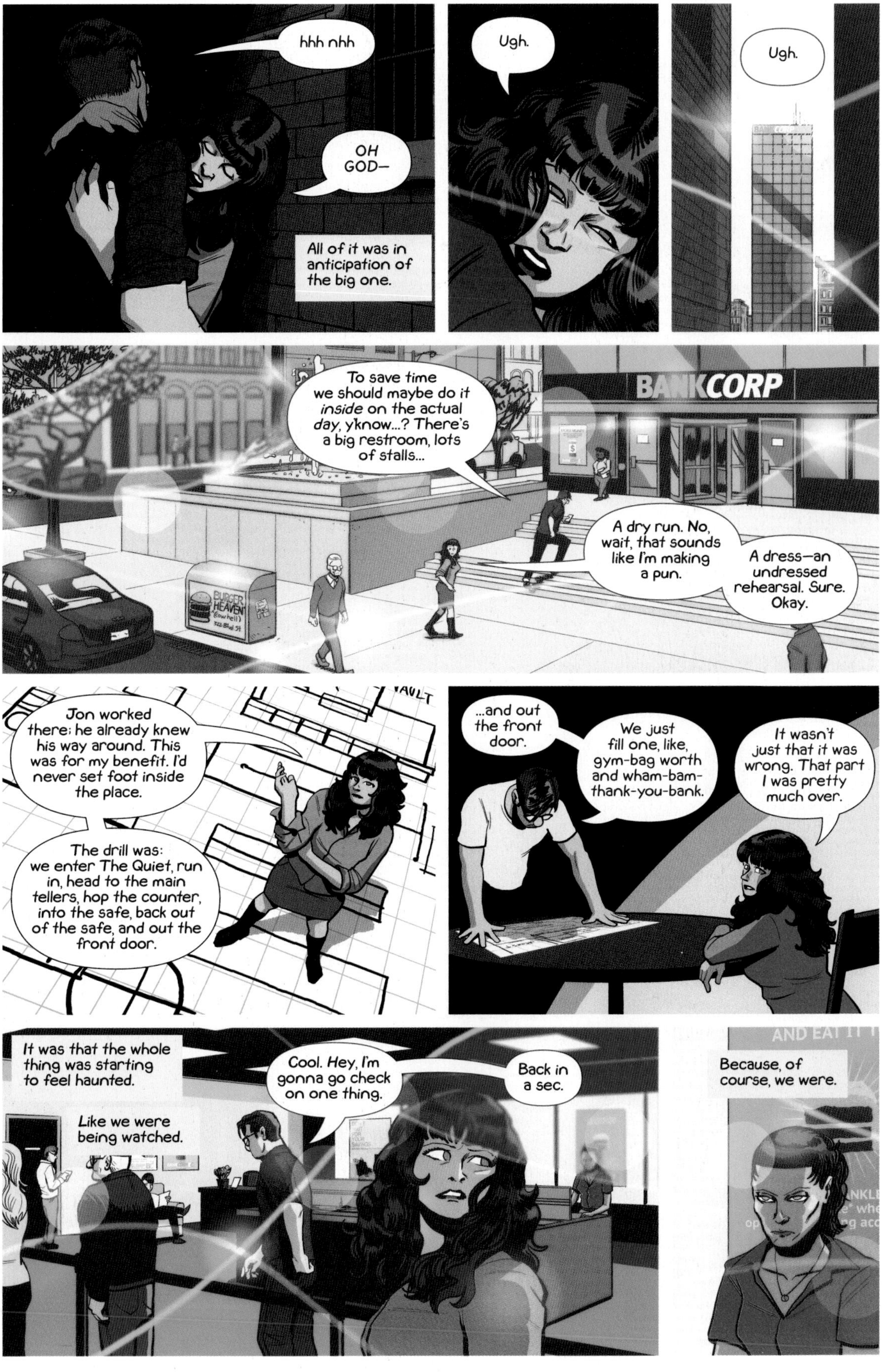
hhh nhh
OH GOD—
All of it was in anticipation of the big one.
Ugh.
Ugh.
To save time we should maybe do it *inside* on the actual *day*, y'know...? There's a big restroom, lots of stalls...
BANKCORP
BURGER HEAVEN
A dry run. No, wait, that sounds like I'm making a pun.
A dress—an undressed rehearsal. Sure. Okay.
VAULT
Jon worked there; he already knew his way around. This was for my benefit. I'd never set foot inside the place.
The drill was: we enter The Quiet, run in, head to the main tellers, hop the counter, into the safe, back out of the safe, and out the front door.
...and out the front door.
We just fill one, like, gym-bag worth and wham-bam-thank-you-bank.
It wasn't just that it was wrong. That part I was pretty much over.
It was that the whole thing was starting to feel haunted.
Like we were being watched.
Cool. Hey, I'm gonna go check on one thing.
Back in a sec.
AND EAT IT
Because, of course, we were.

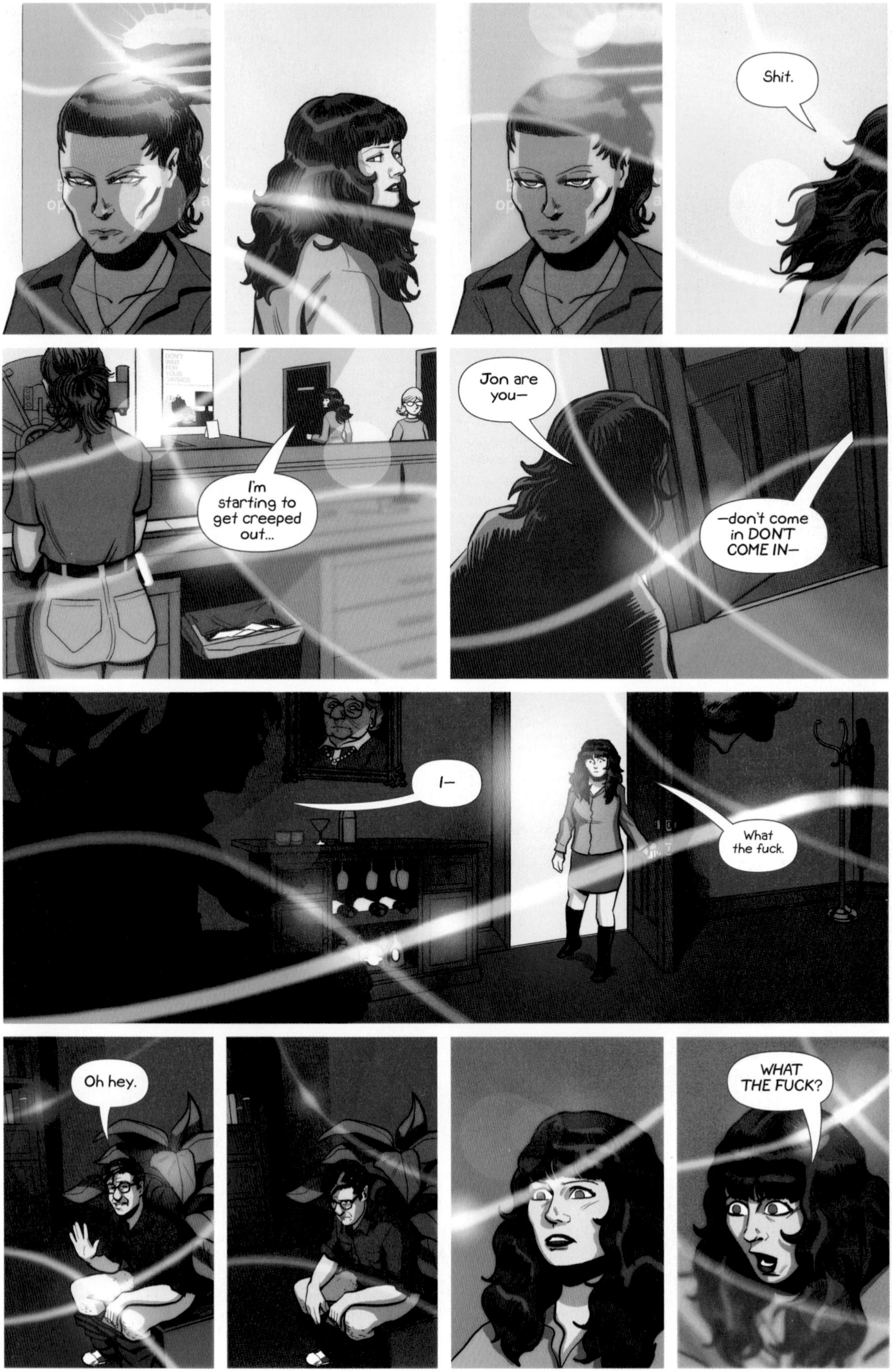
Shit.
I'm starting to get creeped out...
Jon are you—
—don't come in DON'T COME IN—
I—
What the fuck.
Oh hey.
WHAT THE FUCK?

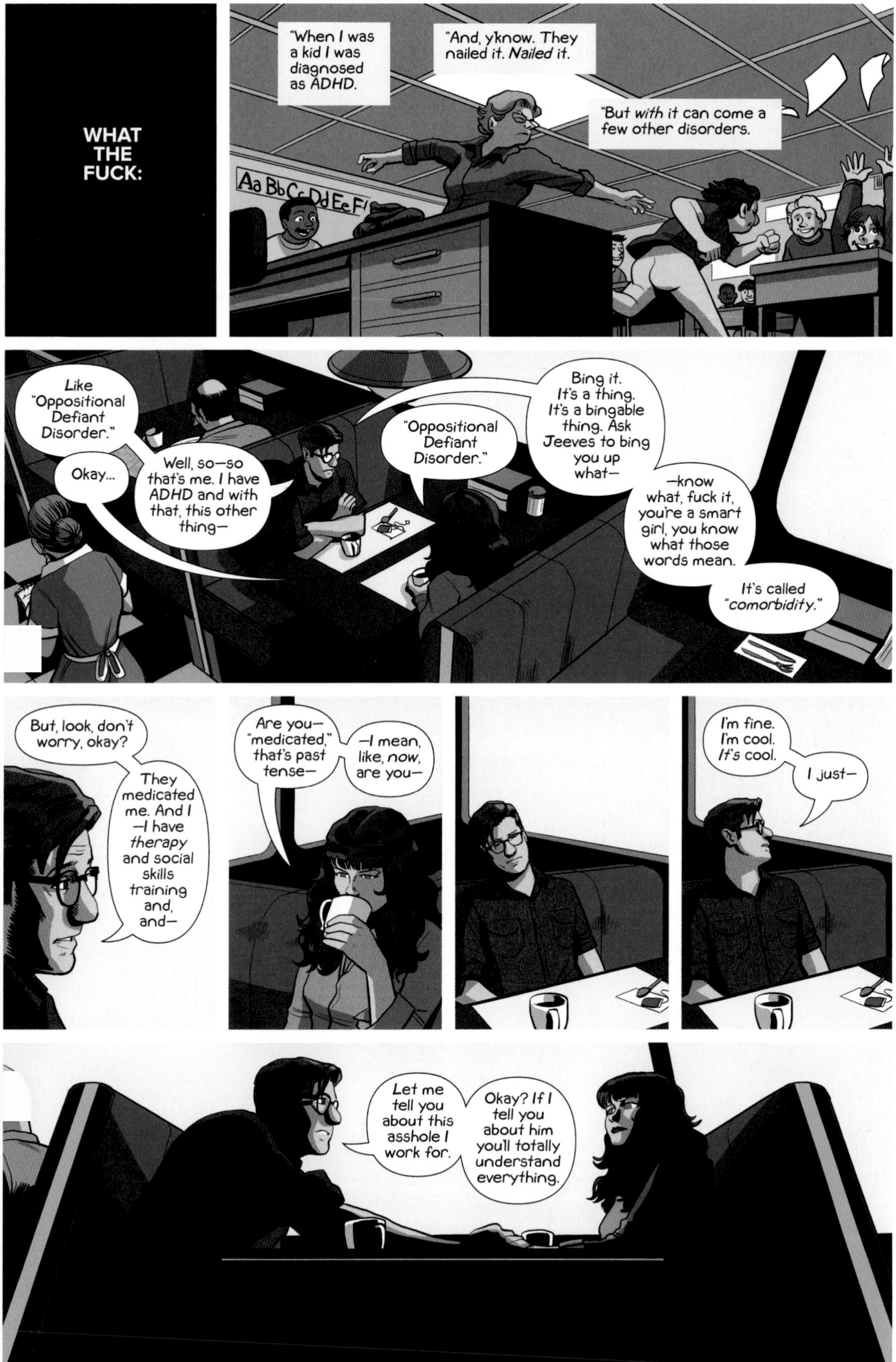
WHAT THE FUCK:
"When I was a kid I was diagnosed as ADHD.
"And, y'know. They nailed it. *Nailed* it.
"But *with* it can come a few other disorders.
Aa Bb Cc Dd Ee Ff
Like "Oppositional Defiant Disorder."
Okay...
Well, so—so that's me. I have ADHD and with that, this other thing—
"Oppositional Defiant Disorder."
Bing it. It's a thing. It's a bingable thing. Ask Jeeves to bing you up what—
—know what, fuck it, you're a smart girl, you know what those words mean.
It's called *"comorbidity."*
But, look, don't worry, okay?
They medicated me. And I —I have *therapy* and social skills training and, and—
Are you—"medicated," that's past tense—
—I mean, like, *now*, are you—
I'm fine. I'm cool. *It's* cool.
I just—
Let me tell you about this asshole I work for.
Okay? If I tell you about him you'll totally understand everything.

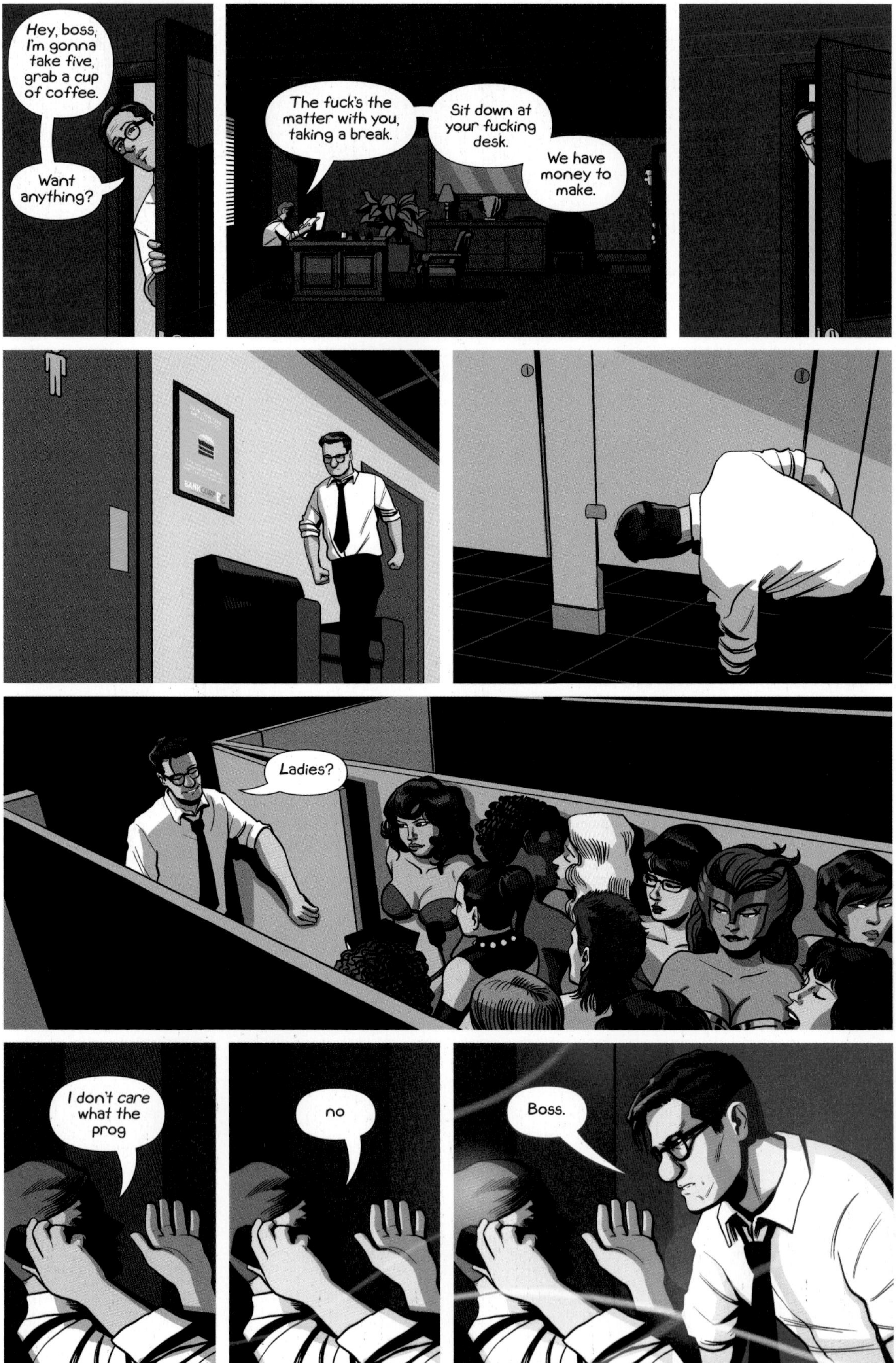
Hey, boss, I'm gonna take five, grab a cup of coffee.
Want anything?
The fuck's the matter with you, taking a break.
Sit down at your fucking desk.
We have money to make.
Ladies?
I don't *care* what the prog
no
Boss.

You fucking prick.

You FUCK—

fflarrble

Hm.

So instead of, like, smashing up the guy's office and losing *another* job and all that—

I started to quietly and consistently drop my daily deuce in his potted plant. Now, the amazing thing is this:

He hasn't gotten rid of the plant. Which is, like, the easy solve, right? Not for him. In fact—

—my boss uses the "Phantom Pooper" to crack down even more on his subordinates.

He even offered a *reward*. People have narced one another out, even trying to get folks they don't like *fired*...

PIN CODES

Come j
an
BOWLI
"Prob
spor

Contac

WANTED
THE MOST DISGUSTING
HUMAN BEING EVER

SOMEBODY *IN OUR OFFICE* HAS BEEN DEFECATING IN THE PLANT OF OUR KIND AND CONSIDERATE BOSS, MR. SHANKWORTH. LIKE MR. SHANKWORTH, THE PLANT HAS DONE *NOTHING* TO DESERVE SUCH ABHORRENT TREATMENT.

THERE WILL BE A REWARD FOR ANY INFORMATION WHICH LEADS TO FINGERING THE CULPRIT AND CEASING THE DEFECATION. PLEASE CONTACT MR. SHANKWORTH'S ASSISTANT, JON, AT X.2435.

Jon.

Are you... on your meds still? Right now?

This guy.

No.

This fucking guy.

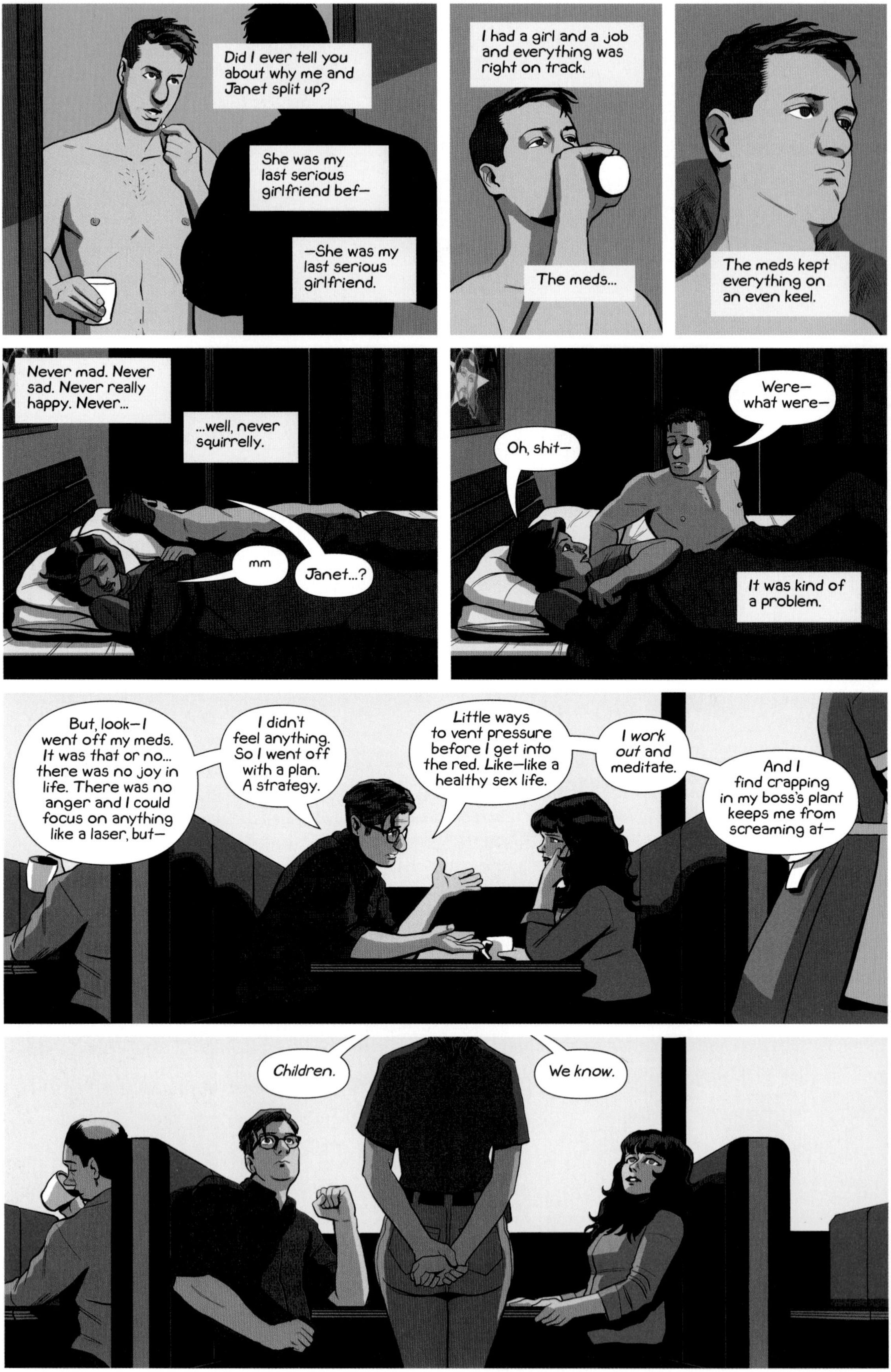
Did I ever tell you about why me and Janet split up?
She was my last serious girlfriend bef—
—She was my last serious girlfriend.
I had a girl and a job and everything was right on track.
The meds...
The meds kept everything on an even keel.
Never mad. Never sad. Never really happy. Never...
...well, never squirrelly.
Janet...?
mm
Oh, shit—
Were— what were—
It was kind of a problem.
But, look—I went off my meds. It was that or no... there was no joy in life. There was no anger and I could focus on anything like a laser, but—
I didn't feel anything. So I went off with a plan. A strategy.
Little ways to vent pressure before I get into the red. Like—like a healthy sex life.
I work out and meditate.
And I find crapping in my boss's plant keeps me from screaming at—
Children.
We know.

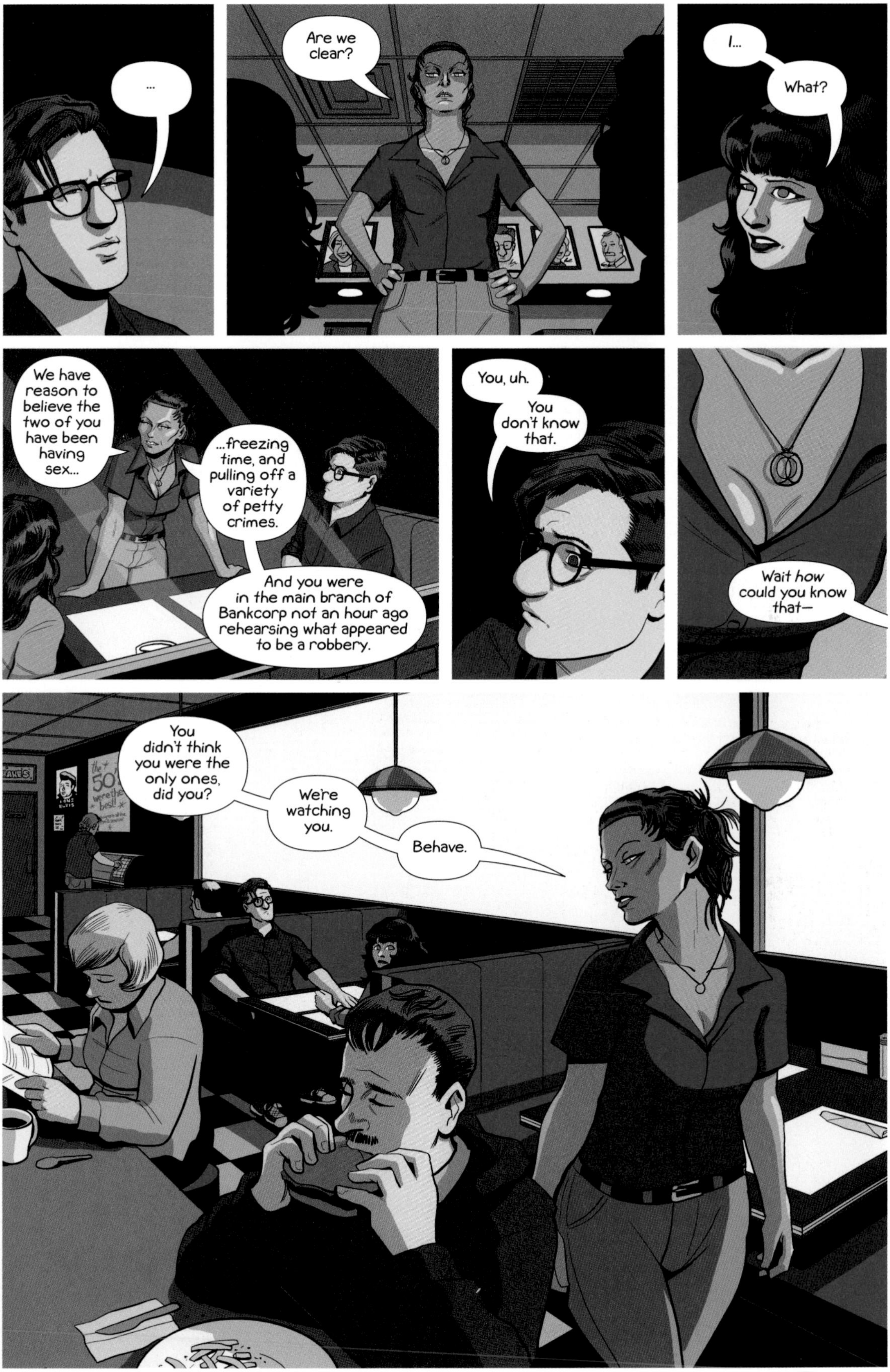
...
Are we clear?
I...
What?
We have reason to believe the two of you have been having sex...
...freezing time, and pulling off a variety of petty crimes.
And you were in the main branch of Bankcorp not an hour ago rehearsing what appeared to be a robbery.
You, uh.
You don't know that.
Wait how could you know that—
You didn't think you were the only ones, did you?
We're watching you.
Behave.

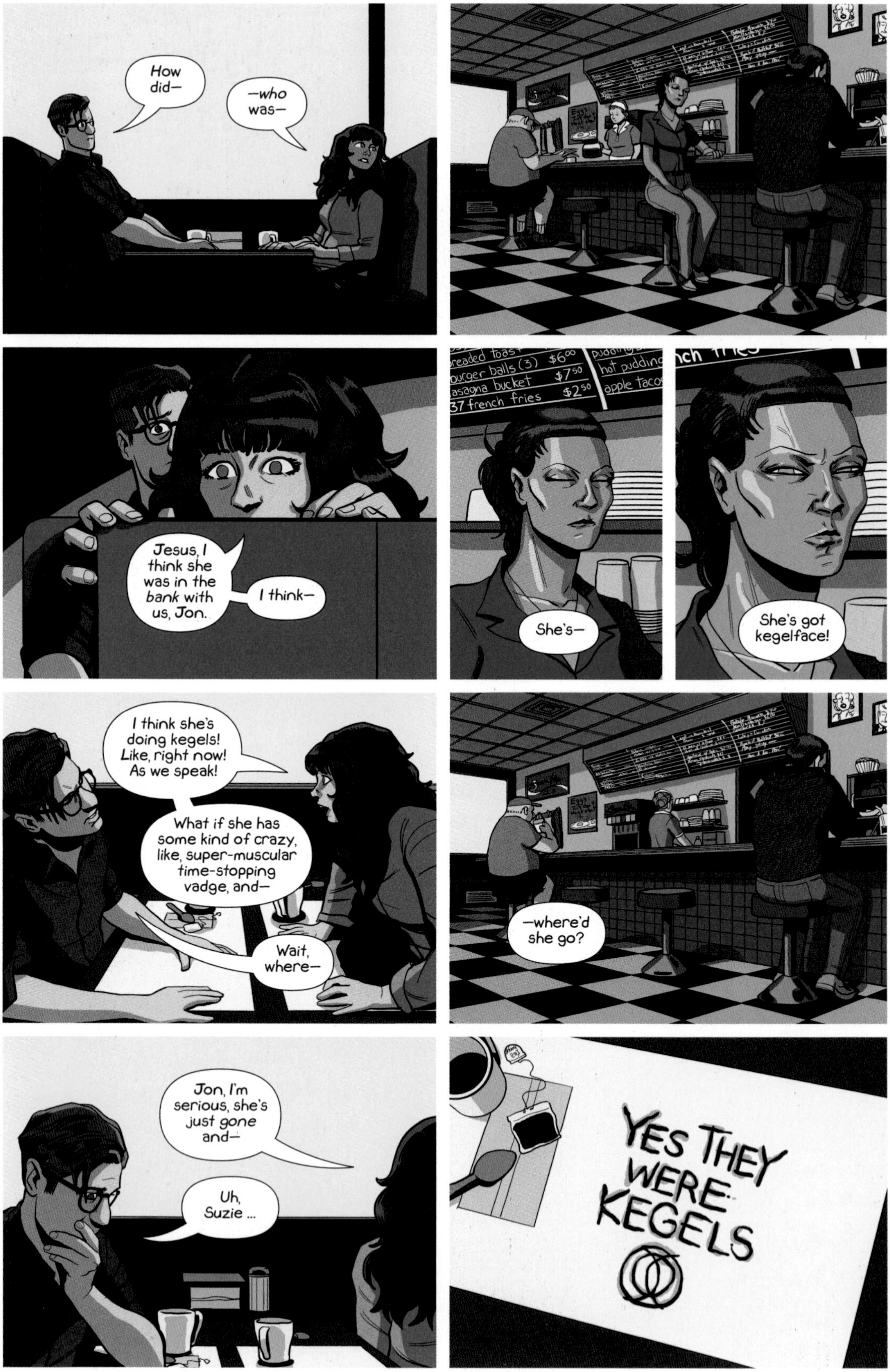

How did—
—who was—
Jesus, I think she was in the *bank* with us, Jon.
I think—
She's—
She's got kegelface!
I think she's doing kegels! Like, right now! As we speak!
What if she has some kind of crazy, like, super-muscular time-stopping vadge, and—
Wait, where—
—where'd she go?
Jon, I'm serious, she's just *gone* and—
Uh, Suzie ...
YES THEY WERE KEGELS

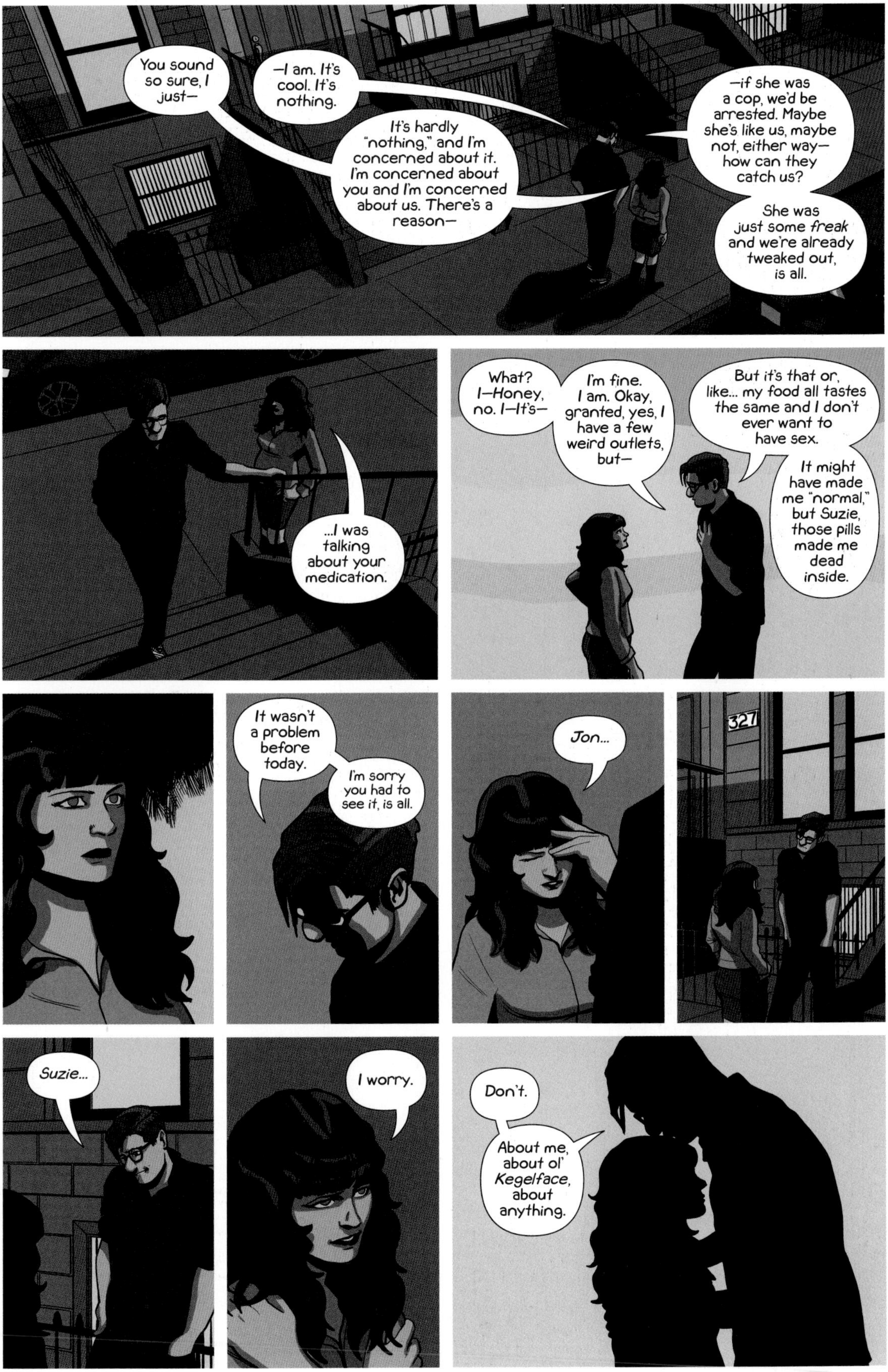
You sound so sure, I just—
—I am. It's cool. It's nothing.
It's hardly "nothing," and I'm concerned about it. I'm concerned about you and I'm concerned about us. There's a reason—
—if she was a cop, we'd be arrested. Maybe she's like us, maybe not, either way— how can they catch us?
She was just some *freak* and we're already tweaked out, is all.
...I was talking about your medication.
What? I—Honey, no. I—It's—
I'm fine. I am. Okay, granted, yes, I have a few weird outlets, but—
But it's that or, like... my food all tastes the same and I don't ever want to have sex.
It might have made me "normal," but Suzie, those pills made me dead inside.
It wasn't a problem before today.
I'm sorry you had to see it, is all.
Jon...
327
Suzie...
I worry.
Don't.
About me, about ol' *Kegelface*, about anything.

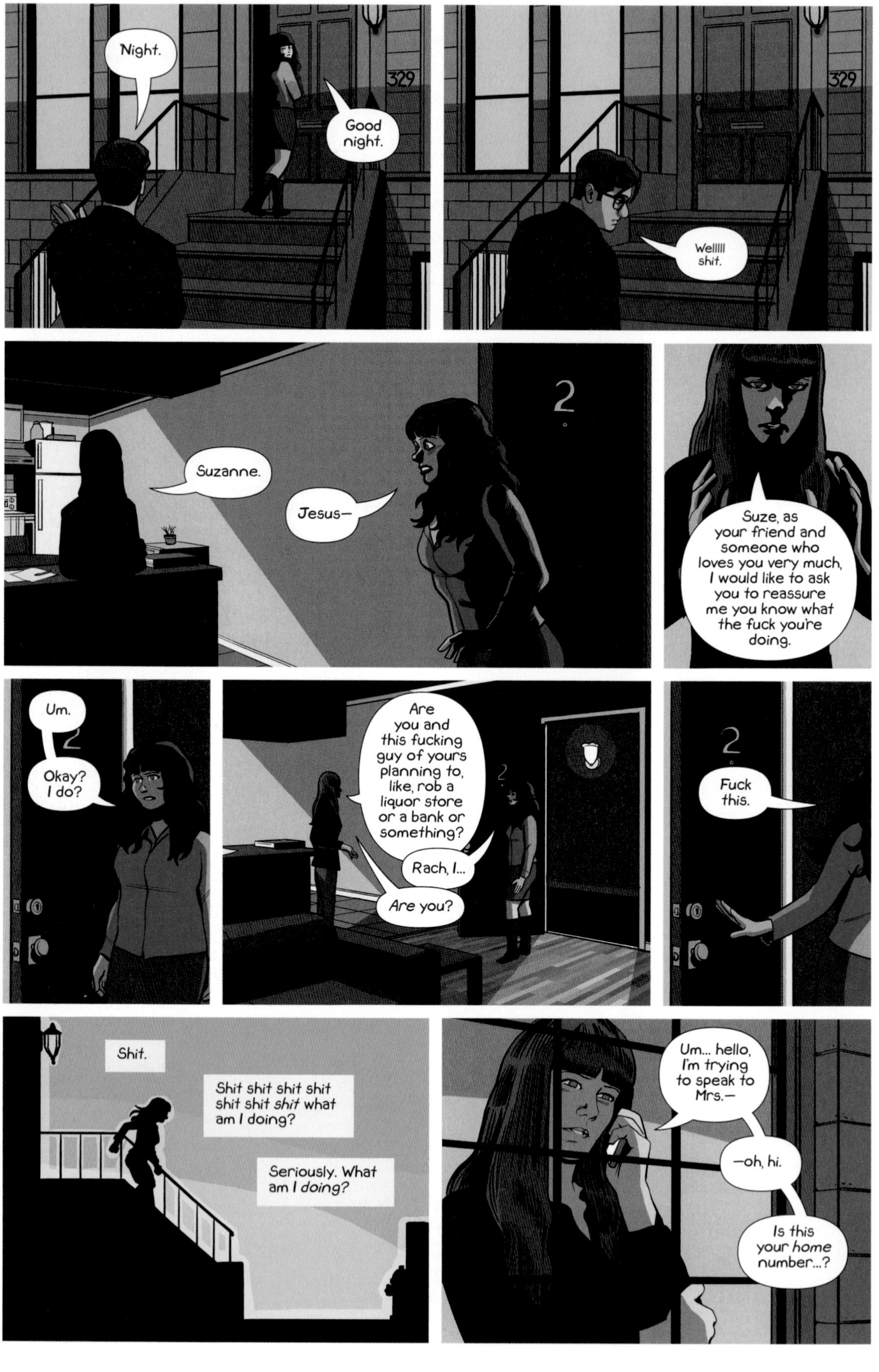

Night.
Good night.
329
329
Wellll shit.
Suzanne.
Jesus—
2
Suze, as your friend and someone who loves you very much, I would like to ask you to reassure me you know what the fuck you're doing.
Um.
Okay? I do?
Are you and this fucking guy of yours planning to, like, rob a liquor store or a bank or something?
Rach, I...
Are you?
2
Fuck this.
Shit.
Shit shit shit shit shit shit *shit* what am I doing?
Seriously. What am I *doing*?
Um... hello, I'm trying to speak to Mrs.—
—oh, hi.
Is this your *home* number...?

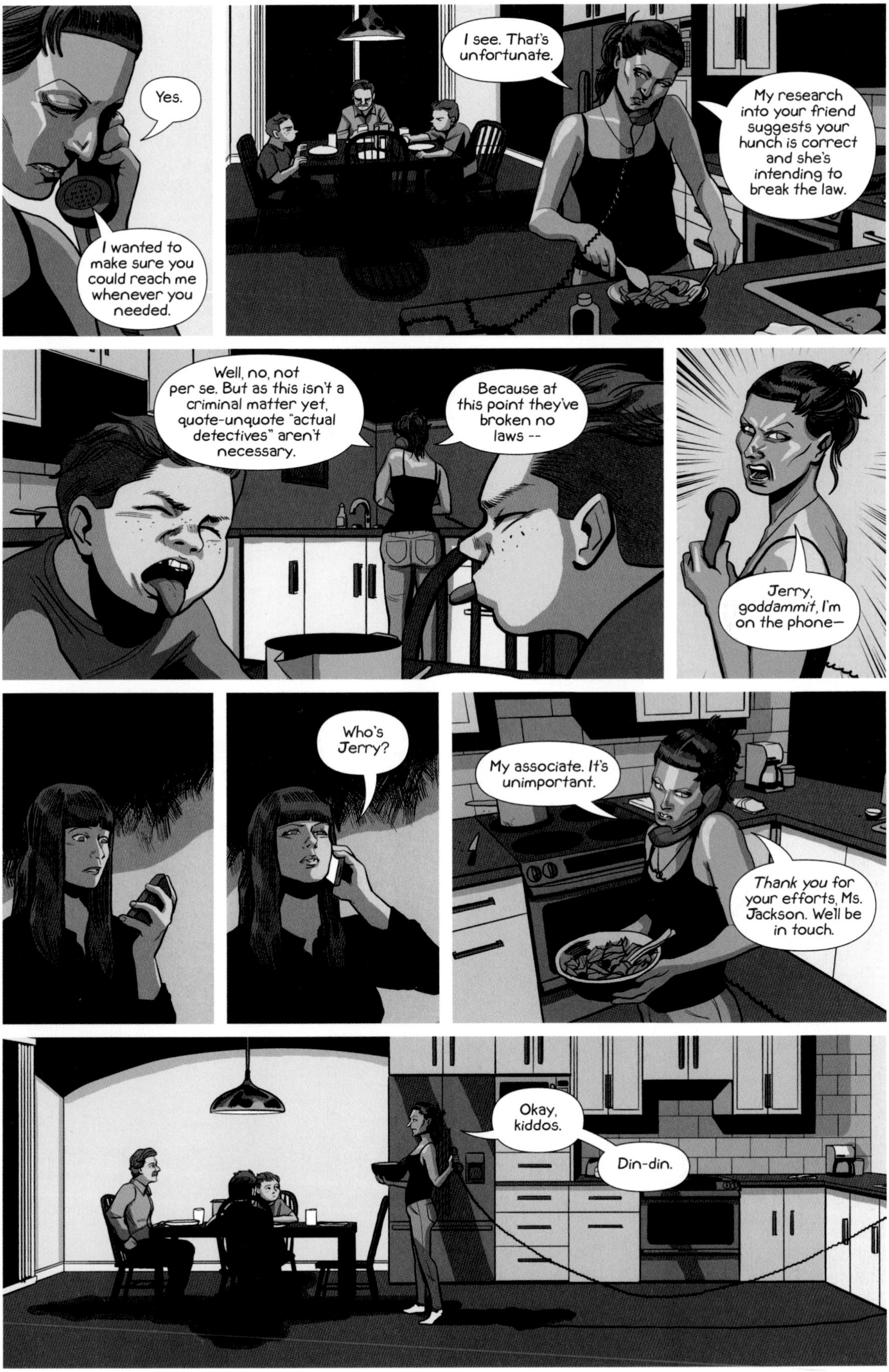
Yes.
I wanted to make sure you could reach me whenever you needed.
I see. That's unfortunate.
My research into your friend suggests your hunch is correct and she's intending to break the law.
Well, no, not per se. But as this isn't a criminal matter yet, quote-unquote "actual detectives" aren't necessary.
Because at this point they've broken no laws --
Jerry, goddammit, I'm on the phone—
Who's Jerry?
My associate. It's unimportant.
Thank you for your efforts, Ms. Jackson. We'll be in touch.
Okay, kiddos.
Din-din.

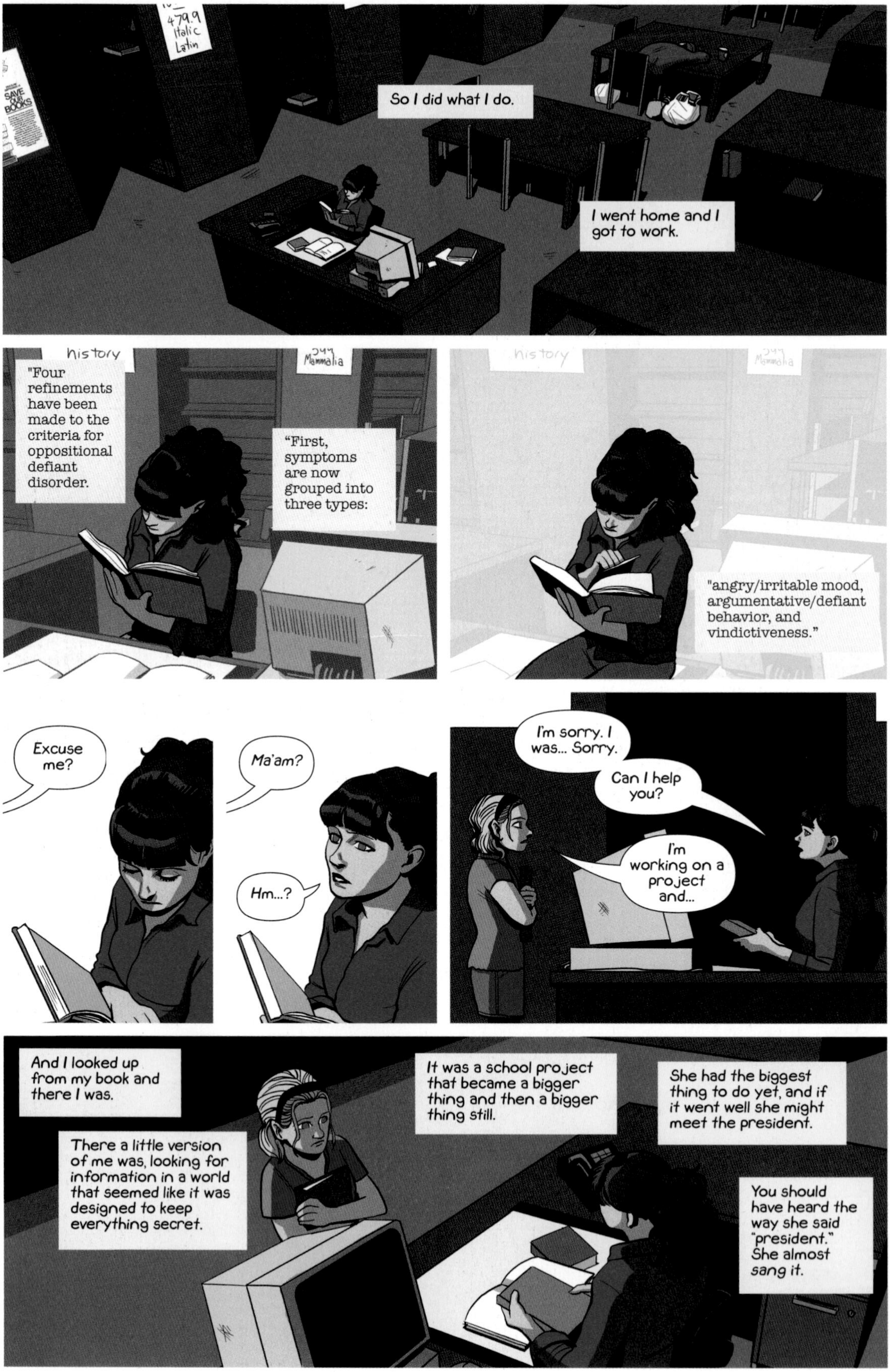
479.9
Italic
Latin
SAVE OUR BOOKS
So I did what I do.
I went home and I got to work.
history
599
Mammalia
"Four refinements have been made to the criteria for oppositional defiant disorder.
"First, symptoms are now grouped into three types:
history
599
Mammalia
"angry/irritable mood, argumentative/defiant behavior, and vindictiveness."
Excuse me?
Ma'am?
Hm...?
I'm sorry. I was... Sorry.
Can I help you?
I'm working on a project and...
And I looked up from my book and there I was.
There a little version of me was, looking for information in a world that seemed like it was designed to keep everything secret.
It was a school project that became a bigger thing and then a bigger thing still.
She had the biggest thing to do yet, and if it went well she might meet the president.
You should have heard the way she said "president." She almost sang it.

This kid.

'...certain batteries made with limited purpose utilize lithium-metal electrodes to prevent...'

This fucking kid.

This fucking place.

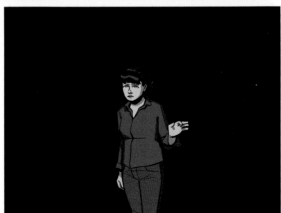

Contacts
Norville
Nuncio
O
Ofelia
Oscar
Reply | Send

Contacts
Oz
P
Pat
Patricia
Patty
Reply | Send

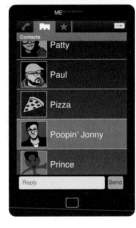
Contacts
Patty
Paul
Pizza
Poopin' Jonny
Prince
Reply | Send

metaphysics
Okay, Jon.

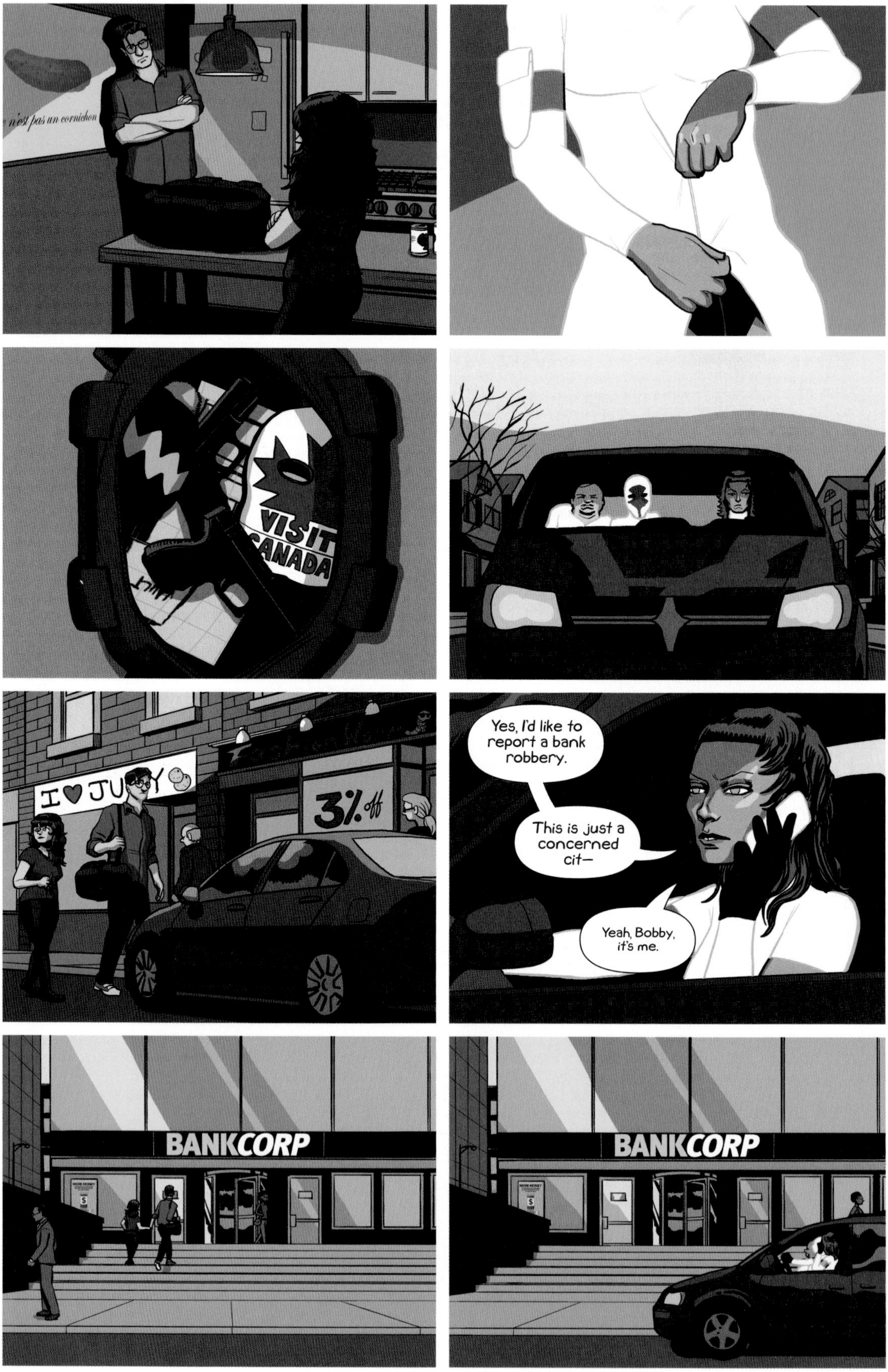
n'est pas un cornichon
VISIT CANADA
3% off
Yes, I'd like to report a bank robbery.
This is just a concerned cit—
Yeah, Bobby, it's me.
BANKCORP
BANKCORP

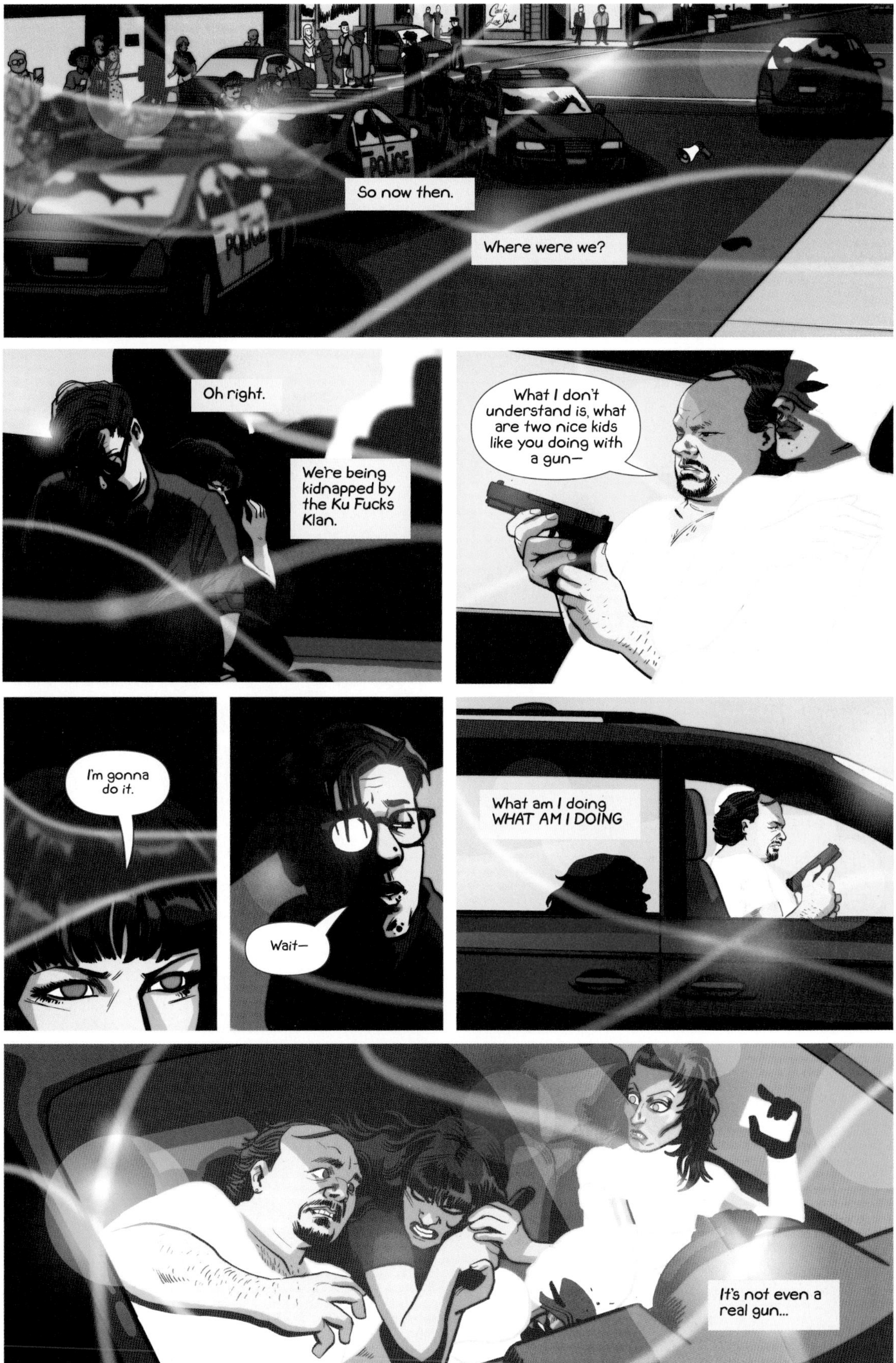
So now then.
Where were we?
Oh right.
We're being kidnapped by the Ku Fucks Klan.
What I don't understand is, what are two nice kids like you doing with a gun—
I'm gonna do it.
Wait—
What am I doing WHAT AM I DOING
It's not even a real gun...

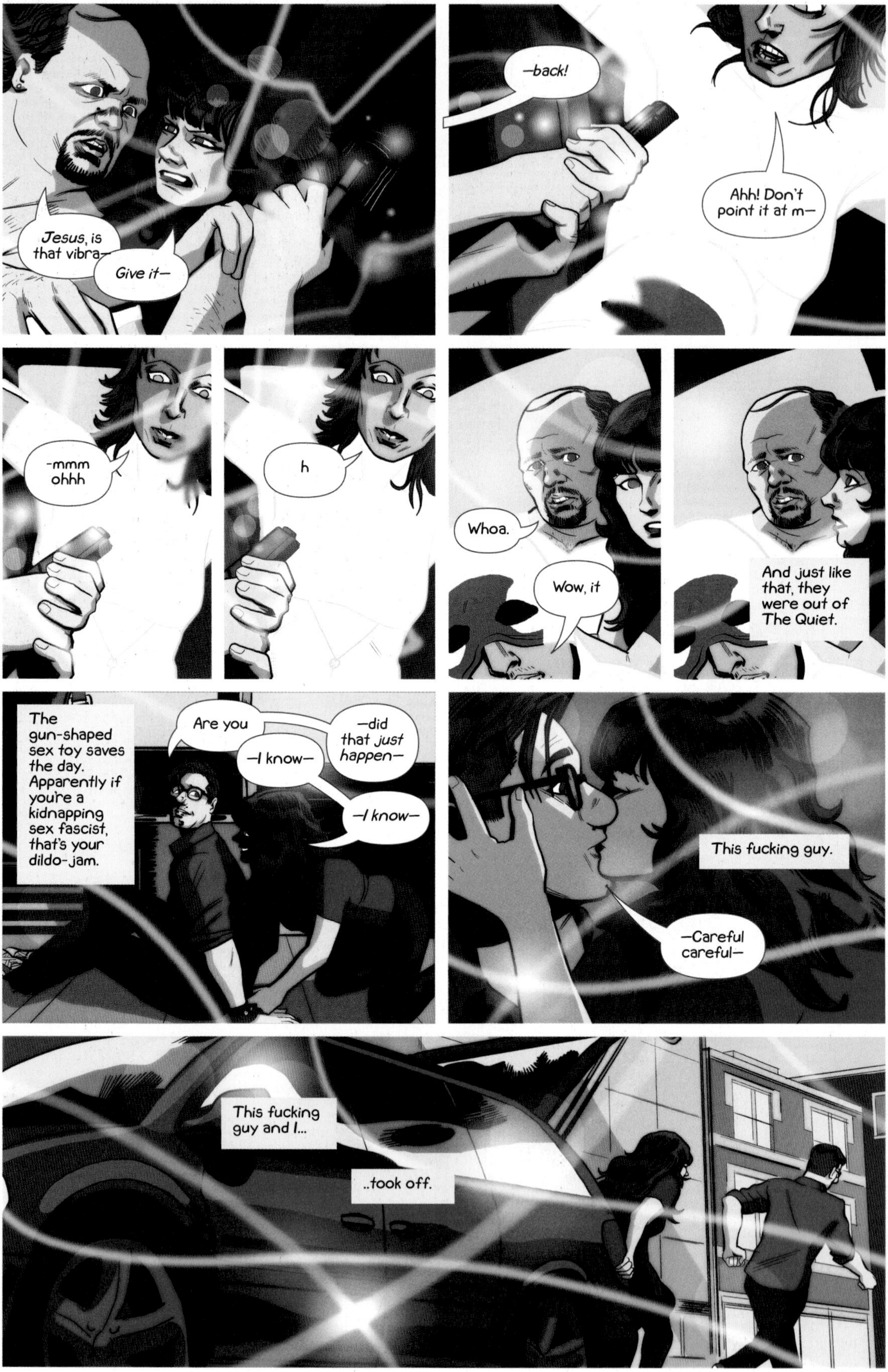
Jesus, is that vibra—
Give it—
—back!
Ahh! Don't point it at m—
-mmm ohhh
h
Whoa.
Wow, it
And just like that, they were out of The Quiet.
The gun-shaped sex toy saves the day. Apparently if you're a kidnapping sex fascist, that's your dildo-jam.
Are you
—did that just happen—
—I know—
—I know—
This fucking guy.
—Careful careful—
This fucking guy and I...
..took off.

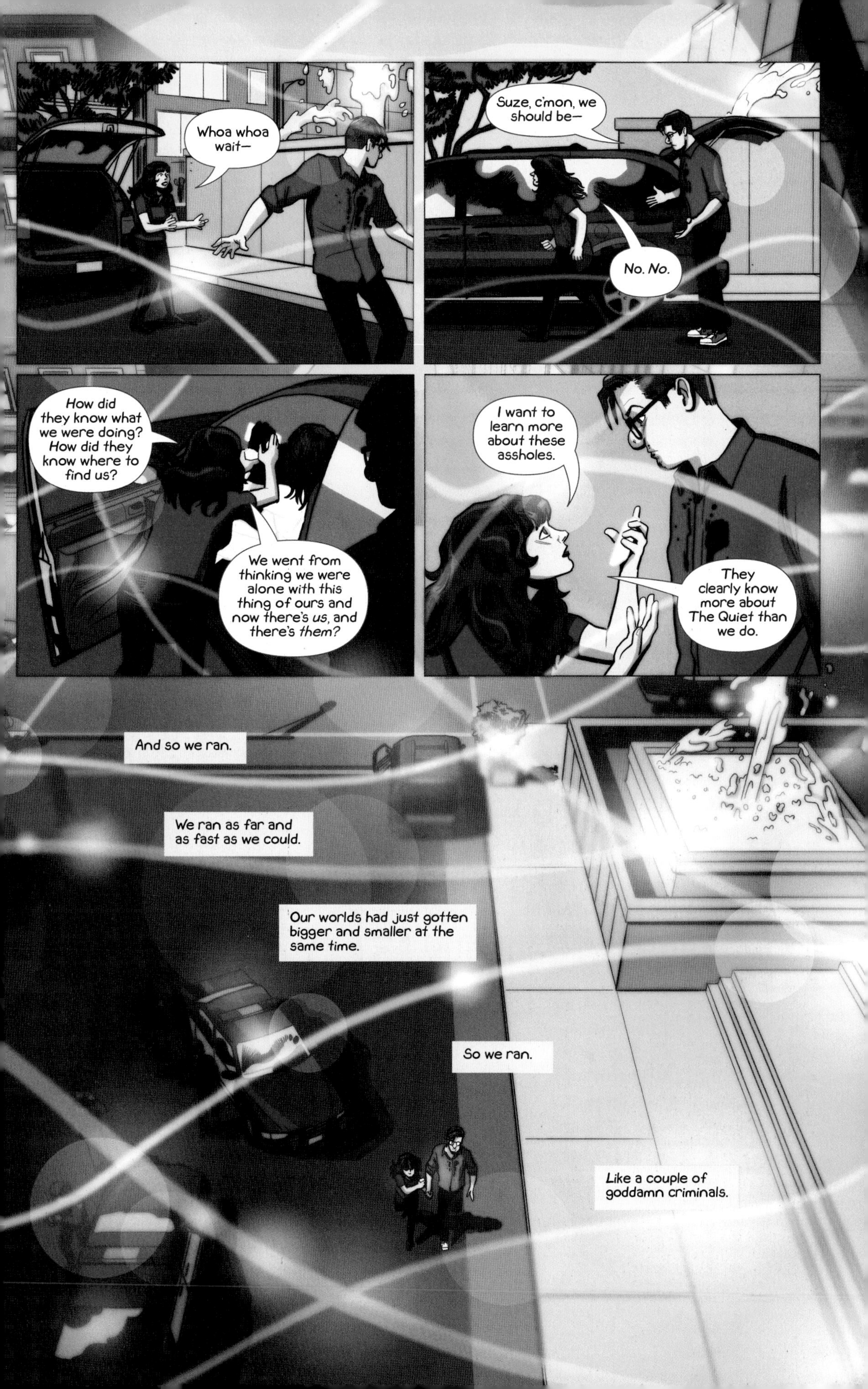

Whoa whoa wait—
Suze, c'mon, we should be—
No. No.
How did they know what we were doing? How did they know where to find us?
We went from thinking we were alone with this thing of ours and now there's us, and there's them?
I want to learn more about these assholes.
They clearly know more about The Quiet than we do.
And so we ran.
We ran as far and as fast as we could.
Our worlds had just gotten bigger and smaller at the same time.
So we ran.
Like a couple of goddamn criminals.

The Cordoba Kegel Tappin' Primping
The World Service
The 3-Second Rule Taco Whisping Slotting
Screebing
Queeps
Shrimping
Strumping Swaffling Cleefing
Crapplich
The Candle in the Wind Gossling

The Second Knuckle Winterizing the House
Goolating
Swundling
Bloobing
The STD test

The German Sex Shocker
Reverse-reverse Cowgirl
Reverse-reverse Cowgirl
Signing The User Agreement
The Dutch Microwave

MATT & CHIP'S ULTIMATE
SEX MOVES
OUR MASTER LIST OF WHAT DID (AND DIDN'T)
MAKE THE CUT IN THE WASHROOM STALL

Assperger's Syndrome
The Why Knot Hambo
Quoontzing
Pillow Cock

The Chocolate McKitten Scrubich
Butt-Nugging Brimping
Brimping Comme Vous L'Aimez
The Swift Gary Beethering
Mr. Brownstone Slimpping
The Tip Top Cheerio Guvner
E.T. The Sex Move Debuquing
Scooting Montezuma's Reward
Blurping/Fingerblurping
Space Waddity Space Mountain(s)

Broops
The Fleshy Lightswitch
Turtlesuiting
The Unrelated Godfather
Gillin'
The Sloopy
Thrushting
Tabbing

Foonting Quirping The Supreme Brifknockin'
Twerging/Auto-Erotic Twerging
Shumping
Breedlery
Fropery Frunging
Brooklyn Walk-up
Zdarsky Procking
Sex
The Pink O
The 1980s Sitcom
Cockguy Bro-cade
Female Injaculation
The Self-Service Gas Station Oh Christ
Peenery Butt-Tunnellin'
The Grand Poonification Theory
Quisping Fudgefist
The 100mm Diet Frosting
The "Love" "Boat"
The Unusual Sandwich
Muffling Balrogging

The Walking Head Blarging
Blurping/Fingerblurping
The Maybe He'll Like Me
Corinthian Lather

BARTON RE-THINK

In issue three, Suzie & Jon partake in the viewing of an erotic film entitled HARD-ON FINK. Matt, being a fan of its non-erotic spoof, Barton Fink*, had a few more dialogue options to use for the scene. Here is what did not make the cut.

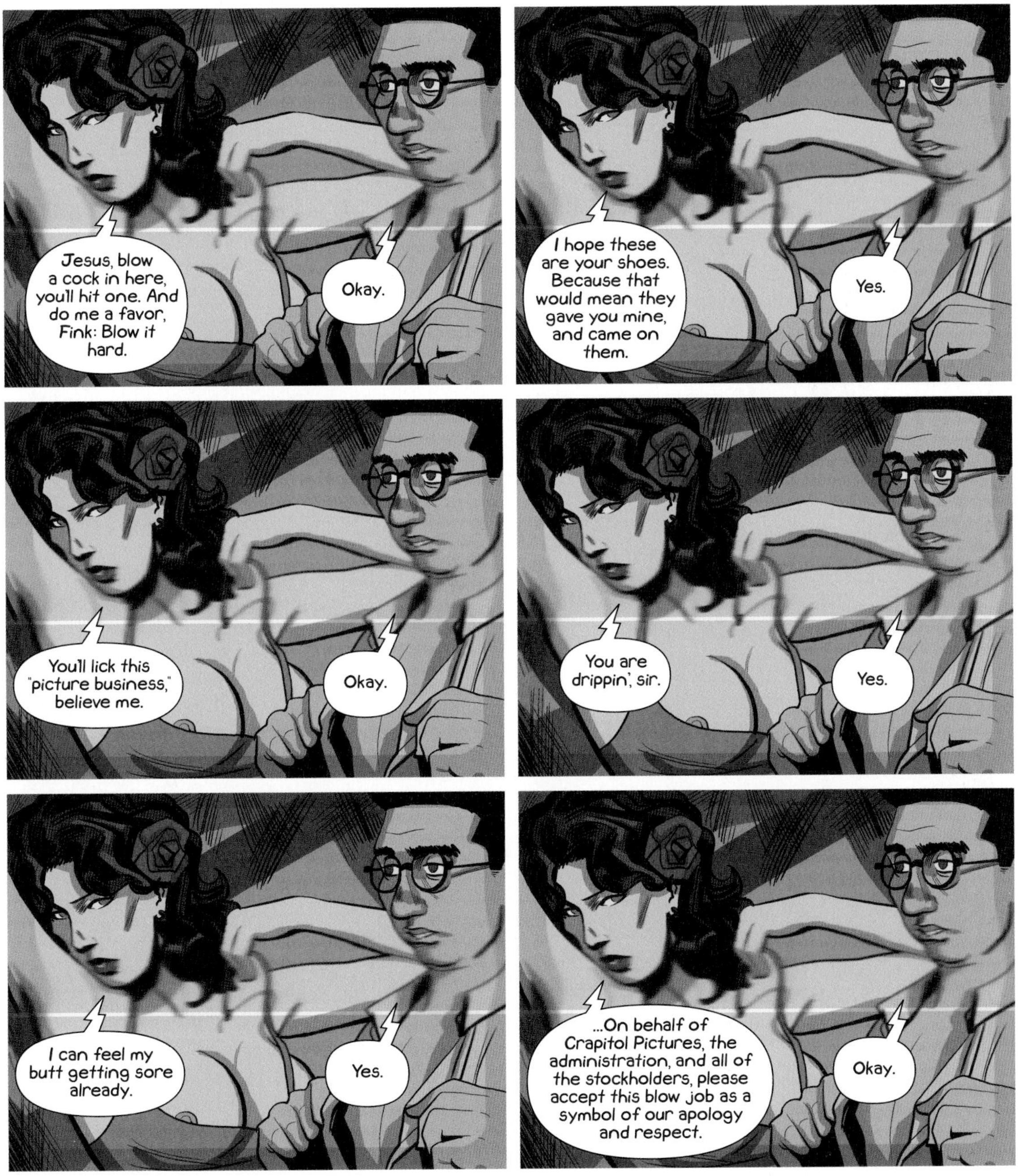
Jesus, blow a cock in here, you'll hit one. And do me a favor, Fink: Blow it hard.
Okay.
I hope these are your shoes. Because that would mean they gave you mine, and came on them.
Yes.
You'll lick this "picture business," believe me.
Okay.
You are drippin', sir.
Yes.
I can feel my butt getting sore already.
Yes.
...On behalf of Crapitol Pictures, the administration, and all of the stockholders, please accept this blow job as a symbol of our apology and respect.
Okay.

*Chip still has yet to see it. Shame him.

STEAMING RADIO

While promoting the first issue of SEX CRIMINALS, Matt & Chip created an original radio erotic drama for the literary website, *Hazlitt.* This is it, I guess.

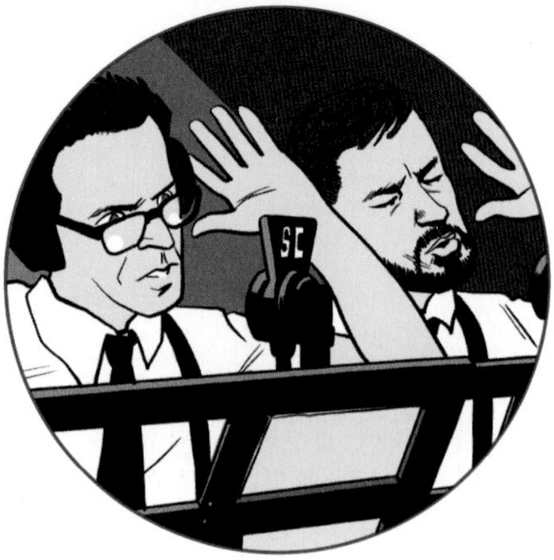
SC

CHIP: (Dialing number (multiple beeps) while softly singing "Tears in Heaven" to self)

AUTOMATED LADY VOICE: Welcome to Night Moves, where sssexy ladies grab you with their sssexy voices and make you dump your stuff all over the darn place. Press 1 for sssexy Linda, an exotic, dark-skinned beauty up all night with a tummy full of gas station dendrobium, locked inside of a Nursing School in Winni—(Beep from a button pressed)

(MATT clears throat)

CHIP: H-hello?...

MATT: What's your name?

CHIP: Hello?

MATT: What's your NAME.

CHIP: ...Steve?

MATT: (On script) Hiii Steve. Welcome to Night Moves, my name is Linda. I'm pretty horny let me tell you, but my dorm room key won't fit in any of these slippery locks. My ulnar collateral ligament, in relation with my tri --

CHIP: Um, excuse me?

MATT: Yeah?

CHIP: Are you L-Linda?

MATT: Sure.

CHIP: I'm ... pretty sure you're a man.

MATT: Ok, first off, that's just straight-up misandry. Second, gender is a societal construct defined by each of us in our own minds and not by society's precepts, and lastly, yes, I'm a man. And now thanks to Affirmative Action, straight white men like me have just as many opportunities in the workplace as lady-women like the "old" Linda. So: is your Dutch Baby buttered and out of the oven?

CHIP: I don't...I don't want this.

MATT: Look, your credit card's already been charged for, like, five minutes. You really want to fight with your bank about it?

CHIP: ...No, I guess not. It just—all right. Okay. Go ahead.

MATT: Okay. Good. ... Here goes ... are you ready? (Clears throat) Hey there. My name's Linda. I've been incredibly naughty. I misplaced all those shiny new highlighters from the office supply store and now Mr. McKelvie wants to "dock" my "pay." Do YOU want to "dock" my wet little "pay?"

CHIP: ...Oooh, yeah. I'd love to just grab your beautiful, shiny lady hairs and toss you onto the bed. Then I'd tear open that sensible Nursing School blouse of yours.

MATT: Oh no! It took sooo long to button!

CHIP: —And under it I see your huge nipples ready to just BURST out of your custom leather bra, you—

MATT: Wait, is that a thing? Leather bras?

CHIP: I...yeah. Yeah.

MATT: That sounds like it would be incredibly sweaty and, I don't know, a little *uptown* for a Winnipeggian at Nursing School.

CHIP: A girl I used to date wore them. Not ALL the time, but yeah, they exist.

(long pause)

MATT: (Back on script) Oooh, baby, my basement is tepid and soggy like a terrarium abandoned in the event of nuclear holocaust. Stand over me and demand to inspect my lady-curtains.

CHIP: Shuh ... show me your lady curtains?

MATT: MMM, honey, not only do these curtains not match the carpet, but there aren't even any windows. So I hike up my skirt and I'm just oozing with seriochemicals that drive your inner Asian elephant CRAY-CRAY.

CHIP: Your...your lady curtains are soaking through your

underparts, which are like...like paper towels after you spill your beer, just...just falling apart. Low quality. Discount underpants.

MATT: My student loans are fucking brutal! So I buy them in bulk, but now they're dissolving in my hands, hands which are now free to go inside my eager body and spelunk for feminine doubloons of ecstasy.

CHIP (Into it): Yeah, that's...that's pretty good, Linda.

MATT: Mouth-whoopee or hand-gladdening?

CHIP: I — what?

MATT: Mouth-whoopee or hand-gladdening?

CHIP: I don't know what you're...

MATT: Your man-danglings— would you like me to mouth-whoopee on them or to share with you a festive hand-gladdening?

(Long pause)

MATT: What are you going to do with your dick?

CHIP: I'm, uh, going to pull it out of my pants and...and maybe let you suck it with your...mouth...for a bit?

MATT: (Chewing food) Mmm, yummy yummy in my tummy. Like a $10 fat ballgame sausage. Man, it's even bigger than mine.

CHIP: I...can't! Your voice! It's just...just ruining the illusion. I'm sorry.

MATT: Because you know I'm a man.

CHIP: Yes!

MATT: A man...with a white-hot

t-shirt cannon arming my lower ramparts.

CHIP: ...Yes, sure, that.

MATT: Well, Chip, I'm going to ask you something.

CHIP: I didn't tell you my real na—

MATT: Chip, have you ever... *enthusiastically greeted the bishop after Sunday services*?

CHIP: Do you mean...have I ever manipulated the stock market?

MATT: Yes. Are you a *digital downloader*.

CHIP: A *Fan of Tango and Cash.*

MATT: Have you ever *stabbed Cthulhu with a dirk fashioned from the blackened tears of the ancient elders.*

CHIP: Oh, sure. I beat off like an angry chimp at the porno zoo. It's...kind of why I'm calling you.

MATT: Okay cool, so—so do you define your gender as "male"?

CHIP: Yes?

MATT: And you're a man with your very own "turgid podcast"?

CHIP: Yes.

MATT: And have you ever tickled your little Elia Kazan until he testifies before the HUAC in parabolic arcs of informative white gravy?

CHIP: Well, if you must be VULGAR, yes.

MATT: So you knowingly let a man's hand come in contact with your Yellow Submarine.

CHIP: What?

MATT: You—a man—frequently masturbate men.

CHIP: I don't know if seven or eight times a day qualifies as "frequent" but --

MATT: Don't deny it! Do you, a male man—

CHIP: How did you know I was a mailman?

MATT: —take a penis in your hand and manually manipulate it to the point of orgasm?

(Long pause)

CHIP: Oh my god.

MATT: Yep.

CHIP: I'm GAY.

MATT: We're all gay, Chip. Even me. Even if it's only for seven or eight times a day.

CHIP: I feel so free.

MATT: That's great.

CHIP: So liberated.

MATT: Sure.

CHIP: Maybe I should just get off the phone and go experience some real, genuine man touch—

AUTOMATED LADY VOICE: Your first five minutes are up. If you wish to continue at $3.99 a minute, please press 1, or hang up.

(Pause)

Your first five minutes are—

(BEEP)

MAKIN' SAUSAGE

How do comics get made? Where do babies come from? Surprisingly, both answers are the same: lots of fucking work! Here, Chip breaks down the process for creating a magical panel!

1: SCRIPT

Matt sends me the script and I read it and I laugh and I cry and it becomes a part of me. And then I realize he's set half the story in a cluttered porn shop and I hate him so much but he's so pretty how can I hate him for long?

2: LAYOUTS

I go through the script and make layouts for it in Photoshop. It's relatively easy, because Matt's written the script with a specific eight-panel grid in mind, because he likes to make my job easier except for setting things in that fucking porn shop oh he's so pretty.

3: PENCILS

I have an evening where I shoot as much reference as possible with my two main models, Tiffy and Alex. We drink and eat and laugh and simulate lovemaking. Sometimes I just rely on my own stunning body, as evidenced below for this panel.

For reference I use Google Maps to find buildings and Sketchup to find and arrange cars, then I start pencilling in Manga Studio.

1

2.4
HALF-PAGE PANEL. OUTSIDE THE BANK. TIME FROZEN, COPS and SWAT FOLK around. KEGEL, in her OUTFIT, and her two SEX POLICE, all in white, move through the frozen timescape towards the BANK. She lets the megaphone drop.

    KEGEL   We're coming.

    J (CAP, OP)   "How did I learn I could DO THIS...?"

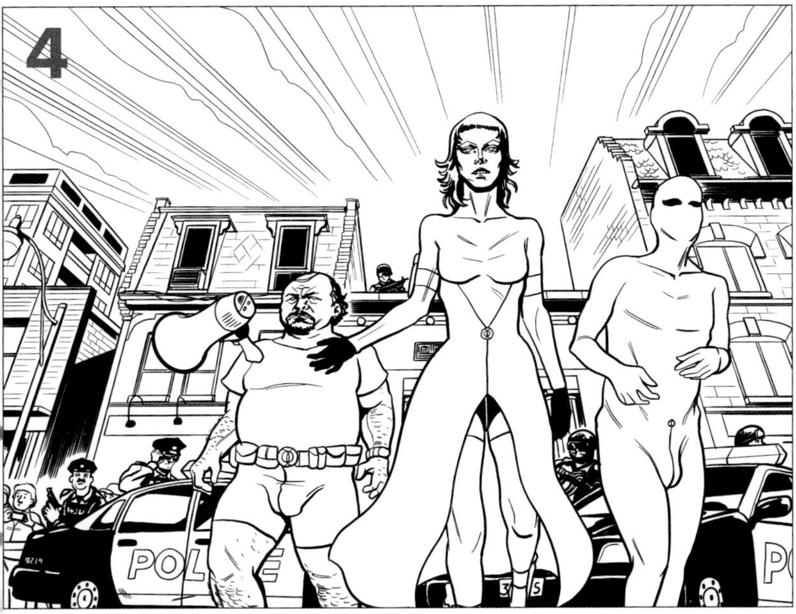
4

I bought a Cintiq pen display and Manga Studio when I realized I'd be doing a full comic project, and they've been craaaazy invaluable. #promotedparagraph

4: INKS

It's so funny to call these "pencils" and "inks," but what else am I going to do? I'm an old man trapped in your fancy compooper age. So, yeah, I ink it in Manga Studio.

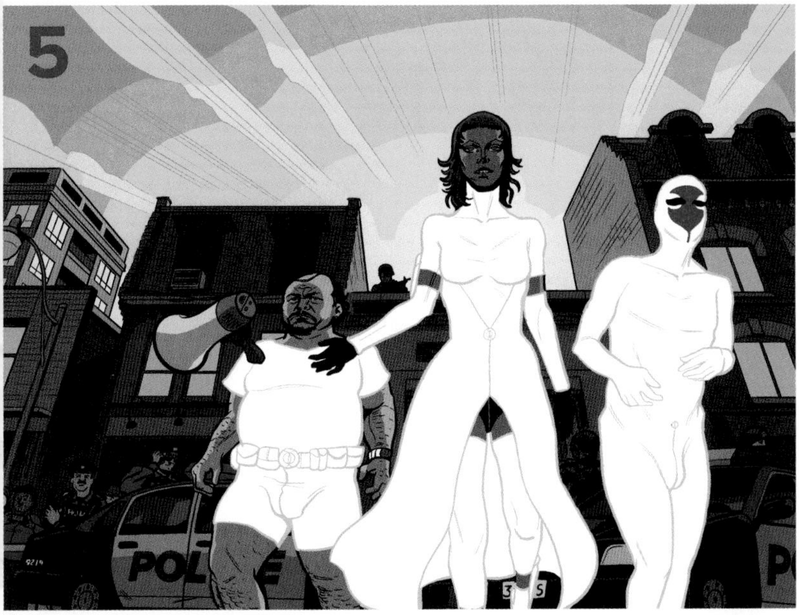
5

5: COLOURS

Yeah, that's right. I just spelt it with a "u." This is my fucking section and I'm a Canadian.

So, I send the inks to a colour flatter, and they assist me by filling in distinct shapes with flat blocks of colour. It makes it a lot faster to colour when you can just select shapes and start colouring instead of trying to draw within the lines. If ever I have a kid I will teach them to hire someone to colour within the lines. Kindergarten Kapitalism.

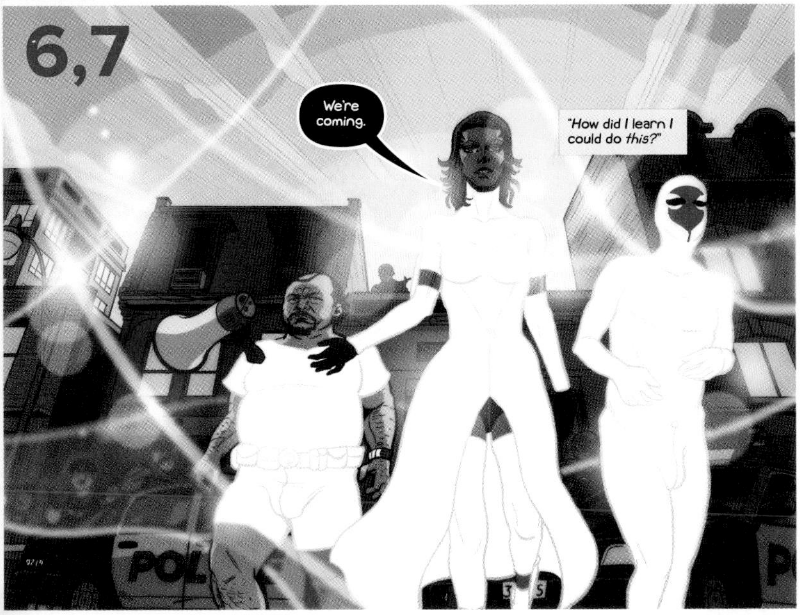
6,7
We're coming.
"How did I learn I could do *this?*"

6: THE QUIET

Once I've coloured it, I then render the effects for The Quiet. It's a ludicrous number of layers, but it's worth it, I guess. I don't know. Maybe it's not. Maybe I'm wasting my life.

7: LETTERING & EDITS

When we started the comic I spent a couple of days turning my handwriting into a font. I call it "Comic Avec." So, yeah, I then letter and send the page to Matt and our editor, Tommy K, with my dumb notes, like, "can we change 'coming' to 'cumming'?" and they just fucking ignore me.

PHOTO SWAP

For the fourth printing of issue one, Matt and Chip decided to try something different: a photo cover of them as proud parents to the first printing. But they live in different cities! How did they do it? Magic? Photoshop? I guess we'll never know unless we read below.

1. Yes, it was Photoshop. Before bed one night, Chip did a rough sketch for Matt, showing him how to pose for the cover, with very helpful labeling.

2. While Chip slept like a bearded Canadian baby on the East Coast, Matt posed with a "friend" he found and sent images to Chip from the West Coast, showing that the great East-West divide could be conquered.

3. Chip woke up to emails from his mommy, a penis pill company partially owned by his mommy, and Matt. After reviewing the photo, Chip got his long-suffering girlfriend to take photos to match Matt's, only the fifth-strangest photo request she's ever had from Chip.

4. A couple of hours later and, voila! Done! Chip is especially speedy at photo manipulation from his years of photoshopping his penis to look "more cool" in online dating profiles (simplyredfan69).

1
MAGAZINE'S 2013 COMIC OF THE YEAR
SEX CRIMINALS
FRACTION + ZDARSKY
1
FOURTH PRINTING
$3.50
you
me
comic

2

3

4

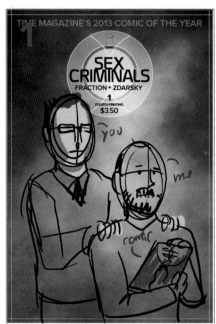

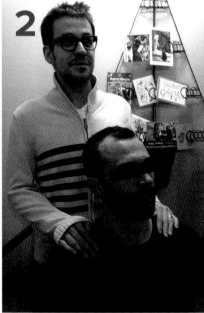

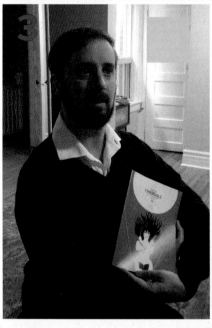

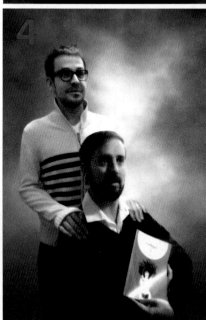

COVER GALLERY!

Starting on the opposing page, we're proud to present some of our favourite covers from the various reprints and variants we've done on our issues to date! In order, they're: *#1 fourth printing (photo cover), #1 Forbidden Planet variant, #1 Ghost variant (Yuko Shimizu), #1 EH! variant, #1 Image Expo variant, #2 fourth printing, #3 second printing (TIME), #3 third printing (Queen tribute), #4 second printing*

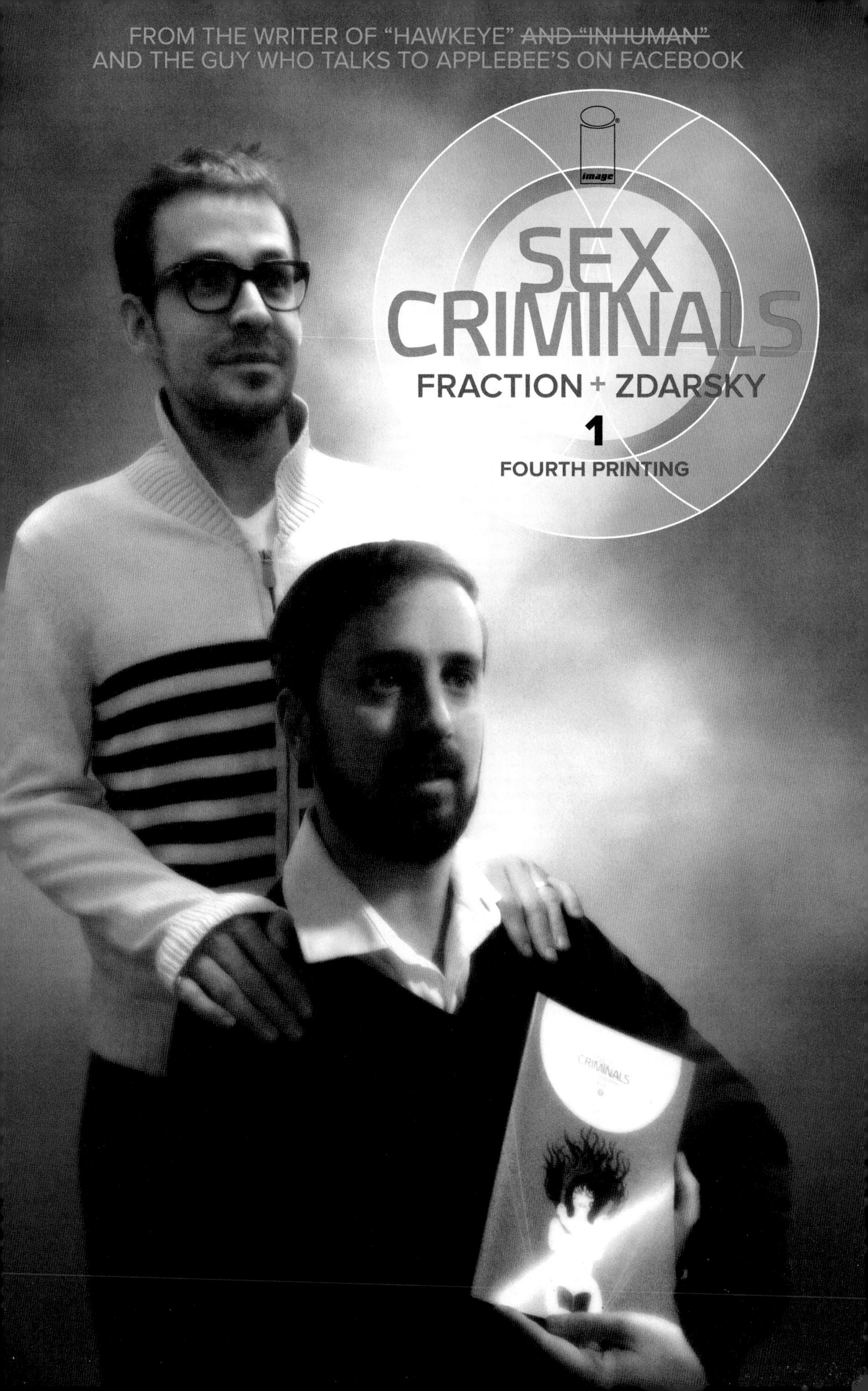
FROM THE WRITER OF "HAWKEYE" ~~AND "INHUMAN"~~
AND THE GUY WHO TALKS TO APPLEBEE'S ON FACEBOOK
image
SEX CRIMINALS
FRACTION + ZDARSKY
1
FOURTH PRINTING
CRIMINALS

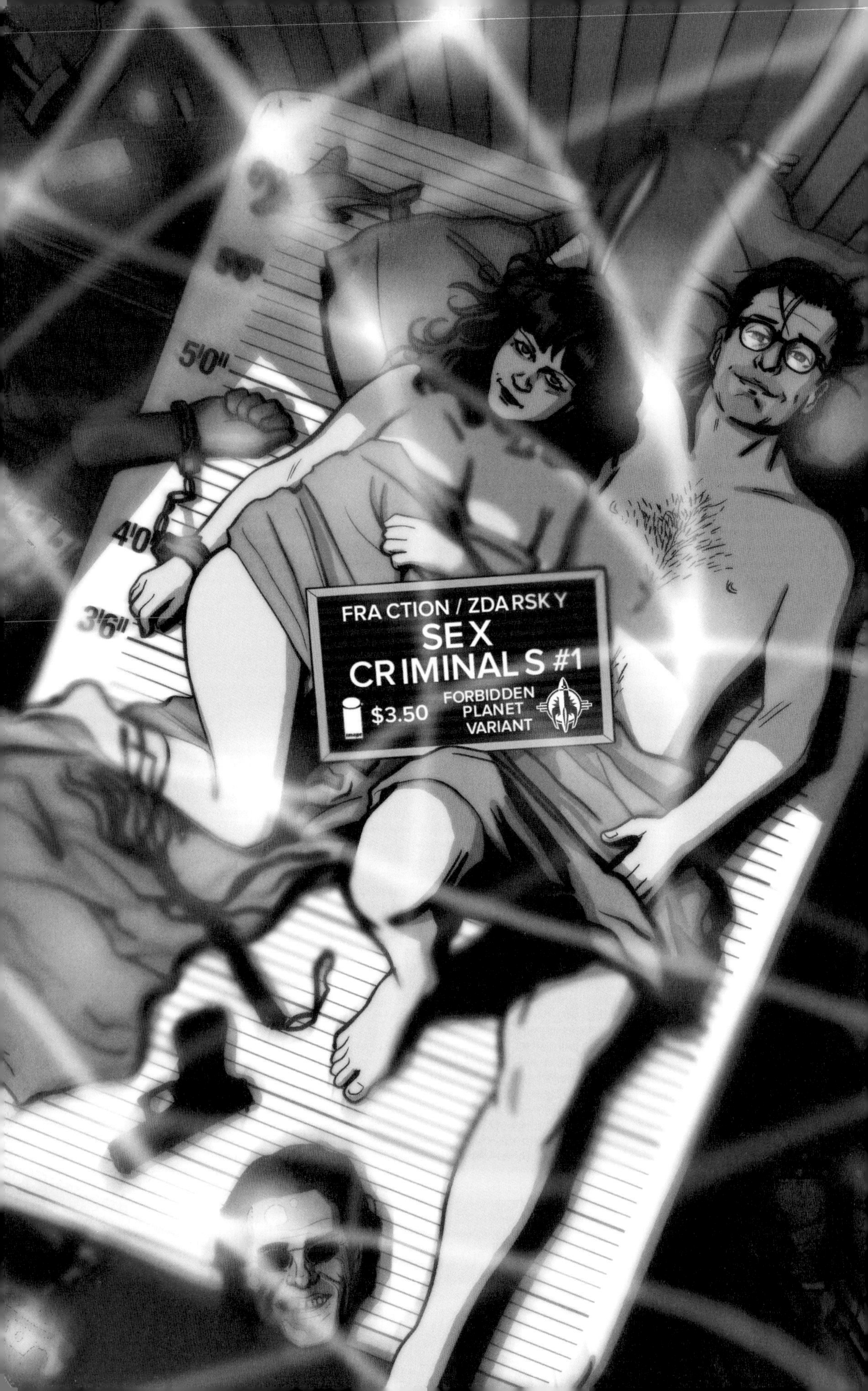

5'0"
4'0"
3'6"
FRA CTION / ZDA RSK Y
SE X
CR IMINAL S #1
$3.50
FORBIDDEN
PLANET
VARIANT

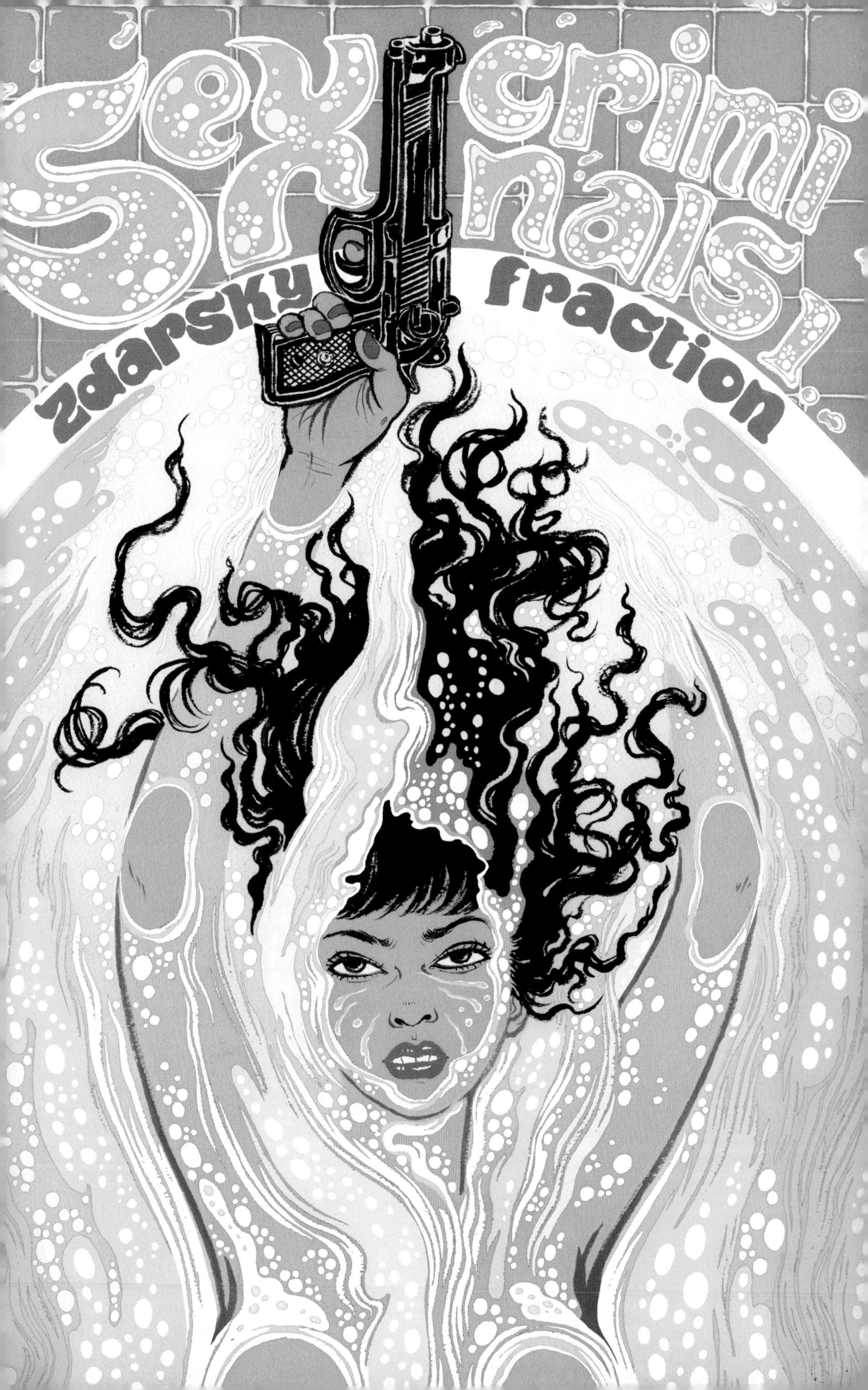
Sex Criminals 1
Zdarsky
Fraction

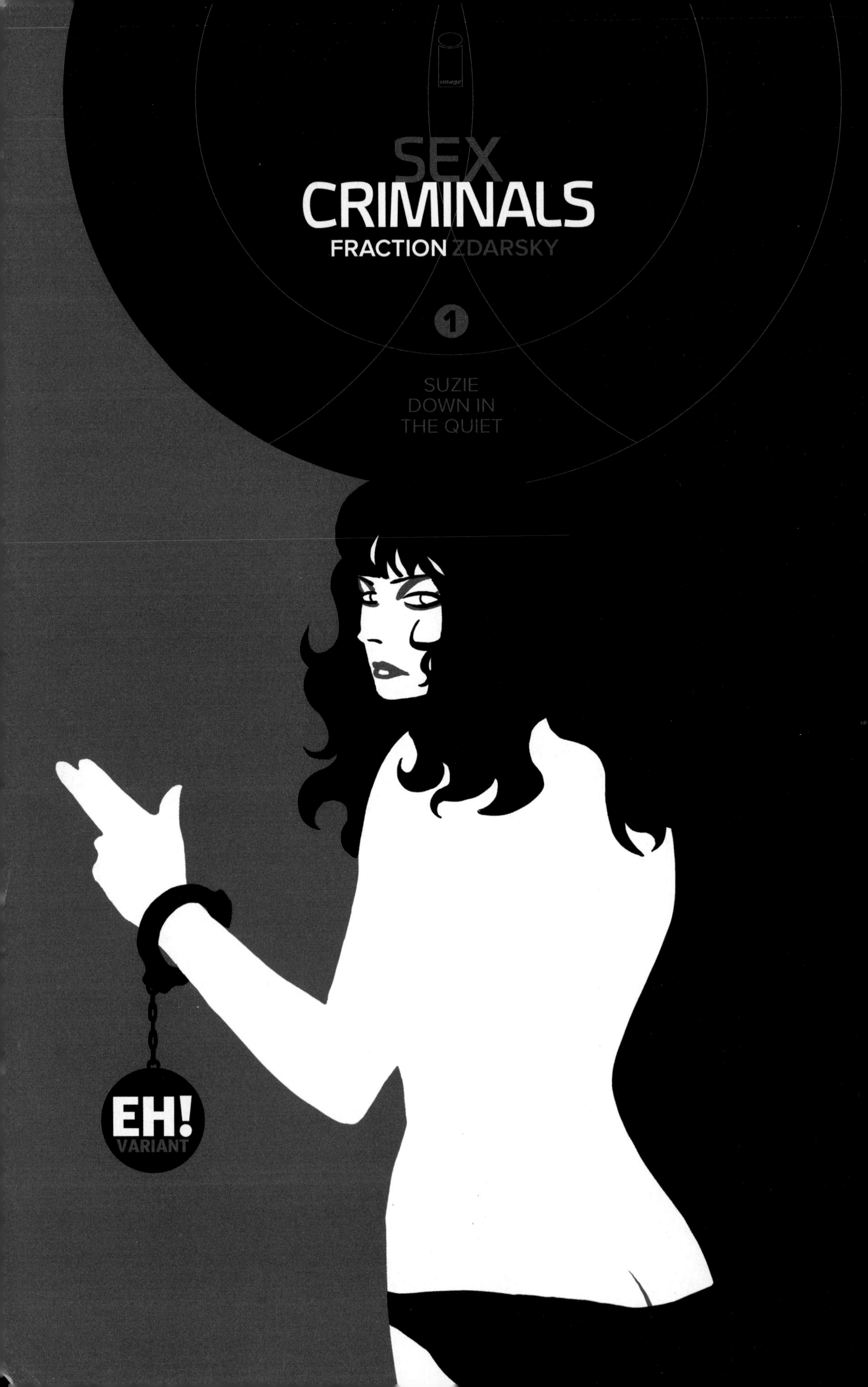
SEX
CRIMINALS
FRACTION ZDARSKY
1
SUZIE
DOWN IN
THE QUIET
EH!
VARIANT

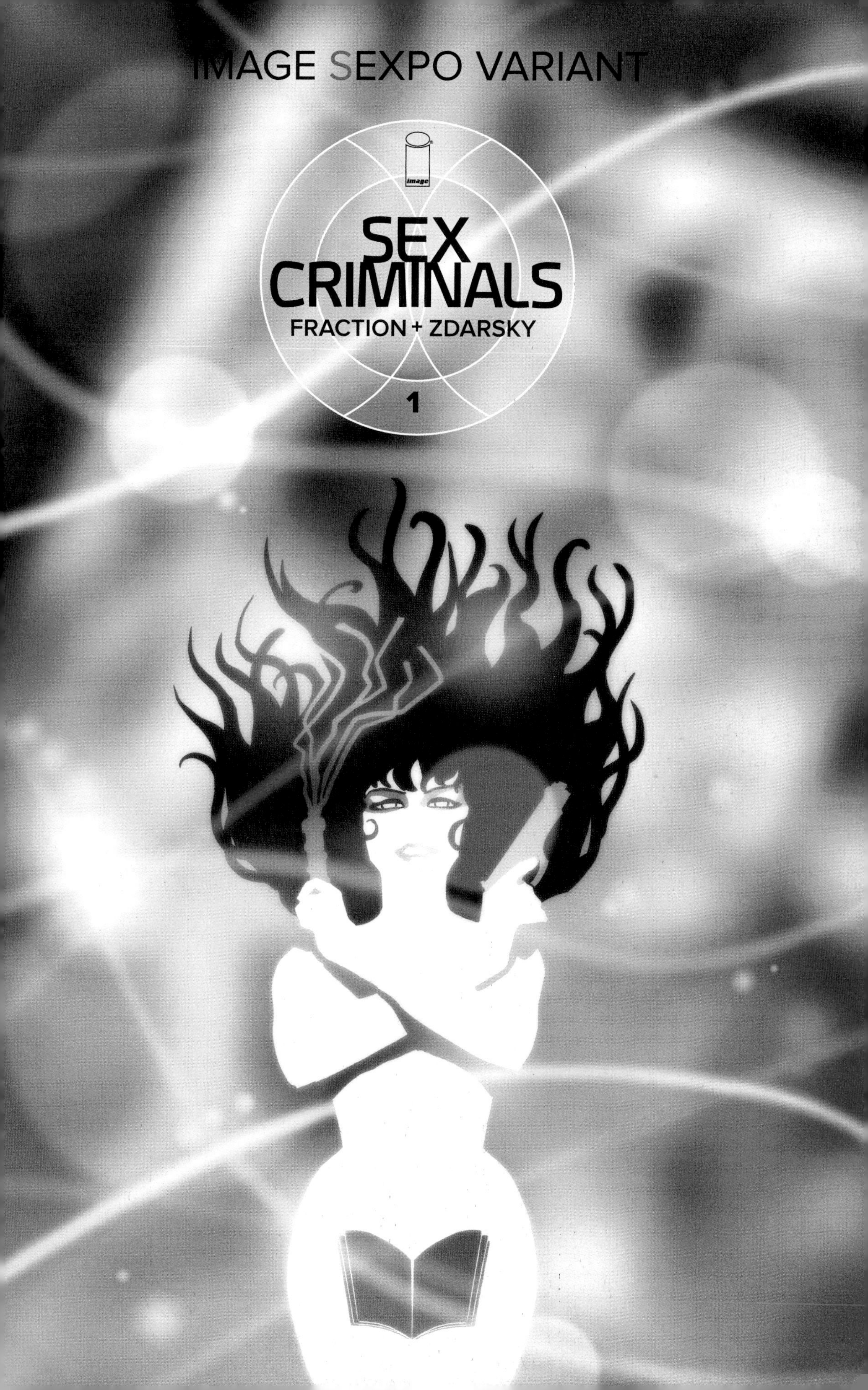
IMAGE SEXPO VARIANT
SEX CRIMINALS
FRACTION + ZDARSKY
1

FOURTH PRINTING

SEX CRIMINALS
FRACTION + ZDARSKY

2

COME,
WORLD

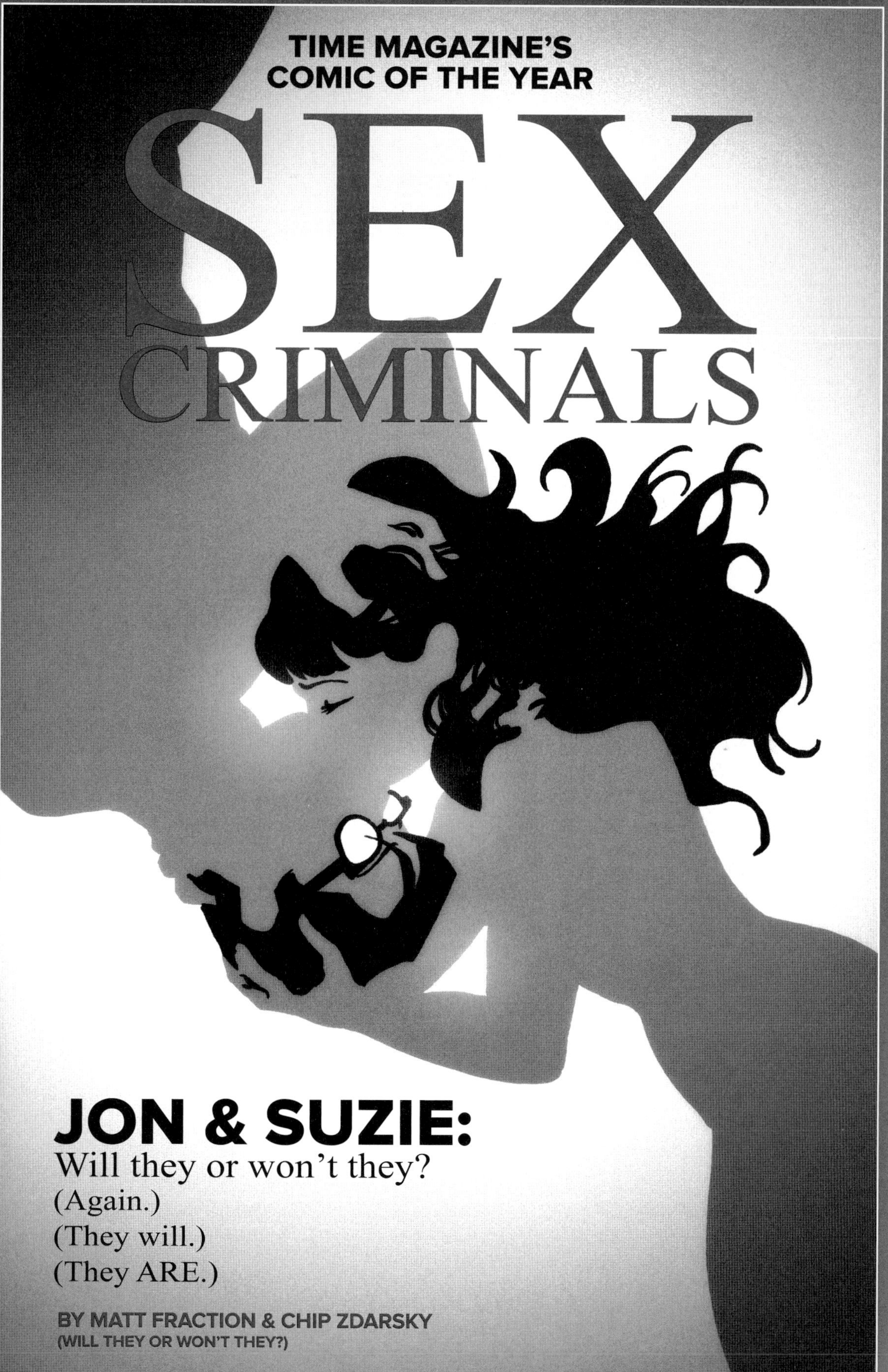
TIME MAGAZINE'S
COMIC OF THE YEAR
SEX
CRIMINALS
JON & SUZIE:
Will they or won't they?
(Again.)
(They will.)
(They ARE.)
BY MATT FRACTION & CHIP ZDARSKY
(WILL THEY OR WON'T THEY?)

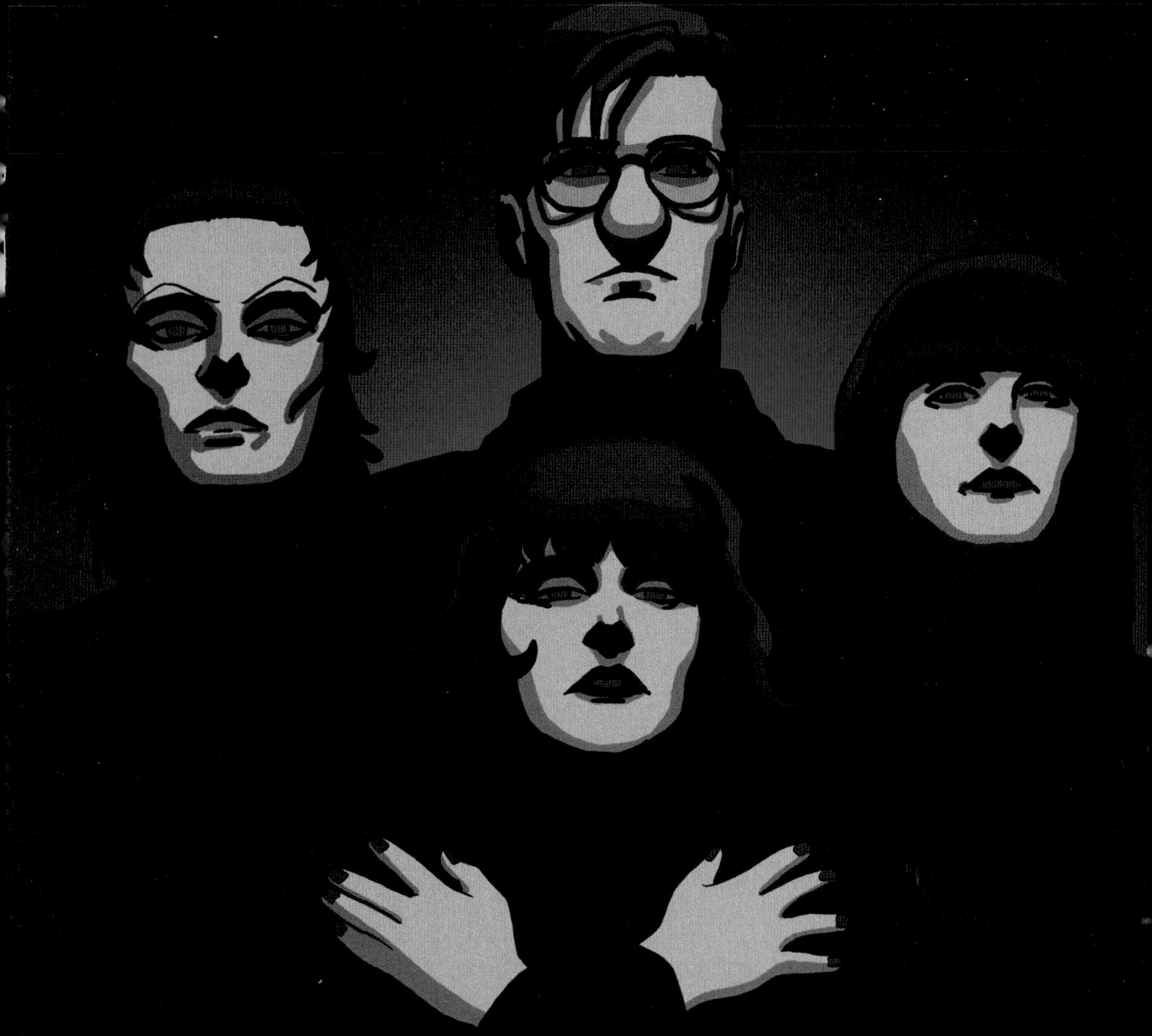

3

THIRD PRINTING

SEX CRIMINALS

FRACTION ZDARSKY